Cases in Small Business Management

A Strategic Problems Approach

John Edward deYoung

Barther, Clark, deYoung, and Associates

Merrill Publishing Company
A Bell & Howell Information Company
Columbus   Toronto   London   Melbourne

Dedicated to
My wife, Barbara, and my mother and father
The three people who have
Had the greatest impact on my life

Cover art: Larry Hamill

Published by Merrill Publishing Company
A Bell & Howell Information Company
Columbus, Ohio 43216

This book was set in Garamond

Administrative Editor: John Coleman
Production Coordinator: Pamela Hedrick-Bennett
Cover Designer: Cathy Watterson
Text Designer: Connie Young

Library of Congress Catalog Card Number: 87—62065
International Standard Book Number: 0—675—20787-8
Printed in the United States of America

1 2 3 4 5 6 7 8 9—93 92 91 90 89 88

Preface

The purpose of this book is to provide students with an opportunity to apply the basic concepts discussed in the Small Business Management course to a wide variety of real-life situations. The 50 cases were carefully selected to cover a wide range of businesses, both in the consumer and industrial fields. There are cases dealing with the retail, wholesale, service, and manufacturing sectors. Most cases deal with the domestic market, but several cases involve international business.

The book includes cases that deal with both large and small companies, and the problems contained cover all the major and minor areas normally included in a Small Business Management course.

The book can be used in one of two ways: first, as a practical teaching aid with any of the leading texts in the field, or second, as the text for a case problems course.

The book is divided into seven sections. Section One has five cases on starting your own business. Section Two has five cases on buying an existing business. Section Three has two cases on franchising. Section Four has five cases dealing with special buy-and-sell situations, which cover problems such as how to buy into a business as a minority stockholder and how to properly sell one business and purchase another. Section Five has seventeen cases focusing on marketing problems faced by the entrepreneur. Section Six has eight cases dealing with financing problems and methods. Finally, Section Seven has eight cases dealing with management problems.

While the cases focus on a particular area, in most instances a case can be used several times. For example, a case might focus on a marketing problem, but also be used later to discuss management approaches used by the owner.

The questions at the end of each case focus on all the important topics in small business and will challenge students to apply what they have learned. Furthermore, students will frequently have to research certain areas to solve some questions. However, the information needed can be found in any college library. Detailed answers for all questions are given in the instructor's manual to the text.

While all the cases are based on true situations, all names of companies, individuals, and locations are fictitious. In addition, the financial data and other details have been modified; however, the basic facts remain the same. Any reference to names of companies or persons living or dead is purely coincidental.

Finally, a large number of students always complain that the cases they must read are boring. With that in mind, I have presented all the necessary facts in each case, but modified incidental details surrounding many of the cases to make them easier and more enjoyable to read.

Acknowledgments

It is impossible to fully acknowledge and express my gratitude for the generous support and assistance I have received from so many people in the preparation of this casebook. However, I would particularly like to thank the staff of Merrill Publishing Company, including John Coleman, Administrative Editor, and Pam Hedrick-Bennett, Production Coordinator, Larry Qualls, Product Manager, and Colin Kelley, Sales Representative, for their expertise, constant guidance, encouragement, and understanding in making this casebook a reality. I would also like to thank the following people for their individual contributions:

- John P. Kunz, President, and Joseph O. Miles, Director of Industrial Services for Dun & Bradstreet Credit Services, for going out of their way to supply financial data for a number of cases.
- Terrance J. Dolan, Marketing Manager, Northeast Region for the Foreign Credit Insurance Association, for his up-to-date information regarding insurance and exporting to the international market.
- Art O'Bester, Senior Public Affairs Officer of the United States Export-Import Bank, for sharing his knowledge in international financing of exports.
- William Martini, C.P.A. for Martini and Martini, P.A., for his advice and recommendations on various segments of the casebook.
- Bruce Carson, Assistant Vice-President, New Jersey National Bank, for his efforts and special assistance regarding banking situations.
- Frank Crawford, General Manager, Frankel Associates, Inc., Financial Consultants, for his special insight and advice.
- Louis Rubino, Attorney and Partner in Milstead and Ridgeway, for his valuable expertise concerning certain legal questions and research.
- Robert Anthony, Attorney, Legal Interpretations Department, United States Securities and Exchange Commission, for sharing his expertise on stock offerings and investments.
- John McCarty, C.P.A., McCarty Associates, P.A., for his suggestions and recommendations in various case situations.

- Russ Mass, Associate Director, Rutgers Small Business Development Center, whose constant assistance, advice, and cooperation over many years had a great deal to do with this casebook.
- Joseph D. O'Neill, and Linda T. Pirolli, Attorneys, Joseph D. O'Neill, P.A., for supplying me with legal information on several areas as well as some interesting suggestions.
- Larry Rabun, Partner, Deloitte, Haskins and Sells, for sharing his expertise with me on voting trusts.
- Robert Zuckerman, Attorney Securities Examiner, Bureau of Securities for the State of New Jersey, for his information concerning public offerings.
- Michael T. Manning, Senior International Trade Specialist, Department of Commerce, ITA/United States and Foreign Commerce Services, Trenton, New Jersey.
- Cesar Ballester, Officer in Charge, and Whit O'Neal, Business Development Specialists for the Small Business Administration, in Camden, New Jersey, for their valuable cooperation and assistance and input in keeping me abreast of current SBA practices.
- Kathleen Hartman, Vice-President of Marketing, Aetna National List Company, for her suggestions and advice concerning direct mailing lists.
- Donald Clark, my associate, for his encouragement and many valuable suggestions on the various stages of this project.
- Professor Nancy Kozak, to whom I am especially grateful for reviewing and editing the entire manuscript, and for her many valuable suggestions and recommendations.
- Beverly N. McFadden, for her expertise and persistence as she plodded day and night through what seemed like a mountain of endless materials with her usual energy, enthusiasm, and good humor.

Contents

Starting Your Own Business

The Integrity Automotive Center

For many years Tom has been thinking about going into business with three of his friends, Matt, Jim, and John. They had all grown up together, and each had gone into a different area of the automotive field with a different company. They all think that they could pool their resources and start an automotive center that would be economical and efficient—not your typical "rip-off" joint that consumers think of when the words *service center* are mentioned. Their skills are diverse, and put together, Tom and his friends feel they have what it takes to run an efficient, honest operation that takes care of the customers. Tom is a good administrator as well as an excellent mechanic; Matt is an excellent painter; Jim is an outstanding body and fender man and can repair anything that comes down the road; and John knows exactly where to get parts for any type or model car.

Finally, they agree to start an operation together. They estimate that they will need about $50,000 to get started, so they each agree to put up an equal share of the money. They also agree that each will take out of the business only $400 per week until the business starts making money. Their wives agree to help with clerical work and other office assistance, each working part-time as much as possible without compensation.

The group then searched and found a good location, obtaining a one-year lease with a renewal option for three years plus another renewal option for five more years. They also obtained a purchase option to buy the building for $100,000 if bought within two years. The present market value of the building is $60,000.

Because the partners all know one another, they decide that they do not need a lawyer, thus cutting down on expenses. Since Tom's wife, Cathy, took a bookkeeping course in high school, she agrees to handle all the accounting records. After much discussion at Murphy's bar, their favorite hangout, they decide to draw up their own agreement for the "making of a new automotive empire." The partnership agreement, as drawn up by the four friends and future partners, was *exactly* as follows.

THE PARTNERSHIP AGREEMENT

We, Thomas Dooley, Matt Boyle, James Reynolds, and John O'Toole, hereby agree to call the new undertaking The Integrity Automotive Center. It is all agreed between each of us that as friends and partners we will all take $400 a week out of the business and not one penny more until the enterprise is out of the woods. As soon as the business makes a lot of money, then and only then will all partners of the first part be able to take money out of the business. Further, it is agreed as friends that all decisions will be made as we have done since we grew up, and that is we will discuss what has to be discussed and then agree. If someone does not agree, then the others will try and convince the disagreeing friend and partner and, it is understood that there will be no fighting to make the disagreeable partner agree to whatever is being discussed. Further, it is understood that there will be no drinking on the premises to be rented in the city of Chicago and especially Matt will not bring booze or whiskey to work and will not drink on the job. Each partner will put up $12,500 in cash in the business tomorrow after we sign this paper tonight and the money will be kept in a bank account. Since we are all friends and partners, each of the partners will be able to sign checks because of the mutual trust we have for one another. However, we all agree to tell Cathy, who is going to handle the books, how much we made out the check for so she can keep the books straight. Each friend and partner will tell Cathy how much to charge for the work on the cars and trucks and Tom, who knows about how to manage a business, will prepare bills for the customers and see they are paid.

At the end of each month Cathy will tell us how much money the enterprise has made, and at the end of the year or sooner, we will all take out our share of the profits from the pot that will be building up with profits from the endeavors of the four partners. If the friends and partners think that the money should stay in the company or enterprise because it needs it, then everyone will have to wait until we can get the money out.

Each wife of the partners and friends will try to do her share of work in the business and offer her services without charging a dime for what she does. Cathy will handle the books since she took a course in bookkeeping years ago. Debbie Boyle will answer the phone since she has a nice voice and used to answer the phone for a big company when she used to work before she married Matt. Eileen Reynolds will meet people who come in to pay their bills and help in the cleaning because she is good at meeting people and likes to talk. And finally Jane O'Toole will help everybody any way she can and bring lunch and dinner since she is the best cook of all the wives. When the business can afford to employ people, each wife will be allowed to stop working.

Everybody agrees to get to work early in the morning and stay as long as they can at night. The enterprise will remain open every day of the week except on Sundays when it will not open until after church services. Finally, no vacations will be allowed until we all make money and it is now agreed that the party of the first part will now affix their valid signatures or "John Henrys" to the line at the bottom of the page and we all agree to be friends and partners in the new enterprise The Integrity Automotive Center. One last thing we forgot to mention is that we will charge prices that will be pleasing to the public and we all will turn out good work. After we affix our names we will all be partners.

_____   _____
Tom Dooley   Matt Boyle

Jim Reynolds	John O'Toole

Paddy Murphy (witness)

Each of the partners put $12,500 in the local bank under the name of The Integrity Automotive Center, and they all signed the signature cards giving them the right to sign checks. After doing this, they each quit their jobs and started getting the location ready for business. Tom purchased a sign and told the others that it would be ready in about two weeks. According to Tom, it was a big beautiful sign that would clearly advertise their name to consumers, and anyone driving down the street on either side could not miss it. All the partners seemed to be quite pleased.

Each of the partners stuck to their specialties and purchased whatever they needed for their respective departments. In about two weeks they had the business stocked with parts, tools, and all the necessary equipment. They also had business cards and stationery made for use in the business.

Just before opening day Tom went to the local newspaper, and the staff prepared a full-page ad announcing the opening of The Integrity Automotive Center. The ad stated that the new business offered full services to the public at reduced prices. The ad promised guaranteed efficient service.

After the ad was placed, the traffic was tremendous and the business brisk. Customers flocked in and all four men were constantly busy. All the wives were enthused, each taking care of her individual assignments and more. At the end of the first month Cathy presented a statement that showed sales of $25,000 and a cash balance of $900. Needless to say, the partners were disappointed and could not understand how they could be so busy and end the month with such a small profit of $900.00. To make matters worse they received a letter from a lawyer stating that because they had not answered his correspondence asking them to desist from using his client's name in the Chicago area, he was filing suit against them within 20 days. He stated that this was the final opportunity to discuss a possible settlement with his client regarding the name. Further, the City of Chicago informed them that the sign violated zoning laws and must come down.

As it turned out, Cathy had not thought it was important that another company already was using the name The Integrity Automotive Center and had thrown all the notices away without bringing them to anyone's attention. This other company is a small parts store on the other side of town, and would be willing to sell the name for $10,000.

During the month Cathy called everyone into her office and insisted on knowing who was writing checks because some were missing from the checkbook. Everyone cooperated with Cathy, although Jim and Matt could not remember all of the checks or the exact amount of the checks they had written.

At the end of the month Tom found that some customers who were supposed to have paid cash owed money, a situation for which Cathy had no explanation. After investigating, she found that some of the clients had picked up their cars but not paid for one reason or another. In one situation, a client had come when Matt was alone and working on another car; the client left without paying the bill, telling Matt he was charging the bill. Cathy also could not reconcile the accounts payable because each of the partners made purchases for cash or on account, and purchase invoices were lost or misplaced. However, they think they owe $37,900 to various vendors.

At this point the partners are a little depressed, and yet they still want to continue. They had thought that all they needed was cash, determination, and honesty to make a fortune in business. In any case, they know they have some problems and don't know where to turn. They come to you to get advice on what went wrong and what to do to correct the problems.

QUESTIONS

1. What mistakes did the four partners make when they decided to go into business (before they entered the business and after)?

2. Do you think it is possible for friends to be successful in business? What special problems can this create?

3. What is wrong with the partnership agreement? Outline all mistakes and indicate what you feel should have been included in the agreement.

4. Do you think the partners should pay the company that owns the name $10,000 or do you think they should change the name? How would you deal with the company that owns the name?

5. What advice would you give the partners to straighten out the business and get it back on track? How would you handle the zoning problem?

6. What lessons did you learn from this case to help you when you start your own business?

CASE 2

Deliciosa Ice Cream Parlor

For some time Janet and several of her closest friends have been talking about going into a small business that would produce additional income and have possibilities of growing into a chain of stores. However, they did not know what type of business they should enter nor where to get the capital to start it. They figured that between the four of them they could split the working hours so they would not have to hire outside employees. Also, their husbands and kids also were willing to help occasionally.

Finally, Janet called her friends together and said "I have a terrific idea that I think will make money." Her friends were fascinated when Janet told them she had surveyed the entire area of Bueno, and that there was not one ice cream parlor in the entire town. She felt that if they started an ice cream parlor like those of years ago which sold homemade ice cream and candy they could make money.

The idea sounded ideal to her friends. To begin with, Beth Farrell made delicious candy, a skill which she had learned from her mother. Beth felt she could teach everyone how to make candy within a few weeks so they all could eventually pitch in with the candy making.

Sherry and Tracy said they would look for an appropriate location in the area. Tracy was a real estate agent and felt she could be very helpful in that direction. Sherry worked for a plastics firm in the purchasing department, so she offered to contact all the vendors who sell the basic materials needed to make candy and the other items they expected to produce. Sherry also offered to contact all the ice cream companies, including some of the bigger ones in the state, to see if they would sell to them wholesale. Janet offered to calculate all the finances and work on the marketing package since she had some experience in that field.

After several weeks everybody got together to discuss their progress. Tracy had found a lovely location in a small strip shopping center. The location was surrounded by other stores including a supermarket, news stand, small department store, liquor store, camera shop, and drug store. The location was in the middle of the strip and would cost $750 a month. The owner would not give more than a one-year lease, but assured them that this location was a good bet since all the present tenants have been there for seven years, as long as the strip had been there. Sherry told of how one of the new ice cream companies taking the country by storm would be interested in selling them their ice cream in bulk. This company would even put in the refrigerators and counter cases on a rental basis if they would use their ice cream exclusively and feature their ice cream in all advertising and promotion. Sherry told the company officials she would get back to them. The company, which produced new European ice cream, was selling its product at an astounding pace throughout the country, so they were all excited about landing a deal with the company. Beth had given Sherry all the ingredients needed for making candy, and Sherry reported that she had numerous vendors eagerly lined up to do business. She could not get any of them to buy the machinery to make the candy, but Sherry did find some used equipment with a six-month guarantee which they could purchase for $3,500. The price included all the other pieces of equipment and utensils needed to make the candy. Sherry brought up the point that two of the major costs would be shopping bags with the shop's name printed on them and containers for the candy and ice cream.

Janet estimated that $35,000 was needed to get started in the business. This would cover start-up fees, equipment, furniture and fixtures, signs, uniforms, deposits for utilities, and telephones. Janet also included money for materials and supplies to get the business started. In addition, Janet set aside $5,000 for a one-month advertising campaign to start the business with a bang. The campaign would include some local television spots she had obtained through her friends who were willing to give her special rates on time slots that were not already sold. While these might be 10- or 20-second spots for as little as $30 per spot, they almost certainly would not be prime time slots. However, Janet felt it was a terrific idea because it would give them exposure. She intended to make up her own television commercials in the TV studio featuring each one of the owners doing something that would get everyone's attention.

Janet estimated that around $10,000 would be left over for working capital to tide them over for at least three months. The only problem they had now was assigning the time slots for each to work during the day. They were all working during the day except Janet, who left her job a few months ago. She was all set to take another job when this project started to materialize, and she decided to wait and see what happened. The other three asked Janet to work during the day five days a week, and they would take over the nights and weekends. Janet agreed, with the stipulation that she be paid a reasonable salary; she was earning $27,000 in her old position as assistant to the marketing manager. Her friends agreed that she was entitled to a good salary, but felt she would have to take less than $27,000 until things got going. Janet agreed to take a $20,000 annual salary since she felt optimistic and believed that if they all cooperated in this enterprise they could eventually establish a basis for franchising other stores in the surrounding area. They decided to call the candy "Beth's Old-Fashioned Candy" and Janet agreed to design a box that would really be a standout.

Janet informed them that each would have to put up $8,750. She stated that any two of the owners could sign checks and felt that, since she was going to be the main person running the business, she should also handle the administrative part of the business. However, Janet felt that they should have a local accounting firm come in monthly and prepare an income statement and balance sheet for the business. Each of the partners agreed, so they decided to formalize everything in a legal document. The following partnership agreement was drawn up by an attorney who lived in the same neighborhood.

Partnership Agreement

I.   Introduction
     <u>The parties to this agreement</u>, Janet Conway, Beth Farrell, Sherry Parotti, and Tracy Cohen all of Bueno, New Mexico, hereby agree to enter into a partnership agreement on the terms and conditions set forth in this partnership agreement.

II.   Purpose of Partnership
The partnership shall be formed for the purpose of engaging in the business of selling Ice Cream and Candy to both retail and wholesale trade and in any such other business as the partners may agree upon in the future.

III.   Name of the Partnership
The name of the partnership shall be the "Deliciosa Ice Cream Parlor."

IV.   Place of Business
The principal place of business for the partnership shall be in Bueno, New Mexico, and any other place or places as may be agreed upon by the partners.

V.   Duration of Partnership
The partnership shall commence on April 28, 1987, and shall continue from year to year until dissolved or terminated in accordance with the subsequent articles of this agreement.

VI.   Capital Contributions
Capital contributions to form this partnership will be $8,750 for each partner. Additional capital contributed as needed will be made equally by each partner. If any of the partners cannot or will not make any further contributions, then that partner or partners who do make the contributions will then own a greater share of the business and will share in profits and losses based on their total contribution to the total contribution made by all partners.

VII.   Partnership Property
All property paid for or brought into the partnership shall become the property of the partnership. Specifically, the name "Beth's Old-Fashioned Candy" shall be considered as part of the partnership property.

VIII.   Partner Rights, Duties, and Liabilities
a. No partner shall, during the term of this agreement, become involved either directly or indirectly in any business or occupation which is in conflict with the purpose of this partnership.
b. Each partner shall devote all the time possible to this partnership. It is agreed that Janet Conway will be the General Manager of the firm and that she will devote full time to the business at an agreed annual salary of $20,000 per year. She will be expected to handle the company during the day and each of the other partners will make arrangements to cover the operations of the business during the evenings and weekends.

IX.   Management of Business and Voting Rights
Except as otherwise provided in this agreement, each of the partners will have an equal vote in the management and conduct of the partnership. All decisions shall be made by a majority vote.

X.   Profits and Losses
a. The partners shall be entitled to the net profits of the business that remain after payment of all expenses from gross revenues. Each partner shall be entitled to an equal share of the profits.
b. All losses that occur in the operation of the business shall be paid from the capital of the partnership and profits if any exist, or, if such sources are deficient in funds to cover such losses, by the partners equally, or based on their proportionate share of the ownership in the partnership.

XI. Retirement

Any of the partners shall have the right to retire or terminate their relationship with the partnership at the end of any fiscal year. However, written notice of the intent to retire shall be served upon the other partners at the office of the partnership at least two months before the end of the fiscal year. The retirement of any of the partners shall have no effect upon the continuance of the partnership unless all of the partners desire to terminate the partnership. The remaining partner or partners shall have the right to purchase the retiring partner's interest in the partnership, or to terminate and liquidate the partnership business completely.

XII. Death of Any of the Partners

Upon the death of any of the partners, the surviving partners shall purchase the entire interest of the deceased partner in the partnership, and the heirs of the estate of the deceased shall sell such interest to the partnership. The purchase price for the deceased partner's interest shall be whatever the deceased partner's equity interest is determined by the auditor in the partnership as of the date of her death. It is agreed further that the total amount to be paid to the deceased partner's estate shall be paid within 60 days from the date that the value of the deceased partner's equity has been determined.

XIII. Entire Agreement

This agreement sets forth the entire understanding between all the partners mentioned in this agreement and it shall not be amended, modified, or terminated, except in a written statement signed by all the partners in the partnership.

XIV. Interpretation

This agreement shall be interpreted according to the laws of the State of New Mexico.

IN WITNESS WHEREOF the parties have signed this agreement made on the 28th day of April, 1987.

Signed, sealed and delivered in the presence of

_____
Janet Conway

_____

_____
Beth Farrell

_____
Sherry Parotti

_____
Tracy Cohen

After the partnership agreement was signed, each of the partners put $8,750 into the bank and the firm was on its way. The lease was signed, and after three weeks of hard work by the partners and their husbands, the Deliciosa Ice Cream Parlor was open. By this time Beth had been teaching the others how to make candy, and, while not totally proficient, they were all doing well. Beth was confident that in a short time they would be experts in candy making.

The advertising program was a smashing success and in a short time the business started picking up more sales than expected. However, during the day Janet found that there were too many people coming into the store, so she decided to hire two part-time people to help her during the busy hours.

At the end of the first month the accountant prepared the following income statement.

Total sales		$25,000
Cost of sales		14,500
Gross profit		$10,500
Less: operating expenses		
Salary (Janet)	$1,666	
Salary (part-time)	867	
Payroll taxes	304	
Advertising	3,500	
Supplies	1,250	
Rent	750	
Insurance	300	
Utility expense	350	
Legal and accounting	150	
Telephone	85	
Miscellaneous	225	
Total operating expenses		9,447
Net profit		$ 1,053

When the partners saw these figures they were excited. This was the first month of operation, and considering that they spent $3,500 for advertising (which was more than the normal monthly projected advertising expense), they felt they had done an excellent job. As a result, they attacked the enterprise with renewed enthusiasm so they could make additional profits.

During the ensuing months business was brisk, but problems started to develop. During the summer months they had to hire additional part-time help as well as one full-time person to make candy in the back room in advance. Before, they used to make the candy only a few days in advance, but because of the popularity of the candy they needed to make at least two to three weeks' supply in advance. This meant that the other partners had to work longer than usual, and Sherry and Tracy finally said that they could not keep up with the hours. Their husbands were becoming impatient with the fact that this new enterprise kept them away from home so much. Thus, it was agreed that Janet would hire a full-time manager as well as one additional part-time person for the night shift.

At the end of six months the accountant prepared the following income statement.

Total sales		$175,000
Cost of sales		101,500
Gross profit		$ 73,500
Operating expenses		
Salary (Janet)	$10,000	
Salary (others)	15,800	
Payroll taxes	3,096	
Advertising	8,500	
Supplies	8,750	
Rent	4,500	
Insurance	1,800	
Utilities	2,100	
Legal and accounting	900	
Telephone	750	
Miscellaneous	1,350	
Total operating expenses		$ 57,546
Net profit		$ 15,954

Each partner earned a total of $3,988.50 on her investment of $8,750, or a 45.5% return on her money. While the rate of return on the investment was good, Beth, Sherry, and Tracy felt that since they did not get a salary as Janet did, the return was not as great for them. However, each agreed to remain in the business for another six months. Janet asked the partners for a salary increase since she felt she was not earning as much as she could outside the business. In addition, she felt that she had the entire load of the business on her shoulders and she was spending more time than she expected at the store, causing friction in her marriage. The other partners agreed that she could raise her salary to $27,000 a year, which was what she was making at her old job.

Business was a bit slower during the winter months, with people spending a lot of their money for Christmas gifts. However, they still managed to increase sales each month and Janet was beginning to feel that they might be starting to turn the corner. Then Beth informed the partners that her husband was being transferred to Butte, Montana, and she would be leaving at the end of the month. She stated she would like to sell her interest back to the other partners. When the accountant calculated the value of her equity in the firm, he came up with a figure of $13,250. Beth was quite upset, for she felt her share was worth more. However, Janet pointed out that the business had to hire more personnel and spend more money on advertising to keep business up. However, she felt that if Beth left her money in the business her equity would be worth a great deal of money in the future. But Beth wanted out and asked for her money. None of the other partners wanted to put up the money, and Janet and her husband had to borrow money from the bank to pay Beth for her interest. This meant Janet now owned 50 percent of the business, and Sherry and Tracy both had a 25 percent interest in profits and losses. Tracy and Sherry also had stopped coming to the store and were merely investors. They were not as friendly toward Janet as they used to be in the past.

At the end of the 12 months the accountant prepared the following annual income statement.

Sales		$320,000
Cost of sales		185,600
Gross profit		$134,400
Operating expenses		
Salary (Janet)	$23,500	
Salary (others)	32,000	
Payroll taxes	6,660	
Advertising	15,000	
Supplies	16,000	
Rent	9,000	
Insurance	3,600	
Utilities	4,500	
Legal and accounting	1,800	
Telephone	1,900	
Total operating expenses		113,960
Net profit		$ 20,440

The net profit of $20,440 meant that Janet earned $10,220 on her interest in the business and Sherry and Tracy each earned $5,110 on their investment of $8,750 in the business. Tracy and Sherry were not satisfied with the figures even though the $5,110 was a 58.4 percent on their investment. When Janet pointed out that they were now merely investors and not working as they did before, they still felt it was unfair that she should earn as much as she did from the business. Sherry pointed out that next year if the business made the same amount of profit Janet would earn $27,000 plus another $10,220, or a total of $37,220. They felt this was very unfair. Janet pointed out that they could have purchased a portion of Beth's share of the business, and also that she was making the greatest sacrifice in working for the business. However, Sherry and Tracy felt the business should be liquidated and the relationship terminated. Janet pointed out that they had a lease and other obligations, but Sherry and Tracy would not listen. Sherry then said that she would not be surprised if Janet was stealing. A furious Janet asked them if they would sell their interests in the partnership to her, to which they replied that they would get back to her within a few days. When they did they stated that each wanted $25,000 for her individual equity interest in the business. They also stated that they wanted the money in full and would not accept any notes or give Janet time to pay off the money.

Janet was up against a wall. The business was really beginning to get on track, and she had learned a great deal about the business and how to make it more successful. Janet talked to her husband, and they concluded that they could not come up with more than $10,000, leaving them $40,000 short. Janet did not know how to solve the problem. She went to the bank and found she could get a $15,000 loan, which still left her $25,000 short. She sees no solution but to liquidate the business.

QUESTIONS

1. Could anything have been done to prevent the conflicts that arose in this case?

2. Should the partnership agreement have contained other clauses which would have prevented the necessity to liquidate?

3. What options does Janet have at this time? What would you advise her to do? Do you think there is anything that can be done to change Sherry and Tracy's minds? What sources of financing would you suggest to Janet?

4. Do you think that the business of franchising Beth's Old-Fashioned Candy has a genuine chance of success? Do you think that the business was turning the corner? How would you start the franchise process? When would you start? What methods would you use? Outline in depth.

Andy's Home Remodeling & Improvements Company

Andy Taylor worked for a small manufacturing company for seven years, but was not happy with the job. His supervisor was jealous of him because he could fix anything and seemed to have a special knack for knowing how to make work easier and more economical. Thus his supervisor had it in for him. Because the company is small, Andy knew he did not have much of a future and so decided to enter his own business. All he has are tools, a pick-up truck, and determination. He does not know much about business, but has attended some of the seminars given by the Small Business Administration, and so feels he can make it. Andy and his wife have $5,000 total capital. Andy feels that if he can get some work, he will be successful.

Andy asked his wife to handle the phone and the books, and she agreed. He had business cards and stationery made up. He then placed an ad in the paper, as shown at the top of page 14.

Andy got a few responses from the advertisement and went out to give the clients estimates. Because Andy was eager to get started, he quoted ridiculously low prices to the homeowners. One homeowner made him sign a letter stating that Andy would put on a new roof, paint the entire house inside and out, and repair the screens of the porch enclosure for $1,000. Andy took the deal, but

---

ANDY'S HOME REMODELING AND IMPROVEMENTS
Anything for the home at
prices anyone can afford

Additions	Siding	Chimney Cleaning
Roofing	Painting	Window Replacement
Extensions	Bathrooms	Wallpapering
Porches	Kitchens	Cement Work

ALL WORK GUARANTEED/FREE ESTIMATES
THE BEST PRICES IN TOWN AT TOP QUALITY
CALL: ANDY TAYLOR
444–6666
Any day in the week 8 a.m.—5 p.m.

---

immediately saw that he was going to lose money. However, he persisted in the deal and made the homeowner happy. When the job was completed the owner gave Andy a check, which he deposited immediately. About a week later the bank notified him that the check had bounced. Andy called the owner, who told him a mistake was made and that he should redeposit the check the following day. This time the check cleared. Andy learned two lessons: to be careful quoting a price and to be careful taking checks.

Andy had a reputation as a good carpenter. He managed to pick up a few jobs here and there, but he was not getting enough business to make up for what he lost in salary when he quit his old job. In addition, his wife and he were having problems because she had to stay home all day to answer the phone, and she was having trouble getting her other work done. She felt her life was totally disrupted and did nothing to encourage Andy in his work. She also complained about the unsteady work and all the problems Andy was having. Andy told her that he wanted to make a go of this business, to which his wife replied that she just wanted out of the marriage. Andy purchased a telephone answering system and hooked it up to the phone so she could be relieved of some of her responsibility to the business, and hoped things would improve.

Andy was determined to stay on the job. He managed to get another client who wanted a bedroom added to his house. Andy told him it would cost $8,500. The client agreed and Andy went ahead with the task. After he was well into the job, the owner was notified to cease immediately because he failed to get approval from City Hall. The owner came back to Andy and asked him why he did not get the addition approved, but Andy was unaware he needed to do this. By this time Andy had already spent about $4,000 in materials, and spent many hours working on the project. Andy went to City Hall and, through some friends, managed to get the matter resolved. However, when Andy got back to the job he found that approximately $800 worth of materials were missing. When Andy completed the job, the owner gave him a check for $5,000 and told him he would pay the balance in 30 days. He stated he was "short, but the money was good." Andy agreed to these terms because there was nothing he could do. At the end of the 30 days the amount was paid in full. From this job Andy learned a few more lessons about zoning, pilferage, and credit, and wondered how many more he would have to learn before he was a success.

Andy got another job that involved installing siding on a house. Andy had bid against others and so the profit was not huge, but Andy felt that if he kept at it he would get things rolling. Andy needed a helper and hired a friend of his to work with him. While working on the job the helper fell and hurt his back. Andy rushed him to the hospital, and it appeared he would be there awhile because he had hurt himself badly. The hospital staff asked Andy if he had insurance, and when he said no, told him he would be billed for all the charges. Andy agreed and signed the necessary papers. Andy finished the job and was paid, but the hospital bills came to more than $8,000. In addition, his helper sued him for $10,000. Andy learned another lesson—to get an insurance agent and proper coverage.

At this point Andy needs to know how to get more business. He knows he is handy and that he can do almost anything around a house or in a plant. Andy was always a great help to the plant when it needed additions and he handled the entire projects from start to finish. However, the plant had money and handled all the necessary legalities and paperwork.

The strain of an unsteady income finally became too much for Andy's wife, and she filed for divorce. Andy wanted to continue in his business, but the two could not reach a compromise and were soon divorced.

QUESTIONS

1. Was Andy prepared to enter this business venture on his own?

2. If Andy wanted to go into this business, how should he have approached it? Outline in depth.

3. Do you think it was fair for Andy to quit his job and give up a good job just because he did not get along with his supervisor?

4. What suggestions would you give to Andy to market his services? How should he conduct the business with respect to bids, deposits, credits, checks, materials storage, employees, insurance, and advertising?

5. How could Andy and his wife have compromised so that their marriage could be saved?

Funnsy Video Center

Marty Horner decided that it was time for him to open his own business. After much thought, he decided that the best business to enter was the video-cassette rental business. Marty was presently making $32,000 a year working for a local company in a small town outside of Des Moines, Iowa. Marty felt he could easily keep his job and in his spare time run the video rental business. He would hire some reliable part-time help and his wife could also assist when she had time. Marty checked with some video wholesalers and found that each cassette cost about $55, and that he should have at least 1,000 video-cassette movies to have the basic inventory needed to handle the various marketing segments. The wholesalers told him that he needed films for children, family, and adults, including those with "R" and "X" ratings. The wholesalers pointed out that they could keep him supplied with current films, and thus his firm would always retain clients since new films would always be available to them.

Marty calculated his investment as follows:

Library inventory (1,000 cassettes @ $55.00 each)	$55,000
Renovating of location	5,000
Advertising and promotion (start up)	5,000
Video-cassette recorders to rent out (10 units)	2,500
Start-up expenses (legal and accounting)	2,000
Working capital	15,000
Total investment	84,500

These investment figures were based on the wholesalers' estimates of what the typical video store costs to open and operate. Marty had approximately $40,000 to invest into a business, and was able to borrow another $25,000 from the bank against his home equity. He also contacted some of his relatives, and between his father-in-law and sister, was able to come up with the balance of the money needed to open the store.

Marty looked for a location and finally found one in a middle-class neighborhood not far from his residence. There were literally hundreds of homes surrounding the store, and the area was constantly growing. The area's crime rate was the lowest in town, and people with high incomes were moving to the area. The location was formerly a restaurant, but it was closed down due to health violations. The location was in a small strip of stores, but because the supermarket and department store were very aggressive and advertised heavily, the parking lot was always full. Marty felt that this was the right location and signed a five-year lease at $1,800 a month. The owner agreed to clean out the location, but Marty would have to renovate. Marty took his wife and the people who loaned him money to see the site and they were all satisfied with the location. The only one who did not care for the location was his father-in-law, Hubert, who believed that once a location got a "bad name" people usually avoided it. However, he felt that since there was not another video store in that area and because it was an entertainment business, Marty had made a good decision.

Marty immediately hired contractors to renovate the location. Within 30 days the store was ready to open. The inventory had been received and placed on beautiful and strategically placed displays around the store. The wholesaler visited the store and made several suggestions, which Marty followed.

Marty calculated hypothetical revenues, as follows:

Average daily charge or rental per cassette	$2.99
Maximum potential for 1,000 films for 360 days per year at $2,99 per day	$1,076,400
Operating at 50% capacity, or 500 films per day per year	538,200
Operating at 30% capacity, or 300 films per day per year	322,920
Operating at 25% capacity, or 250 films per day per year	269,100

Marty decided it would be better to use the conservative 25 percent figure. He knew that with holidays, specials, and other promotions, he could boost sales beyond this capacity, but he wanted to play it safe. As far as the projected expenses were concerned, Marty worked up the following annual forecast:

Salary (Marty)	$ 25,000
Salaries (others):	
2 part-time workers at $5.00 per hour	
12 hours per day for 360 days per year	43,200
Payroll taxes (12%)	8,184
Advertising & promotion (start up)	5,000
Advertising & promotion (regular)	12,000
Rental expense	21,600
Insurance	4,800
Supplies	1,200
Utility expense	6,000
Telephone	1,200
Legal and accounting	2,400
Maintenance	1,200
Miscellaneous	2,000
Total estimated annual expenses	$133,784

Marty knew that some of these figures were overstated, but wanted to approach the business conservatively rather than unrealistically.

Marty still had to calculate the depreciation for the films. The wholesaler told him that he could get about 200 rentals from each cassette. Marty decided instead to use a factor of 10 percent of the rental fee, which was on the average $2.99, as a more accurate depreciation figure. He also decided to set up a separate bank account and deposit the 10 percent depreciation amount from each rental to pay for new films as they came out and to repurchase the basic films for his library that would be overused. Marty also knew he could sell the much used films for a small price or could even use them as specials when people came in and rented films.

Therefore, Marty calculated his projected annual income statement as follows:

Estimated revenues (at 25% capacity)	$269,100
Less: depreciation of films at 10%	26,910
Gross profit	$242,190
Less: operating expenses	133,784
Estimated net profit before taxes	$108,406

Based on this projected net income before taxes, the return on Marty's investment looked exceptional.

Finally, opening day came. Marty had advertised in all the papers, as well as on the radio. He had also sent out mailings in the neighborhood offering prizes. To top it off, he had two people with sandwich boards covered with advertising on both sides walking back and forth announcing the opening of Funnsy Video Center, and offering prizes to all who came.

Marty's business was such a tremendous success that he even thought about quitting his job, but after discussing this with his wife, he decided against it. Instead, he hired four part-time helpers, mostly younger people, who each worked six hours a day seven days a week. Marty also had his front door fixed so that people who rented cassettes could put them in the drop in the front door so they didn't have to worry about getting the films back the following day at 8 A.M. when he opened.

At the end of the first three months, sales had already reached $100,000, and it looked as if Marty's business was going to exceed his forecasts. Then something unexpected happened. Two stores in the same area, one a drugstore and the other an all-night deli, both started to offer video rentals. Thus they were in direct competition with Marty. However, the drugstore advertised that customers did not need to make deposits or pay membership fees, and rented films for as little as $1.99 per day. Although the drugstore was renting many old films that nobody wanted to rent anymore, some videos were priced about 25 percent less than those in Marty's store. The deli advertised films for as little as $0.99 a film, although it had a limited stock and could not really be much competition for Marty. Marty called his wholesaler, who stated that while he was not selling to Marty's competition, that Marty had to expect to compete as in any other type of business. So Marty got back to work. He advertised that he was no longer requiring a deposit and that he would rent films for as little as $1.50. He emphasized his tremendous inventory, which by this time had swelled to 1,500 cassettes.

Business, while steady, was beginning to slip. Sales for the next three months totaled $62,275 and the advertising costs had risen an additional $3,500. Marty had decided to stick in there when something else happened. One of his part-time workers (he could not determine which one) had been renting X-rated films to 13- and 14-year-old kids. Quite a few parents came to the store to complain and demanded to talk to the owner. Marty was shocked, and told the parents that he had a policy of not renting X-rated films to anyone under 18 years of age. He assured the parents the matter would be corrected. However, instead of things quieting down they got worse. Some of the local church members started picketing in front of his store with signs that said:

"Funnsy is not for Babies"
"Children are not safe with Funnsy"
"Funnsy get out"
"Dirty Films by Dirty People"
"Rid the neighborhood of filth"

Marty tried to talk to the picketers, but this backfired. When photographers from the local newspapers came and took pictures of picketers talking to Marty, a picture of him alongside some of the signs appeared on the front page. Marty was given space in the newspaper to explain his side of the story, but this didn't help. Business came to a halt and sales were next to zero. Marty, who lived in the same neighborhood, was plagued at home with so many calls that he had his phone number changed. His wife and kids were being harassed. Nancy, Marty's wife, was devastated and told him to get out of the business. Marty wanted to stay and fight because he felt that an honest mistake was made and people would come to understand this. However, Marty could not find out which employee had made the mistake, so he fired all the part-time people. Then he found he could not get anyone to work for him. Finally, Marty went to a local real estate agent and asked if she could sell the business for him. Marty asked for an early vacation and his firm gave it to him. He had a letter of apology explaining the mistake printed in the newspaper which stated that his business would no longer carry X-rated films. After a while people started coming back, but many were irritated when they could not get X-rated films. Business was fair; during the first month after the X-Rated War, Marty's sales amounted to $8,000.

Finally, the real estate agent found a buyer for the business. Although Marty had wanted $150,000, the buyer was offering $70,000 cash for the entire store, inventory, and equipment. Marty would lose money on the deal, but he would be finished with the business venture. He hated to quit, but his name was mud in the neighborhood, his kids were being ridiculed, and his wife wanted to sell the house and move to another area altogether.

The real estate agent came back to Marty and asked him for a decision. She told Marty that it was the only offer on the table and she needed a "yes" or a "no."

QUESTIONS

1. Do you think Marty should have quit his job to devote full time to the business? Do you think that if he had been there, things would have been different?

2. What explanation could there be for the employee's "honest mistake"? Would you have fired all the part-time employees? How could Marty have prevented this from happening even when he was not there? What type of identification should be demanded of very young people when renting videos?

3. If this had been your store and you were faced with the new competition Marty was faced with, how would you have reacted?

4. Should Marty sell the store and move out of the neighborhood? Do you think that in view of what is happening to his family it would be best for Marty to take the $70,000 and run? If Marty did not decide to move, do you think he would be able to regain his sales position without X-rated films? How would you reestablish Marty's store as a viable operation?

CASE 5

Ludwig and Greta's Crafts

Ludwig Helmholtz and Greta de Dausett were close friends. Ludwig was a civil engineer by profession and Greta was a controller for a paint manufacturer. However, both were also very involved with their respective hobbies. Ludwig was a genius at building scale models of trains, dollhouses, European mansions, castles, and boats. He not only worked from photographs, but also took trips to various cities and countries to get drawings and other pertinent data to enable him to build exacting models of famous buildings, cities, and other sites. From time to time people would come to his workshop and ask to buy some of his models. Ludwig was always hesitant to sell anything because his creations were very important to him. However, because he was running out of space and because some of the people were offering what he considered ridiculously high prices, he decided to start selling a few of them. One model of a famous castle in Liechtenstein sold for more than $10,000. Some of his model boats sold for as much as $2,500. Greta, on the other hand, was into making pottery, sculptured candles, papier mâché articles (that she created, as she would say, "from the depths of the soul"), and costume jewelry. People who came to see Ludwig's models would sometimes venture over to her workshop and see what she was doing. Because of her unique talents, she found that her products were in demand. However, like Ludwig, she was hesitant to get into business commercially. She often remarked that her hobby took her away from the real world and transported her to another dimension where she was happy.

Both Ludwig and Greta were pleased with the results of the past year; Ludwig had sold about $40,000 of his famous models and Greta $23,000 of her works. Because they were neighbors and neither was married, they became friends. Ludwig was 61 years old and Greta was 52. They often wondered if perhaps there might be a chance of going into the business someday on a full-time basis, but both were hesitant.

Ludwig suggested that they merge their activities but remain at home in their respective workshops until they developed an intelligent plan for expanding their business. However, Ludwig said, "Although I know we can make money on our work and probably enough to live on, I would be afraid of giving up my position. I think you should be very careful, too." Greta replied, "Ludwig, I agree we both have great talent, but what we need to do is to find some way of marketing our products so that we can move from part-time to full-time occupations." Ludwig said that nothing would make him happier than to spend all his time working on his scale models. He said he would like to first find out how he and Greta could increase their present business and then how to go about marketing their products to get sufficient volume to leave their present occupations.

Both Ludwig and Greta were unsure of how much to charge for their products. Ludwig estimated that the model of the castle in Liechtenstein cost him approximately $5,000 for travel and hotel expenses and another $4,000 for materials. He said that it took him more than four months to complete the model on a part-time basis, some days spending one hour on it and perhaps more on the following day. In the future he and Greta agreed to keep accurate time records on how much time and labor they put into each project.

Clients kept coming to their workshops, and from time to time purchased their products. However, neither had come up with a marketing plan which would include both a pricing and promotion strategy. Both of them wondered what they should charge for special requested projects. For example, one client wanted an exact replica of Windsor Castle in England and Ludwig did not know how to approach the question of price or costs. He told the interested party that he would get back to him to discuss the project in more depth. Greta also had some requests for unusual papier mâché sculpture, including everything from face masks of famous people to surrealistic art based on fantasies. Greta also was unable to come up with prices and labor figures.

So, here are two people who are very talented and want to expand their part-time business to a point where they might be able to leave the so-called "rat race" and escape into their own world of creativity.

QUESTIONS

1. Do you think that Greta and Ludwig should quit their jobs now and work on their hobbies as a full-time business? Are they prepared to enter the commercial hobby field and make as much money as they are in their present positions? Do you think they should wait for retirement and then devote their time to their hobbies?

2. What recommendations would you make to help them develop a short-term plan to expand

their part-time workshops into a full-time money-making business? Do you think there is a market for their products? Evaluate each of their individual hobbies with respect to potential sales and profits.

3. What recommendations do you have for pricing their works? Consider both items they make for themselves, which they reluctantly might be asked to sell, and items that are custom-made for special clients.

4. If Ludwig and Greta go into their hobbies business full time, do you think they will be able to escape and enjoy the happiness they both expect?

5. Do you think they should form a partnership or operate on their own?

Buying an
Existing Business

McCann's or Pancho Villa's Hideaway

For several years Ernie York has been looking for a restaurant to buy in the Portland area. He has contacted real estate brokers, answered advertisements in newspapers, and talked to bankers about his interest. Ernie feels well qualified to operate his own restaurant because he has been a successful chef for more than 20 years. He presently works for one of the best restaurants in the Portland area, and people are constantly commending him on his excellent cooking. He also is considered somewhat of a wonder at catering functions because he always manages to come up with cuisine and other personal creative specialties that have made the catering business very lucrative for his present employer. Ernie admits that he is weak when it comes to administration, yet feels that his wife and perhaps his grown children can be of assistance. Insofar as capital is concerned, Ernie and his wife have managed to accumulate more than $400,000 over the years as a result of investing in stocks and real estate. Ernie does not want to invest all the savings, but feels that he has enough to start out in a business. Ernie presently makes $55,000 as a chef, and his wife Belinda makes $25,000 as office manager for a local firm.

In the last two months Martin Dixon, a real estate friend of Ernie's, has come up with two possibilities: McCann's Restaurant and Pancho Villa's Hideaway. McCann's, a locally well-known establishment, specializes in steak and lobster. The owner wants to sell the restaurant so he can retire. McCann's Restaurant includes a bar, but no catering facilities. Ernie has tried to avoid purchasing a restaurant with a bar since his religion forbids drinking. His pastor has told him he should avoid purchasing a business that goes against all of the basic teachings of his religion. On the other hand, his wife, Belinda, who belongs to another denomination, feels that it is vital and necessary for a restaurant to have a bar. Their son, George, feels the same way, although their daughter, Melissa, agrees with her father. Ernie does not want to cause problems in the family and feels that his wife should have some input into the matter because she too has worked hard and helped accumulate the capital they now have.

Ernie decided to look at the business. The owner, Harry McCann, informed him that their dealings would have to be confidential because he did not want his employees to become aware of his desire to sell. He also informed Ernie that if he wanted to look at his books he would have to put up a $50,000 deposit, which would be refundable if he did not purchase the business. Dixon, the real estate agent, told Ernie that a deposit was standard when looking at a business of this type and that his lawyer could prepare an agreement that would give him the protection he needed. Ernie talked the matter over with his wife. He told her that the owner said the restaurant was doing approximately $2 million business per year and was making a profit. The selling price was $650,000, which included the property. Belinda knew of the restaurant and was quite excited. She definitely felt that it was worth looking into and that Ernie should give McCann the deposit and have the accountant examine the books and records. Ernie again asked her to reconsider because of the bar. However, she had come up with a solution: if they did purchase the business she would handle the bar and he could handle the food. This would eliminate any difficulty with his religion. Ernie did not like this idea, but decided to explore the business anyway. McCann took the $50,000 and gave Ernie and his accountant all the books of the business.

When Ernie's accountant examined the books and the tax statements, he found that there were some large discrepancies with what McCann had told him. The tax statements indicated that the business was doing only a little over $1 million business a year and that the business was losing about $125,000 a year. The business was a corporation and was solely owned by McCann. McCann was taking $75,000 plus expenses out of the business each year. The business had been operating for nearly 15 years and, from what the accountant could learn, had never shown much of a profit. It was clear that McCann was not reporting all the income, or was constantly investing more money to take care of losses. The accountant informed Ernie that the building was probably worth more than the $150,000 net book value, but that based on the statements he could not see where any goodwill was evident. The accountant pointed out that in his experience when he came across books that were not kept as they should be, it was best to avoid the situation. McCann also wanted to sell the entire corporation intact, however, he did state he would give his personal guarantee for six months to take care of any unforeseen problems that might arise.

Ernie met several times with McCann and they became good friends. When Ernie mentioned the discrepancies in the books, McCann's initial reaction was evasive, and he insisted that the sales and profits were there. McCann stated that he could never have lasted 15 years if he was losing money. But he finally admitted very confidentially that he was skimming cash sales off the top. He told Ernie that he never reported all his sales to his accountant because the IRS would take all the money in taxes. He said that all cash businesses do this, and since his restaurant was a cash business, he had to take advantage of profit any way he possibly could. When Ernie asked him whether he was afraid of being caught, he told him that he never used numbered customer invoices, so the IRS could not track him down. He also said that he hides profits every possible way he can and even keeps money out of the country. Finally, McCann offered to show Ernie a few things which might impress him and help him understand McCann's position.

McCann took Ernie on a tour. First they went through the restaurant, and then he showed Ernie other properties, including his house, which was magnificent. He even showed Ernie pictures of homes he had in Acapulco, where he intends to retire, and a beautiful estate in Lake Tahoe. He showed Ernie lists of stocks and bonds that he had outside the country and, in general, impressed Ernie with his wealth. "Ernie," he said, "I owe everything to my restaurant and you can have the same thing if you want it." He also informed Ernie that nothing could be traced because he had been careful all during the years. Ernie never thought that he could make so much money, but he resolved that if he took over McCann's business he would not operate in the same manner.

When Ernie discussed the price, McCann stated that the corporation had a book value of $250,000 (after deducting all the liabilities from the assets) and that he felt the goodwill was worth $400,000. McCann said that the business was still growing and Ernie could recoup the goodwill within a few years. Ernie pointed out that while McCann insisted that profits were being made, his accountant found absolutely nothing but losses indicated on the books. McCann invited Ernie to come into his business at the end of each business day for a few weeks and together they would add up the cash and the sales tickets. He even proposed that Ernie take two weeks vacation and work in his place as a chef because he had several chefs who needed vacations. Ernie liked that idea and felt it would give him better insight into the business. McCann said that he would take $350,000 down and finance the balance over five years at prime plus three points. He also suggested that if Ernie would come up with cash he would sell him the business on paper for $350,000 and take $200,000 "under the table" to save Ernie $100,000. Ernie thanked McCann for the information and assured him that everything would remain confidential.

Ernie went home and talked to his wife about what had transpired. While they both felt that McCann was a thief in many respects, they felt his business could be viable, and did not want to dismiss it without thought. Therefore, they both decided to use all their contacts and discreetly find out everything they could about McCann and his business.

Ernie did know one of the chefs at the restaurant personally and felt he could go to him for more exacting information, but decided against it because he promised McCann confidentiality. Instead he and his wife relied on friends and other reliable sources. Over the next week they found that McCann was highly respected in the community. He was associated with several charities and was involved in community affairs. They visited the restaurant quite a few times and each time found it busy. All their contacts came back with the same comments—that the business was solid and appeared to be profitable.

Finally, Ernie took his vacation and went to work as a substitute chef for two weeks. The personnel accepted McCann's substitute and thought that Ernie was just trying to make a few dollars while on vacation. At the end of each day Ernie and McCann went over sales and cash receipts and Ernie went away at the end of two weeks convinced that the business was profitable.

Ernie's accountant was still afraid of the business, and the lawyer felt that since McCann admitted being unethical, they could get hurt. Ernie and his wife agreed with all their comments, but still liked the facts that the business was established, the personnel were experienced, the facilities appeared to be adequate, and the catering business could be developed. Ernie also felt that he could add a few items to the menu to make it more attractive.

The only problem that Ernie had was with the bar. He went to his pastor and asked him to talk to his wife. Belinda agreed to a meeting with Ernie's pastor, whom she liked very much. She was very courteous, but informed him that her religion was not against drinking. She said that she understood and appreciated her husband's religion and respected his beliefs, but that the restaurant was not going to be a drunken saloon, but a respectable establishment. She told him that she did not keep spirits in her own house and certainly did not condone drinking, but that in a public business one must respect other people's values. She told him about the solution she had come up with where she would take care of the bar and keep her husband confined to the kitchen. The pastor finally told Ernie it was now up to him and his wife to make the decision together.

The second restaurant that Dixon showed them, Pancho Villa's Hideaway, was a three-year-old Mexican restaurant which was becoming a very popular restaurant in the area. The cuisine was excellent and the atmosphere and decor were charming. Ernie knew a little about Mexican food and at times prepared some of the more popular dishes. The restaurant did not have a bar. Carlos Mateos, the owner, told them that he had been contemplating getting a liquor licence, but because he was returning to Mexico he did not follow through on it. Carlos' father was terminally ill and he wanted Carlos to return to Durango, Mexico, to take over his business and look after the family. During the three years that Carlos had the business he had become quite a personality and personally greeted people as they came into the restaurant. At times he even appeared on local television urging people to come and try out his authentic Mexican food. Carlos spoke flawless English but with a little accent.

Carlos was very receptive to Ernie's desire to take over the business. He informed Ernie that the business did about $1 million a year in sales and that it was making money. He wanted $300,000 in cash for the business and would not consider financing any part of the sales price. The business did not have any property other than the name, the business itself, and the equipment and fixtures. He had a lease with five years left on it, but the annual rental payments were to be increased each year by 5 percent or the rate of inflation, whichever was higher. He felt that the owner would transfer the new lease and even give Ernie a longer one if he wished. Carlos informed him that he was personally taking $60,000 out of the business plus other household expenses. Ernie sent his accountant around to examine the books, for which he did not have to put up a deposit.

The accountant found the books to be in order, nothing like McCann's. Carlos could account for every penny, and the sales last year, according to the tax statement, were $976,000. The net profit after taxes was $20,000 and Carlos did take $60,000 in compensation out of the business. The business was mainly cash, which amounted to about 50 percent of sales. The balance was credit cards as well as some local clients who kept open accounts. At the present time there was about $24,000 in accounts receivable which were between 60 and 90 days old. Carlos stated that the money was entirely collectible because the clients involved were established firms. The facilities were adequate and parking was sufficient for the present amount of business.

When Ernie discussed the business with Belinda, she felt that it looked like a good opportunity, but that it did not have the potential of McCann's. She pointed out that unless the Mexican restaurant obtained a liquor license, the profits would not be promising. She also pointed out that catering would be minimal since only on rare occasions would people order Mexican food from a caterer. She also pointed out that neither of them spoke Spanish and some of the staff was Hispanic. Ernie stated he could learn a few words from Carlos, but Belinda just glared at him. Ernie stated he felt more comfortable with this business than McCann's because it had no bar, but Belinda felt he was being emotional. Finally, Belinda pointed out that one of the main attractions of the business was Carlos himself. Since he was well-known, when he left, the business might go with him. However, she did think the restaurant might have possibilities.

Dixon, the real estate agent, felt that he could get the price on McCann's Restaurant down to $575,000 and on Pancho Villa's Hideaway by $25,000 to $50,000 if they came up with an immediate offer. Dixon felt both of these restaurants were excellent opportunities and the Yorks could make money at either location.

Finally, Ernie and Belinda sat down with their family to thrash out which business to purchase. Both agreed that the prices were a little high, but hoped that Dixon could get the price down on the one they decided to buy. The entire family agreed that they would abide by the majority decision. After much discussion and argument the family decided to buy McCann's corporation, but only if the price was reduced to $575,000 and if the down payment was reduced to $300,000.

Dixon discussed the matter with McCann, and he agreed to a final price of $600,000, but would accept $300,000 down. Ernie and his wife agreed to McCann's terms. They contacted their attorney to make up the agreement, but found that he was on a 30-day vacation. Dixon recommended another lawyer, but McCann offered to have the agreement prepared by his attorney at no cost to Ernie and his wife. Dixon prepared an offer and used the $50,000 as a deposit, with the balance of $250,000 due in 20 days.

QUESTIONS

1. Do you think that Ernie and his wife made the right decision? Explain.

2. Do you think that Ernie was emotional about the bar? Do you feel moral values should have played a role in this decision?

3. Do you think that Ernie was right to have McCann prepare the agreement?

4. Would you have purchased the corporation? Is there some other way that Ernie could have handled the purchase without incurring any future liability?

5. What terms and conditions would you insist upon before you would sign the agreement?

6. Do you feel Ernie made a good evaluation of the entire business?

7. Are there any other areas you would have explored before you would have agreed to purchase the business?

8. Would you enter into an agreement with a business person who has consistently defrauded the IRS?

9. Do you think that Ernie and his wife will have any personal problems with the business as a result of their differences about the bar?

CASE 7

Love and Care Kennels, Inc.

For some years now Jane Graham has worked for Poodle Heaven Inc., where she feels she has learned everything there is to know about the business. Since she has always loved animals, when the opportunity arose to work in a kennel, Jane jumped at the chance to learn the business from the ground floor. In the beginning she was bitten by a few animals (in spite of her natural ability to handle them), but after instruction and experience she finally learned to handle most animals with ease. Jane is proficient in grooming, bathing, and dipping pets, as well as training, and recommending special diets for them.

Now after seven years of learning Jane wants to start her own kennel. At first she wanted to start a kennel in her own home, but zoning laws would not permit it. So she decided to look for an operating kennel that was for sale, or for a location to start her own kennel. Her husband, George, was very supportive and said that he would give her all the help he could if she got into the business.

Finally, after looking for more than nine months, Jane came across a small kennel located about 15 miles outside of Baton Rouge, Louisiana. The kennel needed some work, but could handle about 50 pets at the present time. The kennel advertised that it had air conditioning and heated deluxe accommodations, but Jane discovered that not all the units were functioning properly. Jane discovered that although the kennel had been around for nearly 15 years, the present owner had only had the business for two years. According to the present owner, Max Latimer, he just could not stand the business anymore and he wants to sell and get out of the business. Jane asked him for the financial facts and he gave her the following information:

	1987	1986
Sales	$35,000	$46,000
Expenses	33,000	43,000
Net profit or loss	$ 2,000	$ 3,000

Latimer was selling the entire corporation for $150,000. The price included not only the kennel facilities, but also a house beside the kennel. In addition, the land amounted to approximately 15 acres. The house was not as nice as the one Jane presently owned, but she felt that it could be remodeled and made into an attractive home. Jane talked to George, and while he did not relish the idea of moving into a new home, he stated that if that was what she wanted, then he would go along with it.

Jane went back to Latimer to inquire further about the business. She asked him what the sales had been for Ella, the owner before him. He told her that when Ella had the business her sales were much higher, but he attributed his problems to lack of helpers and the fact that he was getting older—61 years old. When Jane asked what had happened to Ella, he said she had died and he had purchased the business about four months after. Latimer said that he felt his business was not as good because people missed Ella and so made arrangements with competing kennels.

Jane went to both her accountant and attorney for advice. The accountant, Steve Rossi, felt that there were insufficient facts to make an accurate decision. Jane asked him to prepare a forecast assuming that the 50 units were all operational and that she would be receiving an average of about $8 daily for each unit. Jane told him that the busy months would be January, June, July, August, and December. During these months Jane felt that she should have full occupancy and during the other months she would operate at about one-third occupancy. Steve made up a forecast that indicated sales would be as follows.

Projected Sales for 1987

January	(50 units)	$12,000	July	(50 units)	$12,000
February	(16 units)	3,840	August	(50 units)	12,000
March	(16 units)	3,840	September	(50 units)	3,840
April	(16 units)	3,840	October	(16 units)	3,840
May	(16 units)	3,840	November	(16 units)	3,840
June	(50 units)	12,000	December	(50 units)	12,000

Total estimated sales for twelve months $86,880

Steve felt that the $86,000 figure was much too high based on Latimer's present sales and advised Jane to give herself more time to get the business back on its feet and to establish a good name. He felt that the sales for the first year should be adjusted by at least 30 percent, and, in fact, felt that a 50 percent adjustment would be more realistic. However, Jane told him that she intended to change the name of the business and present a new image to the public. In addition, she said that she intended to advertise and mail to every family who owned a pet an advertisement that would prove to them that the new kennel is better than anything in the area. She intended to call the kennel Love and Care Kennel, with the motto, "If you love your pet, you'll board at Love and Care." Jane stuck to her guns about the forecast, but Steve did get her to accept that even if she did 30 percent less the first year in projected sales, or $60,816, that would represent about a 73 percent increase over what Latimer made last year.

Jane did not intend to take out any salary the first year but instead would use all profits to build up the business. She felt that she would need a couple of helpers during the busy months and one year-round. Jane expected her two biggest expenses to be utilities and pet food. She estimated her overall expenses as follows:

Payroll	$20,626
Payroll taxes @ 12%	2,475
Pet food	11,000
Advertising	5,000
Utilities	6,000
Other supplies	5,000
Miscellaneous	2,500
Estimated total	$52,601

Steve looked over the estimate that Jane had submitted and felt that it was understated and should include another $5,000 for additional start-up expenses, making the total estimated expenses $57,601. In summary, he felt the projections for the first year would be as follows:

Estimated sales (accountant's forecast)	$60,816
Less: estimated expenses	57,601
Estimated net profit before taxes	$ 3,215
Estimated taxes	482
Estimated net after taxes	$ 2,733

Steve pointed out that these figures could vary somewhat, but that it was better to be conservative, especially if she wanted to borrow money from the bank. Jane could see that she had her work cut out for her, but she still felt strongly about the business.

When Jane spoke to her attorney, Ellen Rodgers, she was not as optimistic as Jane. She did not want Jane to buy the corporation, but rather purchase the assets only. Jane informed her that Latimer would only sell the corporation, just as he had to buy it when he took over from Ella. Her attorney pointed out that she could be hit with all sorts of contingencies, if any existed, because when she purchases the stock of a corporation she is buying the past, present, and future of it. Jane did not know this, and told Ellen she would discuss the matter with Latimer. Ellen Rodgers also asked about the reputation of the business as well as its competition. Jane said that as far as she could determine, Latimer's reputation was not good. She further stated that as far as competition went, she visited her two main competitors and they were, in her opinion, not much to worry about. One had facilities for only about 25 pets and provided few services, and the other had facilities for about 35 pets, but seemed to be more interested in breeding than boarding.

Jane went back to her accountant, and they discussed the price that should be paid for the business and the property. Steve had a friend in the real estate business examine the real estate. In a "curbside" appraisal he estimated that the property and acreage were worth approximately $100,000. He did not give an estimate for the business. Based on this estimate, Latimer was selling his other business assets for $50,000. Steve did not feel that the business was worth this amount because the average earnings over the last two years were $2,500 per year and sales were decreasing rather than increasing. He felt that much of the goodwill Ella had built up was lost and that Jane was going to have to work hard to get the business back into condition. Also, the business would have to be remodeled so that the air conditioning and heating would be in 100 percent working condition and the house which they would be moving into would also need work.

Jane told Steve that Latimer insisted on selling the stock of the business and would not sell just the assets. Steve felt that she should purchase assets only and avoid the corporation because there were too many unknowns. Steve told her that she would be better off starting a new business of her own from scratch. Jane ignored the advice and asked him what price she should offer for the company if Latimer would not sell assets, but insisted upon selling the entire corporation. Steve did not want to even quote a price and told her that if she must buy the business, she should not pay more than $80,000 for the entire business and then she should make certain that the owner held back part of the total purchase price for unknown contingencies. Steve suggested that Jane offer him $40,000 down and the balance over a period of five years with interest based on the current prime rate plus one percentage point. Steve also told her that he could not understand why Latimer did not have all the records from Ella since that was part of the corporation. He said that if he could see them, it would shed more light on the overall business. Steve pointed out that she might need them later if a tax audit was conducted by the IRS. Finally, Steve pleaded with Jane to be careful and not be so anxious to get this business since there were others around. Steve offered, as had her attorney, to visit Latimer to finalize the purchase, but Jane felt she could handle it on her own.

Jane went to see Latimer and told him that her attorney and accountant both told her that she would be better off and more secure if she purchased assets only and not the stock of the corporation. Latimer swore that there was nothing to worry about and that she was buying a clean business. Jane offered him $80,000 for the entire business with $40,000 down and the balance over a five-year period. Latimer laughed at her and stated that he could get a mortgage on just the property for $100,000 and he would not sell the business for less than $150,000. After much discussion, Jane increased her price to $125,000 and offered $50,000 down with the balance to be paid off over five years with the interest tied to current prime plus 1 percent. Latimer stated he would think it over and get back to her within a few days.

A few days later Latimer called Jane and told her he would take the offer of $125,000, but that he wanted $100,000 down and would take a note for two years at the current prime rate plus 2 percentage points. Jane said that she would get back to him within a few days.

Jane talked the matter over with her husband. They had approximately $60,000 in cash and had been told by the local savings and loan that they could get an equity loan on their house which would give her an additional $50,000. Jane and George talked about the fact that they would have to move and all the inconveniences that it would cause, but George again reiterated that if Jane felt it would make her happy and that if the accountant and her attorney were all agreeable, he would be glad to make the move with her. Jane called her attorney, and Ellen was not too happy with the entire agreement. However, she told her that she would make up the agreement and would carefully check everything out to see if there were any liens or lawsuits pending. In addition, Ellen stated that this would be a bulk sales agreement and come under the Bulk Transfer Act of the Uniform Commercial Code.

Jane contacted Latimer and gave him a deposit, but pointed out that he would be responsible for any unknown contingencies that came up. Jane also decided to ask Latimer to repair all the heating and air conditioning units. Jane asked Latimer to see that each unit was repaired with a one-year warranty on all the equipment. Latimer agreed to give her only a 30-day warranty. Jane accepted this since she did not even expect to get the units repaired. Latimer also agreed to be responsible for any unknown contingencies that might come up.

In accordance with the Bulk Transfer Act, Latimer submitted a list of all the creditors and the amount owed to each one. Jane's attorney wanted this list so that each creditor could be warned of the impending sale of the business. The seller signed the list and it was recorded with the county clerk. Each creditor was notified by certified mail.

Two weeks after all of this had been accomplished, the closing took place. Latimer agreed to the covenant that he would be responsible for any unknown contingencies for a period of one year and a covenant not to compete. In addition, he further agreed to the warranty on the equipment for a period of 30 days at no cost to Jane.

After the closing Jane took over the business, put her own house up for sale, and immediately started advertising. The entire facility was cleaned up— walls were repainted and enclosures were fixed. In general, Jane did an excellent job making the facility into an impeccably clean and attractive kennel that would appeal to all pet lovers who wanted their pets given the best of love and care. Jane managed to get a list from city hall of all the pet owners in the county and also purchased outdoor advertising on several major traffic areas. Within a few months business began to come in and sales started to increase. In September, which is ordinarily not one of the best months for kennels, sales amounted to $5,000 and her appointments for October pointed to a much better month than projected. Jane was bothered by the number of complaints that she received from pet owners who used to bring their animals to the kennel when Latimer had the business. They complained that their pets were not fed properly, and some even stated that it seemed their pets were mistreated. Jane promised them the best treatment and within a short time the word started getting around that her kennel was the best in the area.

Just as things started going well, an agent from the IRS came to the office in response to a letter from Jane's attorney asking for a tax clearance for the company. Jane was very cooperative, and the agent worked on the books for more than a week. He asked for Ella's books, and Jane informed him that Latimer had indicated he did not have them. The agent stated that he would return, but gave no indication that there was anything wrong. However, within a few weeks the agent came back and stated that according to the bank records for Latimer and Ella, which covered a period of three years, there was a difference between deposits made and total revenue reported on the income tax return. The breakdown was as follows.

	Deposits per bank	Reported as revenue tax returns	Difference
1986	$55,000	$35,000	$20,000
1985	64,500	46,000	18,500
1983	75,000	70,000	5,000
Total unreported receipts			$43,500

The agent was extremely cooperative and tried to be of assistance to Jane. He needed an explanation of the difference between deposits and the amount reported as total revenue on each yearly income tax return. Jane could not answer his questions and said that she would get in touch with the former owner to see if he could explain the difference. The agent left, saying he would wait for her call.

On top of this confusion, during the first month the air conditioning units kept breaking down. Latimer sent over a "patchwork" mechanic who managed to get the units running, but all the mechanic really did was keep the units running (not centrally controlled) until the 30-day warranty had expired.

Then, Jane received by mail notification that a former client was suing the corporation for $10,000 because his pet dog Bumpers had died two weeks after being picked up from a 30-day stay. The owners were claiming Bumpers was the object of cruel treatment and physical abuse. Jane contacted the man's attorney and told him that she was the new owner and knew nothing about the matter. Jane also asked why the owners of the pet waited so long before filing suit. The lawyer explained that the suit was perfectly legal because she was the owner of the same corporation and, while he was sorry that it was happening to her rather than Latimer, he could do nothing about it. He also stated that his clients were within their rights to file suit since the time period to sue had not lapsed.

To make matters worse, one of the former employees was filing suit for $450 back wages never paid by Latimer. Jane was now quite depressed. She called her attorney and they met to discuss the problems. Jane told Ellen, "I know what a fool I was to jump into the business and not follow your advice." Jane told her she had contacted Latimer and he told her that he could not account for any differences between deposits and the amount he reported on the tax returns for the corporation. He insisted that he reported every penny that was due. As for the lawsuit concerning Bumpers, Latimer said that that client was a pain in the neck, and his dog was old and did not die as a result of being in the kennel. With respect to the employee who was claiming Latimer owed him money, Latimer stated that he did not owe him any money because the employee did not show up for work and he would testify in court that the employee was a liar. Ellen said that she would do all she could to help Jane out of the problems she inherited.

Jane contacted the IRS agent and explained that the former owner could not explain the difference between the deposits and the revenue reported. The agent was very helpful, but informed her that they must consider the entire amount of $43,500 as income and she would be obliged to pay the tax and penalties on that amount. The agent calculated the taxes owing as well as penalties and told Jane she would have to pay a total of $42,000. Jane nearly fainted and immediately called her attorney. Her lawyer set up an appointment with the IRS agent at his office. Jane's attorney, who was also a tax expert, met with the IRS agent at his office and methodically explained the situation and the fact that the new owner obviously was not trying to avoid taxes because she had requested the tax clearance. The IRS agent was receptive to Ellen's pleas and he finally negotiated a settlement of $26,100, which the IRS would accept for those years for the areas investigated. Ellen agreed to the settlement and informed Jane what she had to pay. Jane was pleased but still shaken by the fact that she would have to come up with the $26,100. Ellen pointed out that at least she still owed Latimer $25,000 on the purchase and she would charge the taxes against the note. Ellen sent Latimer a letter informing him of the tax liability and that Jane had to pay the back taxes. Latimer's attorney immediately replied that he did not feel his client owed anything and that the entire matter was handled improperly. He said his client still expected the $25,000 to be paid when due. Latimer's attorney also stated that even if it was proved he did owe that amount, Latimer was broke and did not have any money left from the sale. Ellen knew it would come down to a battle to recover anything from Latimer as a result of contingencies. She started the battle to try to get the money over and above the $25,000 note from Latimer. But she knew what would be coming down the road— "nothing in the bank, no assets, and possibly an offer of a partial settlement for the amounts owed, or sue me, wait, and pay lots of legal bills."

Just when Jane thought she had heard everything, she received an invoice by certified mail indicating that Latimer owed $4,000 for reconditioning the heating system and air conditioning. The payment was more than 15 months overdue. Jane called Latimer, and he informed her that he did not owe anything and that he had settled in full with the people who fixed the units. He told her that when they gave him the original bill he protested and they agreed they would accept $4,625 for the entire bill. They had deducted $4,000 from the total invoice and Latimer paid them in cash. Jane could not find an invoice or receipt. Jane contacted her attorney and was told that Latimer was liable for the debt, for under the Bulk Transfer Act the Statute of Limitations on Bulk Transfer is six months from closing.

Jane managed to come up with the tax money only because she and her husband had sold their house and they had some money left over. However, she was still in the hole and just when she needed the support of her husband the most he was complaining about the howling and barking that seemed to take place every night. As a consequence, George was upset with the business, and both of them were wondering what would come up next. They were worried that former clients might continue to come back and try to get even for whatever Latimer or Ella might have done in the past.

Jane was sorry she had gotten into this mess, but tried to concentrate on the business. However, every time a person called or walked in without a pet, she expected to be served with a summons or another lawsuit.

QUESTIONS

1. Why do you think Jane jumped into this business and ignored the advice she was given by her attorney and accountant?

2. Do you think her husband should have played a more dominant role in the business venture? Do you think Jane was ready to start her own business?

3. Do you feel that Jane should have started her own business instead of going into an existing business?

4. Would you have purchased the business if Latimer was willing to sell just the assets and not the corporation? Why do you think Latimer insisted on selling the entire corporation?

5. Were there any indicators that Latimer did not have a solid business? Do you think Jane's accountant and lawyer did everything they could to keep Jane from buying the business?

6. If you were the accountant or the attorney and Jane had insisted upon purchasing the corporation, what would you have insisted upon to give Jane more protection?

7. Do you think that Jane should sell the business because her husband is complaining?

8. What lesson did you learn from this case which will help you if your purchase your own business in the future?

Zachary's Pharmacy

Tom and Dale Clark have lived in a small town about 25 miles outside of Omaha, Nebraska, and had been looking for a drugstore to purchase for about six months. Finally, they saw an advertisement in one of the Omaha newspapers that described just what they were looking for. The advertisement was placed under the section headed "Business Opportunities" and read as follows.

SUCCESSFUL DRUGSTORE FOR SALE

A LOCAL DRUGSTORE THAT IS WELL-ESTABLISHED AND HAS AN ENVIABLE RECORD OF SALES AND PROFITS IS NOW FOR PRIVATE SALE. RETURN ON NET INVESTMENT WILL RANGE AROUND 20% MINIMUM. PRICED RIGHT FOR IMMEDIATE SALE, TERMS MIGHT BE CONSIDERED. SEND REPLY TO BOX 123, OMAHA, NEBRASKA.

Tom immediately sent a letter to the box number and promptly heard from a man who said he was Jimmy Travis, the owner of Zachary's Pharmacy. Tom listened while Travis gave him more of the details about the company, and then he inquired about the company's annual sales, profits, and expenses. Tom had heard about Zachary's and was surprised that such a well-established and successful firm would be for sale. Travis said that he would like to ask Tom a few questions to determine if he was a qualified buyer, and if so he would be glad to set up an interview and hopefully start things moving toward a successful conclusion. He told Tom that the net worth of the business was around $350,000, which included considerable inventory, furniture and fixtures, and other assets that could be easily verified. He also said that the building was leased for $2,500 monthly, and that the lease had five years remaining and was transferable. He said that the sales price was $500,000, and that the only reason he was not asking more was because his wife was terminally ill and he wanted to sell the business quickly and spend as much time as he could with her. He asked Tom if he had the financial resources to invest that amount of money. Tom told him that he could raise $300,000 within a few days, but he would need 10 days to raise another $75,000, and that this was the total investment he could make. Tom asked about the terms and Travis stated that if Tom's credit background was clean he would be glad to hold a note for the balance over a period of 5 to 10 years if necessary. Tom asked about the books, and Travis told him that he would bring everything with him for the first interview. He also said he would bring financial statements for the last three years plus a current up-to-date statement. Tom agreed, and Travis stated that he would like to meet Tom the next night at the Carson Club, which Tom knew to be an exclusive restaurant.

Travis asked Tom to keep the interview as well as the fact that the business was for sale strictly confidential. Travis said he did not want his employees, bankers, or suppliers to become aware of the sale until it was consummated. Tom understood and agreed to the stipulation, and said that he and his wife, Dale, would be at the Carson Club the next night.

Tom and Dale both felt that this sounded like the opportunity they had been dreaming about for such a long time. Dale was a pharmacist and would handle that end of the business; Tom would handle the administrative area. Both were college graduates and had experience in the field.

The following night Tom and Dale went to the Carson Club. When they asked for Mr. Travis, they were escorted to a private room just off the main area. Travis was an extremely charming man, conservatively dressed, of average height, with a small goatee and gray hair. Tom and Dale were not used to surroundings like this private club and so naturally were quite nervous. Travis sensed this and immediately put them at ease with some small talk, asking them where they were from and how much they knew about Omaha and, in particular, Zachary's. Travis was a little surprised when he found out Tom did have some knowledge of Zachary's. After they exhausted those subjects, Travis then talked about his own days on a farm in Fremont, Nebraska. He talked about how he nearly ruined his father's tractor and how his father gave up on him and told him that he should stay out of farming. Tom and Dale slowly started to feel more at ease. After the order was taken, Tom was surprised to find out that Travis did not drink and that they had a lot in common. Finally, after dinner they decided it was time to discuss business. Travis took them over to another table and presented them with a complete array of books, ledgers, journals, and statements that would tell Tom anything he would ever need to know. Tom found that the books were impeccably clean, and he had no doubts that this business was being run in a proper manner. After Travis was certain that Tom was satisfied and wanted to buy the business, he suggested the following procedure to Tom.

1. Tom should have his accountant confidentially scrutinize all the books and records of the company. The records had to be returned in three days. If the accountant had any questions he could call Travis at the store after 7 P.M. any night that week. Travis stated that he did not want to talk during the day because he feared that someone in the business might hear the conversation.

2. Tom should visit the store as often as possible and ask friends and others about the business. However, Tom should be sure that he did not discuss Travis' wife's ill health or divulge that the business was for sale. Travis also would not engage in any conversation with them when Tom and his wife visited the store. Travis was quite adamant about this point and insisted on Tom and Dale's assurance that no conversation would take place. They both

assured him that they would be very cautious. Travis stated that he had too much to lose and he had to be careful.

3. If Tom felt that he wanted to purchase the business, then Travis wanted a check for $150,000 as a deposit, which would of course be refundable if Tom could not raise the additional funds.

4. Finally, either Tom or Travis would have a purchase agreement prepared for final signature within two weeks from the present date. Since Tom did not have a lawyer in Omaha, he asked Travis if he would mind having his attorney prepare the agreement. Travis promptly agreed and stated that the agreement would be ready to examine three days after he received the deposit from Tom. Travis also pointed out that if Tom wanted any changes in the agreement, he would be glad to consider them. However, he pointed out the best time to talk would be after 7 P.M.

A few days after the first meeting the accountant informed Tom that the books were in excellent condition and recommended the purchase of the business based on the figures he had examined. Tom promptly gave Travis a certified check for $150,000. Tom told Travis that his bank would have the additional money he needed within a week. Travis was very pleased and said he would have his attorney prepare the buy/sell agreement immediately. Travis and Tom agreed that the settlement would take place in Travis' attorney's office the following Tuesday at 12:30 P.M. At that time Tom would give Travis a $225,000 certified check and Travis would accept a promissory note for $125,000 payable in annual installments with the interest rate based on prime rate plus 2 percent for the term of 10 years.

Travis had the agreement prepared and had a copy forwarded to Tom. Tom went to a local attorney and examined all the documents. The attorney, Harry Seuss, suggested some changes and Tom agreed to take care of them. Seuss advised Tom that he should be represented even if by some other lawyer, but Tom felt the transaction was clean and that he could handle the closing. The sale was being made under the Bulk Sales Provision of the Uniform Commercial Code, and Travis was to submit a list of all creditors before settlement as prescribed under the Uniform Commercial Code with copies of letters to be forwarded to each of them warning them of the impending sale. Travis also had a letter from the landlord agreeing to transfer the lease to the new owner. Finally, Travis agreed to a noncompetitive clause and agreed to allow Tom to use the present company name. After the list of creditors was given to Tom, Travis stated he would take care of the mailing.

When Tom and Dale arrived at Travis's legal office on settlement day, they found a smiling Travis waiting for them in the sitting room. Travis told them the receptionist was at lunch, but the attorney, Diane Webster, would be with them in a moment. After a few minutes Ms. Webster came in and took them to a closing room. All the papers were signed and the checks were given to Travis. It was agreed that since it was Tuesday, Monday would be the best day for Tom and Dale to officially take over the business. Travis wanted to explain what had happened to his employees and make certain they would remain. It was agreed that all sales made from the settlement date through Sunday would go to Tom and Dale. Tom thought it made sense and agreed. After closing, Travis gave Tom the keys and everyone wished everybody good luck.

Tom and Dale opened up the doors to the business early Monday morning. They started to acquaint themselves with the business and waited for Mr. Travis to arrive shortly to introduce them to all the personnel. The employees started to arrive, all indicating surprise and shock when they found Tom and Dale behind the counter. Finally, one of the employees asked who they were. Tom declared, "Why, we are the new owners of the business; I'm sure that Mr. Travis has already informed you we purchased the business and we are taking over as of today." The employees looked at one another and said that Travis never mentioned a thing, but he would be coming in shortly with his wife. In the meantime they introduced themselves and started trying to answer all the questions Tom and Dale had about the business. Finally, Travis and his wife showed up and when one of the employees said, "Well, here are Mr. and Mrs. Travis," Tom and Dale could have fallen through the floor. The man they were looking at was not the Mr. Travis they had dealt with and Mrs. Travis certainly did not look like she was suffering from ill health. When Travis asked what they were doing in his store, Tom and Dale told them the entire story. When they finished, Dale and Tom were in shock. Travis called the police and when they arrived Travis asked them to confirm his identity as the owner of the store. The police then proceeded to get all the details of the obvious "con job."

The police checked out the description of the impostor who posed as Mr. Travis. He turned out to be Horace Pepper, a man who worked for the real Mr. Travis selling over-the-counter products and performing odd jobs for the last two months. Pepper also opened the door in the morning at 7 A.M. and had access to books, records, and other financial data which were kept in the office in back of the store. The police immediately started investigating the case and traced Tom and Dale's canceled checks to an account that was opened up a month ago in Denver, Colorado, under the name James Travis. Further investigation showed that the account did have deposits recorded for the two checks, but the account was now closed. They checked Mr. Travis' attorney's law office, which was a legitimate office, and discovered that the imposter whom they were now able to positively identify was Marcel Duval, also known as "Jake the Fake." Duvall had come into the office with a young woman and asked the receptionist if he could use one of the closing offices for a few minutes on behalf of Mr. Travis. The receptionist agreed because she knew that Mr. Travis was a client of the firm. However, she left for lunch and told them which office they could use. Just before Tom and Dale had arrived Duvall's female accomplice stepped into another office and then within two or three minutes came out and assumed the role of Travis' attorney. As of today the police have not been able to locate Marcel Duvall or his accomplice, and Tom and Dale have lost $375,000.

1. How can you protect yourself against con artists such as "Jake the Fake"? How can you be certain you are dealing with the real owner?

2. What mistakes did Tom and Dale make in this case? How should they have approached this purchase from the beginning?

3. Although the Bulk Sales provision of the Uniform Commercial Code was mentioned in the agreement, was it handled properly or used as it was meant to be? If Tom and Dale had their attorney represent them, do you think they would have been swindled? At which point in the purchase should an attorney have been employed to represent Tom and Dale?

4. Does the accountant have any responsibility in this case?

5. Does the real Mr. Travis have any responsibility in this case since Marcel Duvall was a full-time employee?

6. What other lessons did you learn from this case?

CASE 9

M.M. Advertising Sign Company

Owen Zeno has been employed by the M.M. Sign Company for the last 10 years. During that period he has worked in every department in the organization with the exception of accounting. Owen is considered an outstanding salesperson and has a special talent for designing signs. This talent has made him highly valued by the company. Clients in Orlando, Florida, have a great deal of respect for Owen and when they need something spectacular in the way of signs they call Owen and ask him to design something that will really stand out. Owen has always wanted his own business, but never had the money to invest in starting one.

One day Michael Martz, the owner of the sign company, died and his wife Margaret came into the company and tried to take over. She was only 28 years old and had only been married to Michael for about two years. However, in spite of her attempts to get the business moving as it used to under her husband, things got worse because she did not know the business. Within a few months sales dropped and the cash position deteriorated. She started relying more on Owen each day and finally offered to sell the business to Owen if he wanted to buy it. Owen told her he was genuinely interested, but he would have to talk it over with his wife and her family. His wife, Helen, came from a wealthy family. Her parents never really liked Owen, but put up with him to stay close to their daughter and grandchildren. Owen thought they might buy the business so he could keep his job.

The financial position of the company before Margaret took over was as follows.

Sales	$6,000,000	100%
Cost of sales	4,200,000	70%
Gross profit	$1,800,000	30%
Expenses	1,320,000	22%
Net profit	480,000	8%
*Taxes @ 34% average	163,200	3
Net after taxes	316,800	5%

*Rate is based on new tax scale of the 1986 Reform Act as it would apply in 1988.

The balance sheet for the same period was as follows.

Cash	$ 80,000
Accounts receivable	750,000
Notes receivable	30,000
Inventory	500,000
Other current	150,000
TOTAL CURRENT	$1,510,000
FIXED ASSETS	350,000
OTHER FIXED ASSETS	400,000
TOTAL ASSETS	$2,260,000
Accounts payable	$ 400,000
Bank loans	100,000
Notes payable	120,000
Other current	350,000
TOTAL CURRENT	$ 970,000
LONG-TERM LIABILITIES	400,000
DEFERRED CREDITS	20,000
NET WORTH	870,000
TOTAL LIABILITIES & NET WORTH	$2,260,000

Margaret said she would sell the business to Owen for $1 million and would accept terms, if necessary, for some of the purchase price. She told him that she did not know where to turn and she was afraid that if she remained in the business she would destroy her husband's dream.

Owen told his wife about this opportunity to own his own business. He informed her that if he did not buy the company he would probably lose his job because the company was on its way to going under. Helen was very concerned and called her father, who said he would talk to Owen about the matter. When Owen went to meet with his father-in-law, Clyde, he was quite nervous because of the resentment Clyde had for him. The fact that Owen was making $75,000 a year did not impress Clyde. He looked at the business and agreed that it had promise and could no doubt be developed. However, he was extremely candid in stating that he felt that Owen was not management material and, in his opinion, did not have the ability to successfully run the business. He said he admired Owen's ability to sell products, but that running a business was much different than selling to a client. Owen admitted that he had never managed a company, but felt he could do the job. Clyde agreed to consider buying the business under the following conditions.

1. That the business be purchased at the audited book value as determined by his auditors, who were reliable and established C.P.A.s. He would then only offer Margaret 75 percent of the determined book value of the firm.

2. If Margaret agreed to that figure he would pay her 25 percent down and then the balance over a five-year period in notes maturing each year with interest based on New York prime plus 1 percent.

3. Margaret must guarantee any unknown contingencies for a period of two years. If said contingencies should arise they would have to be paid immediately by her and not the firm. For example if he had to pay $250,000 today for a back tax delinquency, it could destroy his present cash position. Therefore, he insisted that any unknown contingencies that did arise and which the company would be responsible for would be paid by Margaret when due. He would see that she was properly notified of any such problems and would work with her attorneys so that everything possible would be done to eliminate the contingency or reduce the amount.

4. Clyde would appoint his own general manager and Owen would report to him. Owen would have the same position as he has now except that he would be elevated to the position of vice-president and made a director of the firm with Clyde as chairman and his daughter as one of the five directors.

5. Seventy-five percent of the stock would be in his daughter's name, and Owen would be given 25 percent of the stock in his own. Clyde would vote his daughter's stock for her.

6. If Owen left the company or divorced or separated from his wife he would be obliged to sell all his stock to the corporation at the book value of his stock as determined by auditors selected by the firm.

Owen went back to Margaret and made the proposal. It was not what she expected, but she agreed to the terms because she wanted out of the business. The auditors came in and made a complete audit, which also was approved by Margaret's own auditors. The new book value of the stock was $500,000, and, based on 75 percent of the book value purchase price, Margaret would receive a total of $375,000. Clyde had agreed to pay her a total down payment of $93,750 with the balance of $281,250 to be paid in five equal installments of $56,250 plus interest at New York prime plus 1 percent. Margaret was not at all happy with the deal and felt the business was worth more. Clyde, who was handling the negotiations, was quite abrasive and told her, "From what I know about you I would suggest you take the money and run, since before you met Martz you never had it so good." Margaret was furious, but had no choice. She reluctantly made the deal and the business was now in the hands of Owen and his wife's family.

Clyde's general manager was not experienced in the business and started to make drastic changes. First of all, he wanted a 50 percent deposit on all sign orders and insisted that receivables be paid within 30 days. This was contrary to what competitors were granting, and the company got countless complaints from regular clients. As a result, orders decreased drastically and Clyde was quite alarmed. Then the company was served with papers indicating that some children were seriously hurt by a sign that had fallen apart. The welds in certain parts of the sign were not strong enough, and the falling pieces injured several children who were playing near the sign. The company had insurance, but the amount awarded to the children was $400,000 over the amount of insurance coverage the company carried. During the lawsuit Clyde had his attorneys work with Margaret's lawyers so he knew that the suit had been handled properly and effectively. Clyde demanded the money from Margaret, but she said she did not have the money. Clyde then canceled all the notes and sued her for the difference. If Clyde could collect then he would not have to pay the notes of $281,250 and Margaret would pay the sum of $118,750. Margaret just could not believe that this was happening to her. She had experience buying a small business of her own years ago but no experience selling one, and this was a lesson she would never forget.

In the meantime, the general manager quit the firm and Clyde decided to appoint Owen to this position. Owen immediately went back to not requiring deposits from reliable and established firms and granting them the same type of terms that others in the field were extending.

Owen also thought the business should be expanded. He wanted to start securing sites for erecting signs and renting the space to people who wanted advertising space. He would manufacture the basic sign or billboard and lease the space from the owners of the land for a period of years with options to renew. He decided to go ahead with the expansion without discussing it with Clyde. Finally, the company had arranged for 200 sites at a monthly cost to it of $10,000. The signs would cost him around $100,000 to make. Each location could be rented out from $75 to $150 per month. Owen estimated that if they operated at 100 percent occupancy the total rentals would amount to $25,000 a month. Clyde was furious when he found out that Owen went ahead with this venture without consulting him. He would have fired Owen, but he did not have anyone else to take his place. He also complained about the receivables and the increasing inventory of materials. He said that if things kept up, the business would require more funding or investments. Clyde told him that the bank would finance the receivables and inventory if necessary; however, Clyde, who was from the old school, said this was out of the question. He wanted the company back on a solid cash footing and wanted something done about receivables. He also wanted the new venture into advertising sites for rental stopped as soon as the leases expired.

Owens knew that he had an excellent business, and has about $150,000 of his own money. He is thinking that maybe it is time to call Clyde's bluff and force him to stay in the new venture, or to quit the company and start his own business of renting advertising space.

QUESTIONS

1. If you were in Owen's position, do you think you could have found a way to purchase the business under the conditions outlined by Clyde without using Clyde's money?

2. Do you feel that Clyde treated Margaret fairly? Do you feel that Clyde was unethical when he bought the business as cheaply as he did?

3. What could Margaret have done to sell the business more profitably? If you were advising her, how would you have handled the business at the time of her husband's death?

4. When you sell a business, what procedure or methodology should you follow to get the best price and the best conditions? What mistakes were made in this sale?

5. Do you think Owen should have accepted Clyde's terms and conditions? What could Owen

have done to make his situation better? What counterproposal would you have made to Clyde?

6. When the general manager left and Owen decided to enter the new venture, do you think he should have discussed it with Clyde? Do you think that Clyde would have been more willing to accept such a proposal if a proper business plan had been offered for his approval? Outline the type of plan you would have presented.

7. Do you think that Owen should have called Clyde's bluff and told him to get off his back or he will quit? What do you think Clyde would do if Owen made such a threat?

8. If Owen does go into his own business do you think he will be successful?

CASE 10

Fuller's Supermarket

Bob Fuller owns and operates a little supermarket just outside of Philadelphia, Pennsylvania. He started the business more than 20 years ago as a small vegetable stand and, through his aggressiveness, gradually built the company up to the point where its sales are now about $2 million a year. Earnings after taxes amount to 3 percent of sales and Bob takes a salary of $50,000 per year out of the business. Bob has been making money for years, and he has reached a point in his life where he is content and feels he has accomplished something. He knows all the local bankers and other business people in the community and has an excellent reputation. Bob remembers a time when he was considered a nobody and couldn't even get a banker to give him the time of day. But now that he is very successful everyone is friendly and constantly offering him money that he now doesn't need, but which he could have used years ago when he was beginning the business.

Bob has a problem with his son, Damon. Damon is not satisfied with the way his father has operated the company. He feels that the business should have been expanded years ago or that his father should have sold the company and bought another larger one in a bigger marketing area. Bob did not agree with his son and after many arguments Damon finally quit the firm and went to work for a food company in Philadelphia. Needless to say, Bob and his wife, Susan, have been quite upset that their only son walked out of the house and refused to return unless his father met his demands. Finally, after more than a year and much persuasion from Susan, Bob agreed to talk to Damon and explore possible business arrangements to get Damon permanently back into the family.

A week later, Damon and Bob met for the first time in a year and it was obvious to Bob that while Damon wanted to come back, it was only going to be under his terms. Damon proposed that his father sell his present market and purchase another much larger supermarket with about 50,000 square feet and the capability of doing around $12 million in sales per year. Damon had the business in mind and said that it could be purchased for $800,000. Damon was somewhat abrasive and blunt when he discussed his proposal with his father. Bob got the feeling he had the choice to either take this proposal or lose a son. However, because Bob promised Susan he would do everything he could to get Damon back into the family and because he really loved his son, he decided to explore the proposal. Bob was not thrilled with his son's attitude, but he knew Damon was intelligent and knew the business. When Bob could get a few words in, he did find that Damon had done his homework and had the business' financial and tax statements for the past three years. In addition, Damon had layouts of the premises and other information, which Bob found very useful. The terms of the sale were as follows.

Sales price	$800,000
Down payment	400,000
Balance at closing	$400,000*

*The balance could be financed over a period of five years providing the buyer's credit is acceptable and the buyer provides a personal guarantee that is jointly and severally signed by both husband and wife.

Sales for the last three years were as follows:

	1986	*1985*	*1984*
Sales (net)	$8,500,000	$9,000,000	$10,000,000
Gross profit	1,785,000	1,890,000	2,163,000
Net profit after taxes	(250,000)	(160,000)	113,300

Bob had his accountant examine all the statements, and he informed Bob that the business was about average—in other words, he felt that it was well-managed and that the expenses were not especially out of line. He stated that, in his opinion, since the company was a large independent store it could not compete with the large chains in the same marketing area, and thus could not make money. When Bob conveyed this information to his son, Damon said he thought the problem with the business was poor marketing and that, in his opinion, better cost control would help the company be more competitive. Also, he felt that if his father invested sufficient cash into the business he could buy in large quantities from "cash-and-carry" wholesalers and increase the gross profit. Bob did not necessarily agree with his son, but decided to visit the store, examine the facilities, and talk with the owner.

Bob was very impressed with the facilities and felt that the place was well laid out and appeared to be operating very efficiently. Further, when Bob spoke to the owner, Frank Gerk, he was impressed with his knowledge of the business and especially with his comments regarding the problems he was having with his business. Gerk came right out and said that the problem was that his store could not compete with the "big boys." He could not match the money they spent on advertising and promotion, and could not buy as cheaply as they did. He felt that if the business were taken over by an aggressive person who knew the business and who would perhaps add additional profit centers such as a bakery, a well-stocked deli, and ethnic foods areas, which the big chains were too busy to handle, perhaps the company could make money. He also felt that the company needed a large steady infusion of money to take advantage of quantity cash purchases on various products that come along from time to time. (Manufacturers who offer large cash discounts on overstocked items.) Gerk was very honest and answered all the questions that Bob and Damon asked. He said he honestly felt that a lot of money could be made with the business if the new owner had the necessary cash or credit to handle the business.

Damon was very enthused about the business and felt he could make a tremendous success out of it. Bob was not as certain as his son because he felt that it would involve taking a great risk, and he did not think he would have sufficient capital to handle the entire transaction. After their meeting with Gerk, both Bob and Damon visited the other two large chain operations in the area. They were slightly larger than Gerk's and they followed traditional lines of merchandising. Neither of them had a bakery or deli, and only one carried a small stock of ethnic foods. Both supermarkets stuck mainly to products that were staple items. Damon pointed this out to his father and said that if they carried delicacies and other specialties the other stores were not carrying, they could attract a great deal of customers. Bob agreed with him and felt that his son had a good point, but considered the entire deal to be a risk he would not like to take.

Damon agreed that this venture needed more thought, and they agreed to work together toward a sound decision. Bob was not enthusiastic and expressed his doubts to his wife, but Susan felt that maybe her son was onto something and she pleaded with her husband to do everything he could to bring him back into the family again. Bob assured her he would do all he could, and, after talking to his accountant and banker, came up with the following alternatives.

1. He could sell his business, which had a net worth of $300,000. Bob felt that based on earnings his business was worth at least $400,000 because the building was well located and sound, and the goodwill was certainly evident because of the earnings record. However, he would have to find a buyer and perhaps pay a real estate agent. He felt that after all the legal fees and commissions were deducted, he would end up with $350,000.

2. He could keep his business. Then the bank would lend him the $400,000 he needed as a down payment on the new business and he could keep the present business going. The present business would be able to pay off the loan payments on the new business. The bank wanted a personal guarantee plus first liens on all properties owned.

3. He could get the present owner of the business, Gerk, to finance the balance of $400,000 over a five-year period at the current prime rate plus 2 percent and adjust the interest rate annually. The latter financial proposal would mean payments of $80,000 per year on principal without interest. Breaking it down further, Bob was looking at roughly $6,700 per month just for the principal without interest.

Bob was worried most about obtaining working capital. While he could get sufficient funding for the purchase of the business, he still needed $250,000 in working capital to make the necessary changes in the new store and increase inventory to the desired level. He talked to the suppliers, who all knew him, and they offered to give him 30 days' credit in the new operation. The suppliers' credit line would help, but not solve Bob's problem. Bob talked to his friends who were bankers and none of them would give the additional $250,000 he needed for the working capital. As a matter of fact, two bankers felt that the entire purchase was absurd since Bob had a good business that was making money. They felt that because the supermarket business was highly competitive and the new business was losing money, the whole venture was a bad idea. They pointed out to Bob that he was risking too much and could lose everything. Privately, Bob had similar reservations, but he promised Susan he would do everything in his power to get their son back, even if he lost everything.

Because the working capital loan was denied, Bob decided to sell his own business and net at least $350,000 from the sale. He would use the $350,000 as a down payment on the business and ask Gerk to finance the $450,000 balance. He could then go back to his bankers and borrow the $250,000 they would give him on his home and other assets. The $250,000 would take care of the working capital problem. As of this moment the purchase would be handled as follows:

Purchase price of the new business	$800,000
Down payment from sale of Bob's business (net)	$350,000
Note to be held by Gerk on the purchase of the business	450,000
	$800,000
Working capital loan on personal assets	$250,000

Bob had a long talk with Susan and Damon about the risks involved. He explained that they stood a good chance of losing everything if the new business did not succeed. In spite of Bob's comments Susan and Damon felt enthusiastic and were even more certain that the new business would be a tremendous success. As a result of the group decision, Bob decided to go ahead and buy the business. However, before he did, Damon wanted to make it clear that he was going to run the operation since he had more experience in large city operations than his father did. Further, he expected his father to be there to help him if he needed assistance. Reluctantly Bob approved of the idea.

Bob spoke to Gerk about the estimated $350,000 down payment and financing the $450,000 balance. Gerk agreed to the deal and said that he would finance the balance over a five-year period with the interest rate based on the prime rate plus 2 percent. The interest rate would be adjusted annually. Bob gave Gerk a deposit of $25,000 and signed an Offer and Acceptance agreement which gave him 60 days to come up with the balance of the money. If Bob, for any reason, could not come up with the money, then the deposit would be refunded.

Bob then turned over his present business for sale to a friend in the real estate business. After three weeks of parading prospective buyers through his store, the real estate agent finally found one that was a serious buyer. The proposition the buyer made to the real estate agent was as follows.

Sale price of Bob's business	$400,000
Less: down payment in cash	200,000
Balance to be financed by Bob over a	
five-year period with payments to be	
made monthly at prime plus 3 percent.	*$200,000

*The buyer would be willing to give a personal guarantee, but, frankly speaking, it would not be worth much because he used all his assets to borrow the down payment for the business.

Bob took a deposit of $20,000 from the prospective buyer and then contacted Gerk again to inform him of the new situation. Bob proposed that Gerk accept $200,000 as the down payment and a note for $600,000. This new balance would mean that the payments for the principal only for the next five years would be approximately $10,000 per month plus interest.

Bob would be receiving from the person who purchased his business approximately $3,400 per month plus interest, which would mean that the net amount Bob would be paying out to Gerk would be $6,600 monthly excluding interest. Gerk did request that the note for $200,000 that Bob was getting from the buyer of his business be assigned over to him as collateral for the $600,000 he was financing for Bob. Bob agreed to those terms. Gerk said that Bob could collect the $3,400 from his buyer and assign the amounts over to him, or he could just mail in a check for the $10,000 plus interest monthly. However, Gerk insisted that if the person who bought Bob's business became delinquent in his loan by more than 90 days, he was to be notified immediately. Bob agreed to that request.

Finally, the settlement day came for the new business. Damon, Susan, and Bob all showed up for the closing. The agreement contained the usual conditions, except that it included the following covenants:

1. If the buyer fails to pay, when due, any of the monthly payments on the note owing to the seller for $600,000, then the entire balance will become due in full. However, the seller will grant the buyer a 10-day grace period to allow the buyer to pay off any unpaid amounts owing. If said amounts are not paid off after the 10-day grace period, then the seller shall have the right to take over the business, including all inventory, furniture and equipment, and other assets on the premises at the time of the takeover. Further, the seller will have the right, after proper legal requirements are met, to dispose of all of the assets and then proceed against the buyer to recover any amounts still owing after the disposal of said assets. Buyer shall also be responsible for all legal and other costs incurred by the seller to recover the amounts owing the seller.

2. If the note for $200,000 submitted as collateral by the buyer becomes delinquent, which is defined as more than 90 days past due, then the seller will consider that his collateral position is jeopardized and will demand that the $200,000 be paid in full within 10 days from the date the seller is notified of said delinquency by the buyer. If the buyer fails to notify the seller of the delinquency and is quite aware that said note is delinquent, then the entire balance of $600,000 will become due and the seller will proceed as indicated in paragraph 1 above.

   If the buyer cannot pay the $200,000 in full if it becomes delinquent, then the seller will proceed as indicated in paragraph 1 and take over the entire business.

3. The buyer will deposit all the common stock of the new corporation to be formed with the seller, who will retain the stock as collateral for the $600,000 owing the seller.

Bob did not like these covenants in the agreement and asked to be given privacy so Susan, Damon, and he could discuss how to proceed. The attorney and Gerk were quite understanding about the request and provided them with a private room where they could talk over anything they wanted before signing all the agreements. During the conference Bob indicated that he felt uncomfortable with the entire transaction. He said that he was now a rich man, but once he put his name on that paper he would become a man in debt, and that the entire family could suffer. He pointed out that they stood to lose everything, including the house and all their personal assets. In spite of Bob's statements, Damon and Susan insisted that Damon would work hard and knew the business inside and out. Damon again expressed optimism for the new enterprise, and insisted he could make it a big success. Finally, Bob reluctantly agreed and went back into the closing room. All the papers were signed, hands were shaken, and the usual congratulations were extended. Bob now owned a new business.

The next few months produced some interesting results. The buyer who purchased Bob's business was not doing as well as Bob had done because the business succeeded largely because of Bob's personality. However, the payments were coming on time, so Bob was not worried. He felt that the new owner would get things going shortly. As for the new business, it had some personnel problems and a union to contend with, but sales were slowly improving. Bob used about $75,000 to set up the deli and the bakery, which were doing well. The delicacies and specialties were also drawing people in, but it seemed that the two chains in the area were spending a great deal of money on advertising, and Bob could not keep up with them. Bob tried to use personal contact with customers to make up for his lack of advertising. He spent a lot of time around the cash registers to keep lines moving and make certain that the customers were satisfied. However, Bob found that because of the higher volume and the tremendous number of customers, the personal contact did not work as it did in his former business. As far as the inventory was concerned, he and Damon had their differences, but Bob let Damon make the final decision even if they disagreed.

Three months later the person who bought Bob's business walked out. He left the store empty, and sold the stock, equipment and fixtures, phone, and anything else that was salable. Apparently, this person found someone who gave him a bulk price for all the assets except the building. Efforts to contact the owner were futile and Bob was now faced with a new problem. He desperately needed the $3,400 a month plus interest to keep his own payments up to date because, while the new business was increasing in sales volume and showing some profit, its cash position was poor. Bob knew that in 30 days he would have to notify Gerk and come up with $200,000. Therefore, he had to get things arranged before that time. He now had an empty building and a former business that was destroyed. Bob talked to several of his bankers, but they all declined to loan him any additional funds. Bob felt that with an injection of fresh capital, he might be able to spend more money on advertising and promotion to put the new business in a better cash position. However, he remembered what Gerk had told him when he first spoke: you can't fight the big chains because they have too much purchasing power and they spend large sums on advertising and promotion. Bob discussed the situation with Damon. Damon had to agree with his father, but still felt that the business could be profitable providing his father could come up with more money. Finally, Bob went to some of his friends to see if they could come up with the money, and only a few were interested in helping. Then to make matters worse there was a wildcat strike by the employees, caused by a problem Damon had with one of the employees. This strike cost the company four days' sales. When Bob finally got everything back to normal, he came down hard on Damon, but to no avail. Just as Bob was going to throw in the towel, one of his friends, Morris Faber, offered him a proposition.

Morris reviewed Bob's present financial situation, which was as follows:

Amount owed the local bank for working capital loan (estimated)	$250,000
Amount owed to Gerk (estimated)	600,000
Amount owing suppliers	145,000
Total amount owing	$995,000

Bob just could not believe what he was hearing. Only a few months ago he was respected in the community and had all the material resources he could ever want. Now he was flat broke and owed close to $1 million. His only assets were his house, the old and new buildings, inventory, and some stock that was pledged for the working capital loan. Bob and Morris discussed several alternatives and both agreed to meet in a few days.

During that time Bob had discovered that the Board of Education in town was looking for new facilities to lease on a long-term basis for their administrative staff. Bob discussed this with Morris and approached the Board of Education to see if it would be interested in renting his new building. It finally agreed to a 10-year lease at $4,500 per month, making the lease worth $540,000. Bob went back to Morris and was offered the following proposition.

1. Morris would pay off all Bob's debts, totaling $995,000, and assume title to the old and new buildings, which were appraised at a price of $175,000 and $370,000, respectively.

2. Morris would lease the old building back to Bob for $30,000 per year with the rental adjusted annually by the rate of inflation.

3. Morris would take out a mortgage on Bob's house for $200,000, and the payments would be made monthly with interest at the current rate in the market place at the time of the agreement. The balance of $250,000 would be in the form of a demand note. The only obligation Bob would have would be to pay the interest quarterly, which would be at the current prime rate plus 2 percent, and adjusted annually. Morris would expect principal payments to begin within two years after Bob took over the business and then at the rate of 10 percent per year or greater depending on Bob's cash position at that time.

5. Bob would be the Chief Operating Officer of the corporation and his son Damon would have nothing to do with the business until all debts were paid off in full.

6. Morris would give Bob the opportunity to purchase his old building any time after two years at the market value amount appraised by a recognized appraiser. However, in no case shall the price be less than $175,000.

Bob was quite elated about the entire deal. Here was an opportunity to save himself from bankruptcy and get back on his feet. Bob could take the remaining inventory in the new store, which was more than sufficient to stock his old store. He would use all the equipment, shelving, and other fixtures to get his old business back into action. He knew it would not be easy, but it was a chance in a lifetime. He knew Morris was going overboard, but Morris was returning a favor Bob did for him many years ago. Some years ago when Morris was starting his electrical supply company he badly needed money so he went to Bob, who was on the Board of Directors of the bank. Bob went to bat for him (as a matter of fact, he was the only one on the Board who favored the loan). As a result of Bob's efforts, the loan was approved and Morris began his journey to success. Before signing the formal agreement Bob talked to Susan about what would happen to Damon. She declined to make any comments and felt responsible for their present position. Bob talked to Damon who said he could take care of himself. He did state, however, that if his father had been able to acquire more capital the business would have been a success.

QUESTIONS

1. Do you think that Bob investigated the new business venture properly? What areas would you have investigated if you had been in Bob's place? Do you think Bob acted too fast?

2. Do you feel that Bob was right risking everything to get his son back into the family? How would you have handled Damon? Do you feel that Bob could have suggested other alternatives to Damon?

3. Do you think that Bob should have accepted a note from the person who bought his business? What would you have done? Would you have made the deal under the same circumstances? Would you have retained the business?

4. Would you have agreed to the other provisions in Gerk's buy-sell agreement? Do you think that Gerk was dealing from a position of strength or do you think that Bob was in a stronger position? Comment.

5. Do you think that Bob was right making Damon the General Manager for the new company?

6. Would you have opted for voluntary bankruptcy?

7. Would you take the proposition offered by Bob's friend with the inclusion of the provision that Damon could not have anything to do with the business?

8. What other lessons did you learn from this case?

Buying a Franchise

de Beers Foreign Parts Corporation

Sarah de Beers has decided to start her own business selling foreign automotive parts and accessories in Illinois, with headquarters in Chicago. Sarah is twenty-eight years old, married, and a college graduate in Business Administration. She has 10 years experience in the auto parts business. Sarah used to work for her father, a successful parts wholesaler for American cars throughout the state for 35 years. Her father, now retired, used to tell people that Sarah knew the business inside and out and that if she had been a man he would never have sold the business. However, he did sell the business, and now Sarah has to start from scratch.

Although Sarah's experience with foreign cars is limited, she feels quite confident she can succeed because of her solid background. Sarah wants to establish a competitive edge that will make her business unique. While her competition usually carries only fast moving parts and stock minimal inventories, Sarah intends to handle many brands and carry a substantial inventory of parts and accessories that will include both fast moving and slower moving parts. Sarah knows the latter policy will mean higher investments, but she feels that the profits from such investments will be enormous. Sarah knows she cannot carry every item in stock, but she will promise 48 hour delivery and, if necessary, sacrifice profit to make those infrequent sales. In any case, Sarah feels she will have two steps up on her competition, and because of her inventory will even become a supplier for some of her competitors.

Sarah conducted a thorough market study of all foreign cars throughout Illinois. She determined the total number of foreign cars by brand names and types, as well as their location and age. As a result of this study, she was able to determine which brands comprised the major markets and where to concentrate her efforts. In studying trends, she found that the foreign car market was rising with no end in sight. Sarah's market analysis also included a study of her competition. She discovered that while there were numerous foreign parts retailers and wholesalers throughout the state, most of them handled only fast moving parts and that they charged outrageous prices. She also studied the new foreign car dealers and found that they were more interested in selling cars than parts. Further, these dealers carried only fast moving parts and depended mainly on emergency orders to take care of parts not in stock. When she contacted insurance companies, they informed her that, generally speaking, foreign cars are better built, but that the parts are difficult to obtain and are expensive. The insurance representatives also mentioned that many of their clients had become upset because of the length of time it took to repair vehicles that were in accidents.

Sarah feels that if she were to open a complete center she could in no time get the lion's share of the market. Her only major problem is where to get the parts. First Sarah contacted the parts manufacturers, but most of them would sell only to new car dealers. Some did offer to make her their exclusive parts wholesaler for Illinois, but this would mean she would not be able to carry competing brands. Sarah did not like the fact that this would make her dependent on one brand and thus subject to the policy changes and whims of that particular manufacturer. Sarah still feels that her concept of selling parts and accessories of the major brands in the marketplace would have a greater chance of success. Sarah did contact numerous overseas wholesalers and found that by doing business with approximately 80 suppliers she would be able to take care of all her parts needs for the brands she wanted to carry. Sarah felt that while 80 suppliers are certainly a lot to handle, it is the only way she will be able to get all the parts she needs to do a thorough job. All of her suppliers offered to provide her with emergency service within 24 to 48 hours for parts not carried in stock providing she would carry the minimum stock they suggest.

Sarah sent each of the suppliers her study on the number of foreign cars in Illinois by type and age, and each of them calculated the initial stock she would have to carry. When Sarah assembled all the suggested stock requirements, she discovered she would need about $1,500,000 to buy her initial inventory. Sarah had been thinking she would need only $500,000 in stock and $100,000 for other expenses. Sarah asked some of her father's old associates to examine the stock requirements and prices and found that the prices were higher in some cases than dealer prices and lower in many other cases. The prices were lower in some instances because the car manufacturers were purchasing parts and accessories from outside manufacturers and these same sources were available to wholesalers under a private label box. The serial number was exactly the same as the car manufacturer's, but the box had to be private label to protect the car manufacturer. In general all the prices were acceptable, but the investment in opening inventory exceeded Sarah's expectations. Sarah asked the wholesalers for credit and they told her that after the opening stock was purchased they would give her 30 days' credit. Sarah also approached her bank to see if it would finance the inventory either in whole or part. The bank concluded that, while Sarah had a good concept, she would need to have her father and husband co-sign any loan it would give her.

Sarah had planned to invest $500,000 in inventory and $100,000 for opening expenses and working capital. When she discussed the proposal with her husband, Thornton, he flatly said that her idea had too much risk. He told her that he would prefer that she give up the idea of a business because it might drive a wedge in their marriage. They had only been married for 10 months and Thornton is twenty-five years older than Sarah. Before they got married, Thornton was supportive of Sarah's career, but lately he has felt she ought to devote her time to clubs, volunteer work, and raising a family. However, because of Sarah's insistence, he agreed to sign the loan, providing her father would go along with the proposal. Sarah was privately furious with his demands, and felt that it was now more important than ever to establish her own independence.

Sarah contacted her father, but he was against the entire project. He pointed out that she had too many suppliers, and if some of them went out of business or changed prices she could have a lot of financial trouble. He also pointed out that since she could not get a repurchase agreement whereby each supplier would buy back any parts that did not sell, she could lose a great deal of money. In spite of the fact that the bank had checked out all of the proposed suppliers, her father questioned their stability. However, her father did agree that if some of his former associates could make up the beginning inventory, he would go along with the project. He also wanted to be the part-time general manager of the business until it started making money and have 51 percent of the firm's common stock in his name until he felt that the risk in the business was eliminated. He told her she could repurchase the entire amount of stock from him at the same price he paid for it from profits, and if he died, she would get the 51 percent unpaid portion of the stock free of charge.

Sarah contacted the suppliers about the beginning inventory and they had no objections to her selecting the stock as long as it amounted to a certain dollar figure. They did reserve the right to make suggestions if she did not order what they thought were critical parts and accessories. Sarah was quite disappointed with both her husband and father, because she felt that she had proven her abilities after her years of experience.

Sarah has two alternatives at this point: she can either take her father's offer and get the business underway, or she can start smaller and use her own capital. If Sarah does go into business on a smaller scale she will be departing from her basic concept which might jeopardize the entire business. Sarah felt that servicing all the major brands would give her the greatest chance of success. If the business handled only a few lines, she would not be much better than some of her competitors.

Before she decides which course to take, Sarah wants to see if she can tie up all the other loose ends. First of all she has found an excellent location in Chicago. She can obtain a lease for five years with an option to renew for five more years. In addition, the owner is willing to give her an option to purchase the entire facility for $700,000. The market value of the facility at this time is only $450,000, but in time it could be worth more than $700,000. Sarah has asked some of her father's former associates to come to work for her, and she has commitments from some of them. Sarah knows that she will need sales personnel to contact retailers, other parts houses, new car dealers, and large fleet owners, and she has interviewed some salespeople who seem to be experienced and interested. Finally, she intends to call the business deBeers Foreign Parts Corporation. She figures that if there are any legal problems with the name, she will just use another name. Sarah wanted her business to be a corporation with all the stock in her name. However, now that her father wants 51 percent of the business, she is wondering if she wants to enter the arena as a minority stockholder. Just as Sarah was about to make up her mind, she was contacted by a representative from FORPAR, a new franchise operation. The representative explained that FORPAR specializes in foreign parts for all makes and supplies qualified franchise holders with a one-stop purchase center. FORPAR is beginning to award "valuable and profitable" franchises throughout the country, and is willing to explore the possibility of allowing Sarah to represent it throughout Illinois. The franchisor wants $75,000 up front for the franchise fee and 6 percent of net sales thereafter. One percent of the 6 percent is for national advertising. In exchange for the franchise fee and the royalty percentage FORPAR is willing to offer the following:

1. A complete one-stop parts and accessory purchase center for all foreign vehicles.

2. A 24- to 48-hour emergency service where parts can be ordered through branch offices in key locations throughout the country on a toll-free number.

3. Exclusive territory for the state of Illinois. FORPAR guarantees this territory for one year and will renew the franchise on an annual basis, providing the franchisee performs as indicated in the agreement.

4. FORPAR grants the franchisee the right to appoint dealers throughout the state providing they meet the requirements.

5. Prices for all parts are better than Sarah can get from all her other sources and, according to them, in the majority of cases much better than new car dealers pay.

6. Exclusive repurchase agreement on all approved parts in stock at the end of each year. The only expense to the franchisee would be freight back and forth and any damage to the container. In the event that FORPAR cancels the franchise, parts and accessories will be repurchased at the option of FORPAR on the same basis.

7. Credit terms of 30 days to approved accounts. With respect to the beginning inventory, FORPAR will finance 50 percent of the initial inventory up to six months. Interest charged will be two percent above prime.

8. The advertising campaign will be national and will clearly promote FORPAR's name. The company intends to spend $10 million of its own money the first year in addition to the 1 percent collected from the distributors. FORPAR also will have $3 million in cooperative advertising funds available for its distributors. Cooperative advertising will cover the Yellow Pages, trade magazines, local advertising, and billboards.

9. Managerial assistance and training programs will be provided for management and other personnel.

10. Incentives are offered if the assigned quota is reached annually. These incentives could reach up to 5 percent of total purchases.

Sarah likes the franchise concept and feels that it would give her the opportunity to get in on the ground floor of an up-and-coming company. FORPAR seems willing to spend money on advertising, and because it is a one-stop purchase center, would eliminate the need for so many suppliers. FORPAR estimates that a total investment of $1 million would be needed. This works out fine for Sarah because she can finance 50 percent, and thus not have to share her business with her father or anyone else. Sarah does not like the idea of a one year agreement, but the representative has assured her that all their distributors throughout the world operate on the same basis. The franchise representative has supplied Sarah with the disclosure statement, a list of all franchise holders, bank references, and other names to contact. The representative has insisted that Sarah contact any or all of the names so that she is certain FORPAR is a reputable firm and that those distributors now in the FORPAR family are satisfied.

Sarah noticed while reading the disclosure agreement that several years ago the company tried to enter the U.S. market and failed. When questioned, the representative indicated this had occurred because the company had not analyzed all the markets carefully and was not as selective as it should have been appointing distributors. The company felt that its entry into the market was premature and decided to pull out and come back when better prepared. The representative furnished all the names of former franchise holders throughout the United States at that time. Sarah contacted most of them, including the one who had the Illinois franchise. Sarah found that when FORPAR decided to pull out of the American market it offered to repurchase all the parts in inventory for the full purchase price and paid back all the royalty fees collected from each franchisee. The Illinois distributor said that he felt FORPAR was very fair, but he still lost money because he had left a good job to take on the franchise. He told Sarah that FORPAR offered him the franchise back, but he would not go back and start all over again. Sarah found that 30 percent of the distributors were reoffered the franchise and that 25 percent decided to take another chance.

Sarah's attorney examined the FORPAR distributor agreement which she found to be a typical unilateral contract. She recommended certain changes which the FORPAR representative agreed to take up with his company. The other covenants that the franchiser requires are as follows.

1. The minimum beginning inventory of $1 million will be selected by FORPAR.

2. Each franchisee will erect a building and facilities within three years of the agreement that conforms to FORPAR specifications. Franchisee will purchase and use signs and fixtures to be supplied by the franchisor.

3. All parts and accessories must be purchased exclusively from FORPAR. Failure to comply with this covenant will result in immediate cancellation.

4. The franchise cannot be sold, transferred, or divided without the express permission of the franchisor.

5. If the franchisee cancels the agreement, the franchisee cannot engage in the same business directly or indirectly within the state of Illinois for a term of five years.

6. Monthly financial statements will be furnished in accordance with FORPAR's accounting system to be purchased and kept by the franchisee.

7. The franchisee cannot take on any other franchise or line that will in any way conflict with FORPAR. Failure to comply with this covenant will result in immediate cancellation.

8. FORPAR will grant 30 days' credit to the franchisee, but it is understood that if the amount owed exceeds 30 days the credit will be cancelled until such time as FORPAR decides to reinstate the credit terms.

9. The franchisee for Illinois will purchase no less than $1 million of parts and accessories the first year. The second year's quota will be mutually agreed upon 60 days before the present agreement expires.

10. Termination will be made by the franchisor in the event that the franchisee violates any of the covenants of this agreement. If the franchisor terminates, 30 days' notice is required, and repurchase of all parts and accessories will be at the option of FORPAR and at net purchase price less any damage to the containers. Termination by the franchisee can be made by giving 30 days' notice, but in the event that said termination is requested by the franchisee, the franchisor reserves the right to repurchase any or all of the inventory at the net purchase price.

Sarah has checked out FORPAR through her bank and attorney, and everything indicates that the company is reputable and financially stable. However, since it is a foreign company doing business in the United States, Sarah wonders what would happen if it should fail the second time around. While FORPAR had promised to spend a considerable amount of money for advertising and promotion, so far nothing had transpired. The company expects to be completely under way in 45 days and the representative has stated that FORPAR has already established distributors in nearly all the states, and the warehouses are already in place. Still, Sarah feels uncomfortable with a one-year agreement even though the representative has assured her that the company has never made it a practice of cancelling franchises and she should not worry as long as she performs up to par. Sarah's father is solidly against the franchise proposition because he feels that since FORPAR was a failure before, it will take a lot to convince people that they are here to stay. Her husband feels that she should abandon the idea and think more of the family. He has even bribed her with the promise of a new Mercedes convertible if she gives up the idea.

So, Sarah is confused. Should she go into the business herself on a smaller scale? Should she go into business with her father, who would be a 51 percent owner and part-time general manager, and become Daddy's little girl again, or should she take on the franchise which could develop into a major opportunity? Also, how should she deal with her husband who is now making different demands than he did before they got married?

QUESTIONS

1. Analyze all of Sarah's alternatives and advise her on what to do.

CASE 12

Gifts Extraordinaire d' Europe and the Far East

Mary Higgins has worked in the business world for nearly 15 years. She has a background in marketing and feels it is time she makes the move she has always talked about—starting her own business. However, Mary doesn't know what type of business to enter, but she wants it to be in an area that has great chance of future success. Mary lives in Fort Lauderdale, Florida, and would like to remain in that area if at all possible. However, she is willing to relocate if the opportunity is something truly compelling.

After searching, examining, and rejecting a number of business opportunities, Mary is introduced to Harvey Wyndham, an English American. Wyndham has a very close friend, Nevell Tingley, who is a partner and one of the vice-presidents of the firm of Banks and Bidwell, international importers. The firm is selling franchises for their extraordinary gift catalog of original European and Far Eastern goods. The concept is to sell originals only. The firm consists of an established group of knowledgeable buyers who constantly search throughout Europe and the Far East for rare and unusual antiques, furniture, rugs, jewelry, clocks, coins, paintings, sculpture, and hundreds of other products. All are originals and owned by former royal families or prominent families who are willing to part with their prized possessions for a price. Wealthy Americans who are looking for a unique gift that is both rare and extraordinary may search the catalog for a special gift. Each of the gifts carries a certificate of ownership verification and a short history including information on when and for whom the article was made, the names of the owners down through the years and any other enlightening facts that enhance the value and worth to the purchaser.

The Banks and Bidwell Company has just started to do business in the United States, and so far it has had tremendous success. With franchises in New York, Illinois, Texas, Oklahoma and California, in a month's time all of the gifts offered in the first catalog were sold. The least expensive gift in the catalog was $350 and the average purchase was approximately $7,500. The company has toll-free telephone numbers in its catalogs and accepts all major credit cards. As indicated in the catalog, all of Banks and Bidwell's buyers are experts in their various fields. The company also offers gifts from some of the most prestigious auction houses in Europe and the Far East, which are sometimes included in their catalogs. Because the company's reputation is excellent, as set forth by expert references in the catalog, all the gifts are accepted as genuine.

The catalog itself is quite distinctive and elegant. Each gift is displayed clearly and information is presented in a short descriptive narrative about the individual gift. Some gifts cost up to $750,000. Special requests are accepted and the company does what it can to find gifts for the individual client.

The company's owners decided on the franchise system because they felt they would get better marketing coverage in individual states and it would be less expensive than setting up offices around the country. The franchise fee for each state ranges from $75,000 to $150,000. The annual royalty is 5 percent of net sales. The catalogs, which are advertised in all major magazines, each costs the consumer $10, though each would cost each franchisee $3 each.

Mary could not understand why Harvey had not entered this business sooner because she felt it had tremendous possibilities. She thought about the holidays when she frantically sought a gift that was different for her husband for whom it was so difficult to buy. Now, after going through the catalog, she feels this difficulty, as well as that of many other shoppers, would be resolved. Mary felt that if Banks and Bidwell was as reliable as Harvey indicated, this was the opportunity she was looking for. Harvey informed her that he would have entered this business sooner but he had just been divorced and his financial situation was strained. He told Mary that if she were definitely interested he could get the franchise for Florida, and he could save the initial franchise fee of $100,000 and the 5 percent royalty fee for the first year. His old school chum Nevell promised him he would help him get back on his feet by getting the company started. Harvey told Mary that if she would raise the rest of start-up costs, he would be willing to contribute the franchise fee for a 50 percent interest in the company.

Mary decided to explore the proposition. She contacted a prestigious mailing house and asked for market information and costs. The people there informed her that in Florida there were approximately 200,000 households with annual incomes in excess of $75,000. They also indicated that catalog buying was one of the biggest rages in America and about 70 percent of the population was buying from catalogs. Therefore, she would have a target audience of about 140,000. However, they also pointed out that the return on direct mail averaged 5 percent, if the firm were lucky. They pointed out it could vary depending on the catalog, type of products, and the reputation of the company. The charge for pressure sensitive stickers was $53 per thousand so her cost for an initial mailing to this population would come to $10,600. After the first mailing she would be able to determine the number of returns, and if 5 percent of the 140,000 sent in orders, then her next mailing would be only 7,000 catalogs. She would then be able to determine the people who were really interested and adjust her mailing list accordingly. Her next list would cost $371 ($53 per thousand times 7,000). However, the vice-president of Marketing for the National Mailing List Company thought she still might want to continue mailing in certain very affluent areas even though the recipients did not order anything on the first mailing. Alternatively, she could include all these names of purchasers in her own data base and develop her own mailing list.

Mary next considered the mailing costs, envelopes, and the labor costs for distributing the catalogs. In addition, she had to consider the other operating costs that are involved with any business, such as rent, utilities, insurance, and salaries. After checking with the U.S. Post Office Mary found that the cost to bulk mail 200,000 catalogs would be $0.53 per catalog. Envelopes from Banks and Bidwell would cost $0.10 each. Temporary hired help could put the pressure-sensitive stickers on the envelopes and mail them out. Since the firm issues a new catalog every three months and is thinking of making up a catalog every month within a year, the mailers would become full time employees. The accountant estimated that she would need seven people to handle the first mailing, and after she reduced the list would need only two full-time mailers. The expenses could be summarized as follows:

Estimated costs for first mailing

200,000 catalogs at $3.00 each	$600,000
Mailing list costs	10,600
Mailing costs (bulk mail)	106,000
Cost for mailers (seven people)	8,280
Payroll costs	994
Miscellaneous	1,000
Total estimated costs for first mailing	$726,874

The accountant then calculated the anticipated income from the catalog sales based on figures conveyed by Banks and Bidwell and developed the following estimates for the first three months:

Estimated net sales	$3,500,000	
(200,000 on the list x 70% catalog buyers		
x 5% return = 7000 x $500 per avg. purchase)		
Estimated gross profit, 25% of net sales	$ 875,000	
Less: estimated costs for first mailing	726,874	
Estimated profit before deducting operating expenses		$148,126

Less: operating expenses		
Payroll (Higgins & Harvey)	$ 18,000	
Payroll office (not mailers)	9,000	
Payroll taxes, 12%	3,240	
Rent	6,000	
Telephone expense	30,000	
Utilities	1,500	
Advertising expense	12,000	
Supplies	5,000	
Legal and Accounting	1,500	
Insurance	2,000	
Maintenance	500	
Miscellaneous	6,000	
Total operating expenses (estimated)		$ 94,740
Estimated net profit		$ 53,386

When the Banks and Bidwell representative, Horace Sparks, arrived to finalize the agreement with Mary and Harvey, he suggested that they target certain areas and address catalogs only to those known to have a level of affluence needed to buy the catalog's merchandise. They could identify one-third of the population by selecting certain areas. Mary thought it better to send to everyone, and then cut the list to those who respond. She felt they should move immediately to gain visibility. Since Banks and Bidwell advertises in prestigious magazines and publications throughout the country, they could gain from this exposure. All leads received from Florida would be credited to Harvey and Mary's account. The company would sell the merchandise and send the full commission to them since they would be the exclusive distributors in Florida, Sparks explained. He also stated that if an order came in from other states the same procedure would be followed, for they did not want one franchise encroaching on another's territory. Sparks also pointed out that the franchise was being granted solely because Harvey was personally recommended by the vice-president, Mr. Tingley. He understood that the first year there would be no royalty charges and that the company was foregoing the franchise fees. Sparks asked if an agreement had been reached between Mary and Harvey, and she replied that they were now finalizing the contract. However, she expected it to be signed without delay and they would forward the franchise contracts to Sparks as soon as their agreement was final.

After Sparks left, the accountant prepared a second forecast of estimates based on a much smaller mailing list. He suggested that instead of 7,000 they use 10,000 to be on the safe side. The income statement for the second subsequent mailings was projected as follows.

Estimated sales	$3,500,000
(the mailing would be 10,000; but we are	
using 7,000 as purchasers, with an average	
order of $500)	

Estimated gross profit, 25% of sales		$875,000
Less: estimated costs for subsequent mailings:		
10,000 catalogs at $3.00 each	30,000	
Mailing list costs	530	
Mailing costs	5,300	
Cost for mailers (2 people)	2,400	
Payroll costs (12%)	288	
Miscellaneous	1,000	
Estimated costs for 2nd mailing		39,518
Profit before deducting operating costs		$835,482
Operating costs (same as first mailing)		94,740
Estimated net profit on sales		$740,742

The analysis shows that based on four mailings the first year their net profits would look as follows:

Net profit on first mailing	$ 53,386
Net profit on other 3 mailings	2,222,226
($740,842 × 3 mailings)	
Total estimated profits	$2,275,612

The accountant analyzed the investment required to initiate the business and came up with the following figures:

Franchise fee in front	$ 0
Investment for catalogs for first mailing	600,000
Cost of mailing lists	10,600
Mailing costs	106,000
Cost for mailers	8,280
Payroll costs	994
Miscellaneous costs	1,000
Operating costs for the first three months	94,740
Other start-up costs including furniture,	
equipment, deposits, licenses, permits,	
legal, accounting, and other items	25,000
Estimated investment in venture	$846,614

If Mary does give Harvey a 50 percent interest in the company, her profits on the projected earnings of $2,275,612 would be $1,137,806; or based on her investment of $846,614, she would have a return of 134 percent.

When Mary and her accountant looked at the figures they both concluded that something was wrong. They simply could not see how anyone could make that kind of money, and they began to have some reservations. Mary also wondered why Banks and Bidwell would forgo profit opportunities like this when so much money could be made in this area. Why did they need franchises? Banks and Bidwell could develop their own target areas by selecting those known affluent areas in the country, rent mailing lists, and go in and set up their own offices. It seemed too good to be true. Yet, on the other hand, she felt it could be a genuine opportunity, and she did not want to miss it.

Mary met with Harvey again and told him that she was working on the financing and hoped to have a resolution within a few weeks. She explained to him how hard it was to raise nearly a million dollars overnight, and she and Harvey parted in a friendly way.

Mary considers herself an expert in marketing, but because she is so close to this problem she feels she needs outside advice. She comes to you for assistance and you agree to help her.

QUESTIONS

1. What recommendations would you give Mary to determine if this company is a "flash in the pan" or is a serious organization? Outline in-depth how you would check on the company, the people involved with the company, or other necessary facts.

2. Should Mary conduct an investigation in-depth into Harvey and his background?

3. Do you think that the estimate of a 5 percent return on the 140,000 first mailing is accurate? Do you think that Mary and Banks and Bidwell have over-estimated their figures? How could you prove these figures are accurate?

4. What is Mary to do if 7,000 people do call for gifts and the gifts are sold? What would she do if more than one person requested the same gift? How many gifts do you think would have to be offered in the catalog to cover demand? Do you think that the buyers in Europe and the Far East can come up with sufficient extraordinary gifts for four catalogs a year?

5. Do you think that Harvey's contribution is worth 50 percent or do you think Mary should make some other arrangement with him if she does decide to go into this business? What else could she ask Harvey to demand from Nevell Tingley that would sweeten the deal to make it a safer investment?

6. Would you go into this venture? What other recommendations do you have for Mary?

Special Buy-and-Sell Situation

Shamrock Chinaware

Alfred Marcus owns and operates the Shamrock Chinaware Company in Silver City, New Mexico. The company has been in business for more than 50 years, and Alfred is quite proud of his achievements. The reputation of his chinaware has spread throughout America. His products are considered to be of the highest quality in the field as well as among the most expensive. He learned the trade when he was a boy in Germany, and when he arrived in America, as soon as he was able, he started his own small company. It took many years of sacrifice and hard work to build the business, but today he has 800 people working for him—people he views as his own family. Some of the old-timers are still around and he has bestowed on them everything he could in warmth and gratitude. Although Alfred has not "spread the wealth," he has always managed to keep his employees happy. He gives an annual picnic, which he makes a big affair. At Christmas or other holidays he goes out of his way to make his employees feel loved and appreciated. He goes through the plant each day and compliments everyone he sees and sometimes admonishes those he notices doing something wrong.

Today Alfred is a multi-millionaire, and he is very content. His wife, Sharon, died years ago. Their only child, Rosa, was very independent, and Alfred and his late wife had thought she would never get married. However, five years ago she unexpectedly married Warren La Gash, who at the time of their meeting owned a television repair shop in the same town. Warren eventually sold his shop, which was just breaking even, and was brought into Shamrock Chinaware as vice-president in charge of personnel. Alfred's motive for hiring Warren was to assure a good life for his daughter. He chose that particular position because it required little responsibility since most new hires were either friends or relatives of current employees. However, Warren really wanted to prove himself at the job, and even went to school to learn human resources management. But when he suggested changes to Alfred, Alfred would not listen. For example, Warren informed his father-in-law that the company should have an Affirmative Action plan and be prepared one day for a union. Although Alfred listened, he told Warren that these changes were not necessary and that he had everything under control.

A short time later a small delegation of workers asked for an appointment to see Alfred. Alfred, who had an "open door" policy, welcomed them into his office. The mood was cordial, and Alfred asked what he could do for them. They reported that they had been approached by a union that wanted to organize them, but they felt that out of respect they wanted to talk to him first and ask for permission to form their own company union. Alfred was upset and asked them for their reasons. They replied (very respectfully) that while they really liked working for him, they felt they should be making more money and have more benefits. Alfred asked them to specify what benefits they lack, to which they responded with these specific requests.

1. Medical benefits for themselves and their families.
2. A retirement plan that would take effect when they reached 65.
3. A bonus each year instead of a party.
4. Tuition assistance so that they might further their education at company expense.
5. An eye care and dental plan for themselves and their families.
6. A grievance system for hearing their claims, because they have no one to go to when they have a problem when Alfred is not there.
7. A 25 percent increase in salary.
8. A bonus when they come up with ideas that save the company money or when they help improve the product line, as some of them have done in the past.
9. A cafeteria to eat in. Now they have to go outside to eat and they lose time traveling to and from restaurants.
10. A lounge to use during breaks.
11. A two-week vacation for those who have been working up to 10 years, and three weeks for those working over 10 years.
12. A sick leave program equal to competition's.
13. A bereavement period of five days when someone in their immediate family dies.
14. A stock program whereby the employee could purchase stock in the organization.

Alfred could not believe what he was hearing from some of his beloved "old-timers" who had started with him many years ago. After a few thoughtful moments, Alfred asked what he had done to deserve these demands from his employees. The delegation responded that they were grateful for all he had done for them and the community, but that they felt they lacked representation and were not getting paid what some other firms were offering. Alfred asked, "Doesn't it mean anything that when anyone needs money for medical bills I give it to them?" He went on to say that he had always solved problems and kept his door open, just as he did tonight. The delegation replied, "We feel safe with you but what if anything happens to you?" Alfred assured them that they would all be taken care of, but the delegation was not persuaded and asked him to consider their demands for a company in-house union. Alfred flatly stated that he would not consider it under any circumstances. The delegation thanked him for his time and left.

A few weeks later Alfred received a letter from a local union which reported that a majority of his workers had signed up to join and intended to have an election. Alfred immediately called all his workers together outside and spoke to them with a microphone. He told them that from this day forward there would be no more personal loans, picnics, or other special considerations. He went further to say that if they voted in the union they would have a constant battle with him on every issue that arose. Alfred knew he was committing violations, but did not care, totally ignoring the advice of his son-in-law and lawyers. He ended the speech by calling them names and saying, "From now on it is going to be a different company."

Three weeks later the election was held and the union won without any opposition. Now Alfred had a union to contend with, and Alfred told Warren to keep away from any union matters and that he would no longer hold an "open-door" policy. To make matters worse, Alfred immediately fired all the members of the delegation.

The union asked for an appointment with Warren to set up a collective bargaining meeting so that they could present their demands. Alfred agreed to this meeting since he had been told he had to recognize the union. Warren and a few of the other managers attended the first meeting and listened to the union's demands. These demands were essentially the items the delegation had identified, but included the immediate rehiring of the delegation with all back compensation immediately paid. The meeting was concluded without comment from Warren or the other managers.

When the union tried to hold another meeting, it was turned down. There was no question that the company was "stonewalling" and that different measures would have to be taken. Instead of going "on strike," all the workers reported for work, but worked slower. They began improperly packing the products, and customers were complaining that their china was being received broken into thousands of pieces. They were mixing orders so that customers were not getting what they wanted. In general, the union was upsetting the entire organization to get attention, but in reality they were only setting the company back many years. So Alfred decided to close the business. He posted a sign that the plant closed and that all paychecks could be picked up at the front office, which would be open for one month only. He told Warren to look for another job.

When lawsuits started against Alfred, he told his attorneys to attend to them and not bother him. He emphasized nothing would make him open the place again. The stand-off between Alfred and his former employees lasted more than 18 months, and many of them had suffered as Alfred had hoped they would. Some were upset at the turn of events, but most felt that Alfred should have understood their position—that he had conveniently forgotten that for many years they had been very loyal to him while he was making millions.

Meanwhile, Warren found a buyer for the business. By this time Alfred was being sued for violating labor laws, and he decided it was time to get out of the business. Warren told Alfred that the people who were interested in the business would buy his equipment, the name of the business, and lease the property with an option to buy the building for the total price of $2,500,000 cash. Alfred felt that offer wasn't enough, but accepted it with the conditions that the name Shamrock not go with the deal and that all lawsuits would have to be settled as a condition of the sale. The investors, however insisted that they be able to retain the name Shamrock because it was the major asset they were buying. Alfred was also aware that his principal asset was the name and not the equipment or the machinery. However, Warren persuaded him to rescind this request on condition that the new owners maintain a quality product. With the matter resolved, a closing meeting was arranged. However, at the closing meeting, the owners noticed this clause in the sales agreement:

> The buyers of Shamrock Chinaware shall have the right to use the name "Shamrock China" for a period of three years, during which time they will demonstrate that they have lived up to their promise to maintain the high quality, workmanship, and status that Shamrock held before the plant was closed. At the end of the three-year period, if the Seller feels they have lived up to their promises, then the name "Shamrock Chinaware" shall belong to them forever.

The buyers were adamant that they would not accept this provision. They felt that they might not be able to satisfy Alfred and that it was a covenant with too many loopholes. However, Alfred assured them that he was not trying to trick, but was only trying to make sure his products were not sold as junk chinaware or "given away as premiums in a soap box."

The group of buyers asked for a recess to discuss the matter. When they went into the other conference room, they immediately examined the matter in depth. Warren thought that the buyers should not worry about it, for they had every intention of positioning the product where it had always been in terms of price and quality. Warren pointed out to the buyers that Shamrock was Alfred's life and the only thing that would be left of him when he died.

When the group of buyers returned one of them asked what would happen if Alfred died before the three-year period was over. Warren suggested that they request a stipulation in the agreement that Alfred's daughter, Rosa, be given the right to make the decision. Another investor proposed starting a competing line of chinaware that would be slightly different in design but on the same status level as the chinaware Shamrock now produced. Then if they did for some reason lose the name, they would have the new brand to fall back on. Warren agreed that they should have the competing line. The investors then agreed to allow Rosa to decide on the name issue in case of Alfred's death.

Warren and the investors re-opened the business. They first had to resolve the union's renewal of its previous demands. Warren pointed out that the company had been out of business for some time and it was questionable if they could achieve the same level of operation or hire the same number of workers. However, he did agree to the following.

1. A medical plan including dental and eye care coverage, for employees and their immediate families.

2. That a retirement plan would be considered when the company got back on its feet.

3. College tuition and books would be paid for those who maintained "B" average.

4. A grievance system would be established between the union and management.

5. A salary increase to be negotiated at the end of the three-year agreement. (The union was told that there was a danger they might lose the name "Shamrock.")

6. No bonuses for the first three years. However, the company would seriously consider permitting the employees to purchase stock in the company at reduced prices from any bonus plan established by the company.

7. A cafeteria would be built to be operated on a concession basis by an outside firm.

8. A room would be provided during break-time which will contain vending machines and games.

9. A one-week vacation for all five-year employees, two weeks for 10-year staff, and consideration of three weeks for senior employees.

10. A sick leave allowance, as well as a three-day bereavement time period for members of their immediate family.

Everyone agreed to this plan and people were rehired on the last-out, first-in basis. Eventually the company soared to 400 people. The product did well on the market; employees worked with renewed effort and enthusiasm. Alfred watched carefully but would not go near the plant. He appeared to be satisfied with the product and informed Warren that as long as they keep up the quality he would give them the name forever.

In the meantime, Warren, who had been appointed to the position of executive vice-president of the company, experienced a change in behavior. While he had always been conservative and very devoted to his wife, he now was having an affair with his administrative secretary, Loretta Grant. Rumors were flying high about the romance in the executive mansion. While Warren and Loretta always maintained a very businesslike attitude in the office, their private meetings were certainly no secret.

Before the three-year period was over, Alfred died in his sleep and the company shut down for a day to mourn the death. Rosa was devastated and became more dependent upon Warren. But, out of the blue she received a few letters telling her of her husband's affair. When she confronted Warren with these accusations he immediately and vehemently denied them. He assured her that all was well and she believed him. Then other rumors started to reach Rosa, and she began to believe there must be some truth to the stories. She was distraught and angry about Warren's unfaithfulness, who she felt would still be repairing TV sets if it were not for her father.

At the end of the three-year period, Rosa sued Warren for divorce and told the investors that they had violated the agreement and could not use the name "Shamrock" any longer. The new owners were stunned and immediately sued to have the decision reversed. Their competing line, Tarassa Chinaware, had done well, but they felt they needed the Shamrock name. However, after discovering the reasons they lost the name from confidential sources they informed Warren that it was up to him to get it back.

In the meantime Rosa informed the owners that she would sell the name back to them under the following conditions.

1. That Loretta Grant be immediately fired without recommendation.

2. That Warren La Gash be fired immediately and that his stock in the company be repurchased as specified in the corporate by-laws and sold to her. (Rosa had a copy of all the agreements from when her husband lived with her.)

3. That Warren La Gash not be hired in any capacity whatsoever, even at no compensation.

4. That they pay her the sum of $1 million for the name of the company.

The group wondered what to do. On one hand they considered Warren too valuable to lose, as he was a major asset of the firm. But on the other hand, they needed to resolve this name issue as quickly as possible.

QUESTIONS

1. How should Warren have persuaded Alfred to avoid being confronted by the delegation before the union was voted in by the employees?

2. Would it have been better for the firm to have an in-house union rather than an outside union?

3. Were any of the delegation's demands unreasonable? If so, what would you have counterproposed?

4. Why did Alfred close the plant? Do you think that owners of companies who are non-union would react much the same as Alfred in this situation? Is it possible to keep a union out? What are the benefits to the company of a union? Is it possible for management to work in harmony with a union?

5. Do you think that Alfred should have sold the business? Do you think the buyers should have accepted the three-year covenant? What else could they have done to protect themselves if they were refused the name?

6. Do you think it was a good idea to build up the other brand to compete with their own product?

7. Do you think they should continue without the name "Shamrock" and push the other brand?

8. Would you accept the terms and conditions that Rosa handed down? What counter-proposal would you offer her?

9. Assume Warren is terminated and has to sell his stock back to the firm. Does he have a legal defense? If Loretta is fired, does she have grounds for defense?

10. What lessons did you learn from this problem?

CASE 14

Asuer-Sam Importing and Exporting Company

Lee Vincent Eggo has been working as an international consultant for the last 20 years. During that time he has acted as a trouble shooter for many American companies established in foreign markets, and he has also consulted and solved marketing export problems for foreign corporations who wanted to open markets for their products in the United States.

Lee has become a vice-president in the consulting company and is now sharing in the profits. Last year he earned more than $200,000 in total compensation. In addition, he is invited to take his wife with him on many trips, and they can combine pleasure with business. All in all, Lee is pleased with his position.

Lee is also the consultant for Asuer-Sam Importing and Exporting Company which has offices in New York, Los Angeles, and New Orleans. The company has serious personnel problems but if these can be resolved, it can have tremendous potential. They have made contracts, some of which Lee has negotiated, with Japanese, Taiwanese, Korean, European and South American firms for Asuer-Sam to represent them on an exclusive basis throughout the United States. In some cases, the representations give them sole distribution rights for the entire world market. The company has had little success in exporting American products despite the marketing plans prepared by Lee. The firm is presently selling about $35 million annually but could be exporting four or five times that volume. The company is undercapitalized and needs an injection of funds. Recently, the five owners invested $3 million in the company, but much of it was consumed by expenses, advertising, receivable losses, obsolete inventory and materials, warehouse space, and personnel costs, especially from managerial changes made at the executive level. The owners cannot find anyone who really knows and can take hold of the business. They decide to make one more attempt before they fold the business. They approach Lee and ask him if he would like to take over the CEO position for the entire organization. Lee is caught by surprise and tells them that he is satisfied with his present position. He tells them that he has nowhere to go but up and eventually he expects to have part ownership in the company.

The owners of Asuer-Sam, headed by Margaret Wolfington, offer to meet his terms and conditions if he takes over the company on a long-term basis. After several meetings, Lee projects that the company needs an injection of at least $3 million in additional funds to overhaul the entire organization and make the company competitive and viable. The final condition he stipulates is that he operate only under a Voting Trust Agreement to be drawn by his attorney. The owners are not familiar with this arrangement and ask him to explain. He tells them that if he takes this position it will have to be on his terms and conditions. He wants complete authority within certain agreed parameters to operate the business in any way he thinks best. In order to protect this special right he wants all stock put in the hands of a trustee, who will issue trust certificates to each stockholder for all stock. He will be the trustee and have sole voting rights for all the stocks. The stocks would be placed in escrow with a local bank. He, as the trustee, will appoint the board of directors of his choice, and will have complete power for a period of 10 years. He asks that his salary be $200,000 plus a percentage of profits. He also requests that the accounting firm be changed to a National Accounting firm because he will need bankable financial statements to present to banks when credit lines are necessary from different parts of the world. He also wants a stock option plan where he can either buy 51 percent of the business or buy them out completely providing he achieved the profit and investment goals.

The group is surprised by the offer. A Voting Trust Agreement was something they had never seen before, but as Margaret put it, "Why not investigate what it is and evaluate our options before we dismiss it?"

The group asked Lee to make a projection of sales and profits since he is acquainted with the business from a consulting viewpoint. Lee agrees so that he can reconfirm his own views about the company and its potential.

Presently the income statement is as follows.

Net Sales	$35,000,000
Net loss	$ (450,000)

Lee can easily see why they are desperate, for they need someone in the company to assume leadership or they will lose their entire investment. The company made money when they started, but after a while became more interested in representing every manufacturer or line they could, but did little or nothing with them. In addition, they invested in several retail automobile operations and small plants which were not producing profits. Lee had told them to get rid of them years ago, but they refused to follow his recommendations. Consequently, the company is now in a precarious position and needs some sound business planning and management. The business will have to be reshaped, building stone-by-stone to form a solid foundation. Lee knows this will not be easy, and yet if the owners will put up the capital and give him complete control for 10 years he will soon be a millionaire and own the majority of the stock in the company, thus making it his own business.

After much consideration Lee comes up with the following projections.

Year	Sales	Net after taxes
1	$ 25,000,000	$ 500,000
2	50,000,000	1,000,000
3	65,000,000	1,950,000
4	75,000,000	2,250,000
5	100,000,000	3,500,000
6	125,000,000	4,375,000
7	150,000,000	5,250,000
8	200,000,000	7,000,000
9	250,000,000	8,750,000
10	300,000,000	10,500,000

When Lee presents these figures to the owners they are extremely excited. They are willing to invest the additional $3 million provided they can be guaranteed these results. Lee reminds them that his entire job depends on it, for if he does not reach those goals then the Voting Trust will be void and they can come back and take over the business. Lee points out that he is giving up 20 years of success and security for this position, and he will only consider it under his terms. The group is concerned about two points: what percentage of the profits he expects and how they can protect themselves. Lee says he wants one-third of all profits after taxes in addition to his basic compensation and that bonuses will have to be paid to him 15 days after the date the audited statements are submitted by the company accounting firm. Further, he will decide when he will exercise his stock options, which would be based on the par value of the common stock. In response to their second point, he affirms their desire for protection and reminds them that while he will have total control of the business and complete voting rights, those conditions will last only as long as he fulfills the terms of the Voting Trust Agreement. At any time if at least 75 percent of the stockholders want to terminate the agreement, they can, but they will have to compensate him in accordance with the agreement to be signed.

The owners, led by Margaret, meet several times and feel that they have a company with tremendous potential, but that it needs someone competent to run it. They, therefore, decide to agree to the Voting Trust Agreement, but with certain additional provisions. They are as follows.

1. If the company experiences a deficit in any one year, the agreement is hereby canceled and Lee Eggo will cease to have anything to do with company.

2. As long as Lee Eggo is able to produce the profits projected, he will remain in control.

3. Eggo will report to the stockholders the condition of the organization quarterly and permit inspections of the operation from time to time.

4. At the end of three years Eggo will be permitted to purchase stock at par value in the company, but only up to a maximum of one third of the total common stock outstanding unless other stockholders wish to sell their stock to him after first offering it to the rest of the stockholders.

5. Lee Eggo will not sever his employment with the company as long as the Voting Trust is in force. If he wishes to terminate for some reason, he must give one year's notice to the group and will be entitled to no other compensation except his salary. Further, if Lee Eggo severs his employment with the Company, the voting trust agreement will be declared null and void. Then the stockholders can enter the company with complete control to do as they wish.

6. Lee Eggo will acquire insurance on his life (term policy) for the sum of $6 million, which will be paid by the company who will be the primary beneficiary.

Lee reads their stipulations and responds that he feels it is to their advantage to retain him in a stock position, but if they wish he would accept those conditions. However, he modifies their requests by proposing the following.

1. Inspections would be under either his supervision or someone appointed by him.

2. Statements and reports would be rendered quarterly by the company auditors.

3. If the group should terminate the Voting Trust by a 75 percent vote of the stockholders and his performance is in accordance with sales and profit projections, he requests termination compensation as follows.
   a. five years' compensation at the rate of $200,000 a year.
   b. five years' estimated bonuses based on either last year's earnings or the average of past years' earnings from the date he took over, whichever is higher.
   c. a personal guarantee from all stockholders that said compensation would be paid no later than 30 days after the termination of the Voting Trust Agreement.
      In the event that Lee Eggo was not performing as expected or in accordance with his projections, then he would only be entitled to five years' compensation at the rate of $200,000 per year or $1,000,000. This provision will also be personally guaranteed by each stockholder.

After all the discussion and meetings the closing took place and Lee Eggo was now in complete charge of all operations. The capital was increased as agreed and trust certificates were issued to all stockholders. Lee now attacked the problems in the business. During the next three months, he brought in a group of experts in the international field. He hired service staff and field executives who spoke several languages and had experience in foreign markets. He sold all company-owned operations and turned the assets into cash. Focusing on the approximately 100 lines owned by the company, his management team had many meetings and conferences to decide which lines to retain and on which areas to concentrate in the future. Many of the lines were valuable but it would take 20 different organizations to do them justice. They decided to sell off lines of little interest and concentrate on the computer equipment field and telecommunications. These fields were dynamic and future-oriented. They also decided to explore Robotics and other operations that would cut production costs in American factories. Another area of interest was pharmaceuticals. This field held some interesting challenges and they wanted to enter this highly profitable area. They decided to drop consumer goods such as cars and televisions. They sold about 80 lines and received more than $2 million for the representation rights they relinquished. Some of the stockholders were furious with these actions. They felt Lee was giving away the company by selling lines in which they had invested time and money. Lee ignored them and continued with his plan.

For the next nine months business was good. He made better arrangements with the manufacturers they represented, and he established a network for distribution throughout the country. Sales kept increasing and by the end of the first year had reached a total of $45 million. The net profit on sales alone, not including profits from selling lines, was $1,800,000. The stockholders were thrilled. Lee had a meeting with them to present the financial statements, and they were especially pleased with the liquidity of the company and thought that his projections would be on target for the future. Lee kept moving ahead, refining the lines and establishing distributors. Then he decided to start exporting goods from America more vigorously. He had one of his teams develop a list of products for the international export market and they eventually decided to market hi-tech products overseas. Lee had made connections with the U.S. Export Import Bank, the Federal Credit Insurance Association, Department of Commerce and other agencies, and arrangements were made for financing exports to overseas markets without much risk for the company. He also made arrangements with the Department of Commerce to handle bartering or counter trades when necessary, and contacted some experienced barter brokers he had known in Europe. Lee covered as many parts of transactions as possible. If he sold overseas and they did not have money he either arranged financing or if necessary purchased some of their goods and then resold them at cost or for a profit through barter brokers. When Lee purchased goods overseas, he always tried to make barter arrangements with other countries to purchase American products.

The organization was growing, and Lee had opened offices in Canada, Europe, the Far East and South America to be closer to his markets and to have his service engineers within immediate striking distance if there were problems. Lee was service-oriented, having learned from his early experience in Germany that service comes first and the products are second. Concentrating on sales alone is not the proper way to market products overseas. You must also possess the technical know how to handle what you sell.

Lee had legal experts throughout the world protecting the company's rights and checking to see that their position was never in jeopardy. The stockholders were getting used to the dizzy heights to which the profits were climbing, and while he did not expect any difficulty as long as he produced, he discovered there was an undercurrent movement. Apparently a sub-group wanted to come in and take over the business. Lee knew that there was always someone in the crowd you could never please, and he was prepared for this day. Before this group attacked him, Lee had a meeting with all the stockholders and confronted them with the facts he had, including letters and statements from reliable people who informed him that the stockholders wanted to void the Voting Trust Agreement. The group was surprised he knew, but did not deny it. They stated he was now a millionaire because they had given him the opportunity and they wanted an entirely new arrangement. One of the major stockholders, Spencer Denby, reported that he had a son who graduated from the university, with a major in the international field, and after working for the company for six months was terminated. Lee responded that he was not qualified to come into the company in an executive position because he did not speak any languages fluently and he was a disrupting force throughout the time he was employed. He told Denby, "If your son had behaved himself he would still be with the company, but he kept telling people that I was just an employee. So, in my opinion, he had to go." Lee asked the group members if they wanted to terminate his relationship with the company. He told them that if they did, it was perfectly all right with him. However, he reminded them he had done his job and that the company would be liable now for nearly $15 million which he expected promptly after the audit.

The group did not balk at the figure because they now knew the company's potential. However, Denby spoke up, saying, "You might be entitled to that money, but it will be a long time before you ever see it as far as I am concerned." Lee responded that they could do what they wanted, but he was now giving the group one year's notice in accordance with the agreement and he would complete his term. He also said that he had every intention of remaining in the same business and that the entire organization would move with him to other quarters and operate under a different name. There was nothing in the agreement that prevented him from doing this, and now Lee had sufficient capital and all the contacts and networks in place to assume control under a different name. He took the letter of resignation from his pocket and handed it to Margaret. The group was shocked. They expected that they would void the Voting Trust and take over and he would be out and then agree to some settlement. Yet, Denby accepted the notice and adjourned the meeting.

The stockholders were confused and upset by the turn of events. They really had no objection to Lee except that he was making too much money. However, they were confident that Denby could persuade people to remain with the company. The next morning the lawyers representing the Trustee, Lee Eggo, were notified that 100 percent of all the stockholders voted to terminate the Voting Trust. A week later the legal matters were resolved, and Denby told Lee to leave. Lee was prepared, and the moment he started packing the rest of the organization did the same. Denby tried to get some of the other executives together, but none would listen.

Before they all left, Lee called Denby aside and said, "I am going to notify, of course, all manufacturers we represent that I am no longer associated with the firm and that, no doubt, you and your son will be taking over." Nearly everyone left the company. Notifications of resignations from branches all over the world came in to Spencer Denby. Denby quickly informed the other stockholders who were anxiously awaiting to hear what had transpired, especially whether Lee's assistant, Allen, was taking over as he agreed privately. Denby replied that Allen agreed a week ago, but apparently had no intentions of remaining with the company. Allen informed him he was also resigning to continue working for Lee Eggo. The group tried to contact Lee for a meeting. Finally, Lee's attorney made contact and, as Lee expected, they were a different group of stockholders than he had met at the last meeting. Margaret started off the meeting by apologizing for what had happened and informing him that there was a great misunderstanding. They wanted him back and would agree to any terms he offered. Lee informed them that he was already in the process of forming his own company. They pleaded with him to reconsider. Finally, Lee agreed to come back if they sold him 51 percent of the company stock at the original par value of $10 a share. Secondly, he wanted complete control over the company and would tolerate no interference whatsoever from any stockholders in the future. He emphasized that there would be no other offer and if it were acceptable they would meet in his attorney's office tomorrow morning and the stock would be transferred to him. The group left the room and took about 10 minutes to confer. Finally they returned and told him that he had a deal and they were glad to get him back.

The following day the stock was transferred and Lee paid the par value for the stock and became the majority stockholder of the company. The other stockholders were not pleased, but as Margaret put it, "He made money for us and no doubt will continue to do so, but he is the slickest two legged animal I ever met." The rest of the group agreed and walked out the door.

QUESTIONS

1. If you were one of the stockholders of the group that owned the business, would you have agreed to the Voting Trust Agreement?

2. Do you think that Lee Eggo was right to demand a Voting Trust Agreement? Could he have obtained protection any other way?

3. What do you think of the management approach Lee used to get the company back on its feet? Do you think that he made the right choices about directing the company's efforts? Do you think he should have sold off the lines he did?

4. Why do you think that the stockholders who had been almost out of business and now were making millions wanted to terminate an executive as productive as Lee?

5. Do you agree with Lee's tactics to confront the group and tell them what he had heard and what he was going to do? Would you have done the same? Do you think that he handled the company ethically? Would the company have continued to be profitable if Denby had been able to convince the others to remain with the company? If you were in the stockholder's position and you did

want to get rid of Lee for some reason, how would you have accomplished it?

6. If you were a stockholder, would you have agreed to the final terms Lee demanded when he agreed to come back into the firm? Does he really have control of the company now, or can the stockholders still challenge him in the future?

7. Do you think that Lee was devious and used his position for his own gain? Do you think he planned this all along? Do you think this is typical of successful business people?

CASE 15

The Baraboo Advertising Agency

Ever since she can remember, N. B. Nelson has wanted to work for one of the big advertising agencies on Madison Avenue. She has an MBA in Marketing, with emphasis on advertising and communication courses. After looking for a job for several months, she finally accepted a position in the office supplies department with one of the largest agencies in New York. This was the only position she could get in an agency, but she felt that if she were aggressive and friendly, she would eventually obtain the position she wants. She finally managed to get an administrative secretarial position. In that position she was able to participate in some of the "emergency think-tank sessions" where everyone would try to brainstorm ideas for a client.

One day N. B. presented a concept and everyone thought it was terrific. She was made a copy writer and began to advance in the field. N. B. spent long hours in the agency working with artists, marketing research people, the department of public relations, and the traffic division. Then she got the opportunity to work with the international division. The staff in the division were unusually stimulating, for they faced the challenges of different countries each with its own customs, mores, language, and methods of doing business. Eventually N. B. was made an account executive, handling several accounts, including those for a beverage, breakfast cereal, and a cosmetics firm. She was earning $60,000 a year with additional bonuses. N. B. was riding high and felt all the effort she had exerted had paid off. Now that N. B. had reached her original goal and was making money she wanted to go further and buy her own agency.

When N. B. decided she had sufficient capital and the experience to direct her own agency, she started to look for a business to buy. She preferred one that was producing about $2 million a year in revenues. An agency with that volume would be earning at least $600,000 gross, and there would be potential for growth. After a year of searching, she found such a firm in Milwaukee, Wisconsin. After N. B. visited the agency, she was quite impressed. The owner, Bernard Rainier, was growing older and had decided he did not want the pressure of running the firm any more. N. B. met the executive vice-president, the account vice-president, the managers, and other staff including the artists and copywriters. She was particularly impressed with the artists, who had won several awards for their work including some for annual reports for large corporations. The firm was a member of the "AAAA" organization and was highly regarded in the trade. N. B. examined the accounts and found that they were quite diversified. Two big accounts dominated with 50 percent of the business, with the rest consisting of small accounts that each spent approximately $25,000 to $50,000 per year. The accounts receivable were high, but the owner felt that they would be paid, since he would not retain an account that was not creditworthy.

Finally, N. B. decided to buy the business. She negotiated a price of $200,000, or 10 percent of net sales. N. B. took over the business, leaving the name the same. She did not intend to make any wholesale changes at first, but instead would build up the confidence level between her and her employees as well as her clients.

Soon N. B. found herself in the limelight. Newspapers, hoping she might be a source of advertising revenue, began stroking her by running stories about "the single girl who made it good in the big city." Her banker, wanting to keep her in his bank's good graces, became fast friends with her. And because she was rich and attractive, all the most prestigious social clubs in Milwaukee wanted her to become a member. N. B. was so taken by this sudden burst of attention that she became more interested in her social life than her career. In the meantime business was brisk. Her employees were good except for the marketing research manager. He did not know the business well, his contribution to total revenues was low, and his work was of low quality. She contacted her former business associate, Jan Krupp, and persuaded him to come to work with her. With his appointment to marketing research manager the agency started to take on a different look.

N. B.'s two major account holders were an industrial company selling farm implements and other products to farmers and a large industrial chemical company that distributed its products over a 12-states region. The latter used several advertising agencies, but N. B. managed to get most of its business. However, N. B. worried that if she lost these two accounts, she would lose about $300,000 in gross profits which would destroy her business. Therefore, she wanted to acquire other large accounts to replace these in case she lost them. On Madison Avenue, accounts switch agencies all the time, so her fear was well founded.

In the meantime, N. B. met Cornelius Tillstrom, the president and owner of one of the largest corporations in Milwaukee. He was 55 years old, had never been married, and up until he met N. B. was a workaholic. He and N. B., who was 35 years old, began to date, and after four months were married. They went on a 30-day cruise for their honeymoon. When they got back they both returned to work. In the meantime, because of the publicity surrounding her marriage, she picked up more than $10 million in additional revenues, and her business was ranked among the best in the state. N. B. increased her staff, trying to bring in people with experience working for bigger New York agencies. She lost the two accounts she expected to lose and concentrated on the new accounts that had developed since her marriage.

Corny wanted to have a child and talked to N. B. about it. Although she feared the consequences of having a child on her career, she agreed. N. B. had a difficult pregnancy and missed a great deal of work. The business began to suffer from her absence. Her executive vice-president left the company, taking some of her people including Krupp, and opened his own agency. He also took with him about $3 million in revenues, which meant N. B. was losing $900,000 in gross profits a year.

Finally, N. B. gave birth to a son, Cornelius Jr. N. B. stayed home for a few weeks and then returned to her office, determined to get the business back on its feet. Her husband did not mind, but he started to become concerned with the excessive turnover of governesses. The governesses found N. B. and Corny too demanding. Finally, Corny asked N. B. to sell the business and come home and care for the baby. He told her he would give her anything if she would. N. B. refused, telling him that she had to work, just as he did, because it was a major part of her life. She told him she just could not waste all those years studying and learning her trade to leave it for the baby. She insisted that she loved her child, and felt he would be all right with the right governess. Corny was upset with her refusal to quit.

Soon after, N. B. started losing some of her accounts. N. B. lost more than $6 million of business, and her revenues fell to slightly more than $1 million a year. Consequently, she had to drastically reduce her organization, facilities, and services. She found herself doing much of the copy work, marketing research, and public relations. Then, one day she met George Calvert, the owner of a former account, who asked her to lunch. He obviously had something he wanted to discuss, and N. B. hoped that he wanted to talk about taking on his account again. However, Calvert wanted to explain that he did not give up her agency because of anything she had done, but because his bank had put pressure on him for his demand loans. All of the pressure came from her husband, who was chairman of the board of directors at the bank. He said that he would have stayed with her if he could have, but the bank made more liberal financing contingent upon his leaving her agency. Apparently, Corny was out to destroy N. B.'s business as well as her confidence.

It had been some time now since she and Corny had talked. The new governess he hired, Francine Gardin, had been on the job for six months, and the baby was fine, and Corny was unusually happy. When N. B. confronted Corny about his scheme (she did not mention Calvert's name), he did not deny it. He told her that he had wanted her home, but now that Francine had taken over he no longer cared. He went on to say that Francine and he were in love and that she was expecting a baby. Nothing could have hit N. B. harder. Corny told her later that he was sorry everything worked out this way, and that he was sorry about her business. He told her it would be best if she left town. N. B. replied that she had every intention of leaving the house and taking the baby with her, but she was not leaving town and she was going to stay in business despite what he would try to do to her. Corny looked at her and said, "We will see, my dear; we will see."

As expected, because of Cornelius' power, he won custody of little Corny. The court also granted Cornelius and N. B. a divorce, and she refused any settlement whatsoever. N. B. decided to return to her business with a fervor she never had before. However, the business was slow to recover. She could never seem to pass the $1 million mark, and it was getting to be a battle for survival. She was also dropped from her clubs and removed from the Milwaukee Social Register. This cost her business because she made many of her first contacts in these clubs. Finally, someone asked her if she would be interested in selling her business. She was offered $150,000 cash for the agency and a three-month retainer of $25,000 to acquaint the owner with the clients.

In the meantime she bumped into Corny a few times and they were cordial to one another. One day he asked her to lunch and they talked about Corny and visitation rights. He agreed that she could see the baby when she could and when Francine would permit. N. B. had to admit to herself that she still had a special feeling for Corny, but did not think it was love. He told her that Francine had a false pregnancy and that they were fighting all the time. N. B. expressed sorrow at this, although inwardly she rejoiced that he was unhappy.

N. B. and Corny started to see one another more often. Corny told her that he was sorry for what he had done. N. B. said she blamed herself for the failure of her marriage. Finally, he asked her to marry him again, and N. B. agreed. Corny managed to get a divorce from Francine, who became a wealthy woman and was all too glad to leave Wisconsin for the south of France.

After returning from their second honeymoon, N. B. sold the business and told Corny that she would be making a career out of their marriage. He was pleased with her decision.

QUESTIONS

1. Would you have advised N. B. to take a job in the supply department of an advertising agency to get her foot in the door after all the studying and preparation she had undergone? Should she have gone to work for a smaller agency?

2. What was N. B.'s approach to learning the advertising business when she got out of supplies department? Do you feel this is the best preparation for owning your own business?

3. When N. B. made her decision to go into her own business should she have moved to Wisconsin in a town where she was not known and to an agency that admitted they had two major accounts which accounted for the bulk of their profits? What are the things to look for when you buy a business of this type? Do you think that her business had the opportunity for growth without Cornelius's assistance?

4. Do you think it is possible to hold on to an account for a long time in the advertising business? What would you do to try to retain those large and small accounts?

5. How does an agency get new accounts? If you knew that a company was changing agencies and that it would soon be available, what method would you use to obtain the account? What type of promotion could N. B. have done to promote her own agency?

6. Do you think N. B. considered the impact upon her business when she decided to marry an older man and have the baby? How could she have avoided these problems?

7. Do you think Corny was right trying to force N. B. out of business and back into the home? What methods could he have used that would have helped him avoid divorce?

8. Do you think N. B. was right staying in Wisconsin and in business? Do you think she was right to remarry Corny and sell her business?

9. Would you have sold the business and come home to take care of the baby?

CASE 16

Morgan's Garden Center

Roger Davis has been working as the sales manager for Morgan's Garden Center for 12 years. Morgan's Garden Center is located just outside Phoenix, Arizona, which is a rapidly growing area. The firm has an excellent reputation and Frank Morgan, the owner, and Roger have become close friends as well as business associates over the years. The garden center sells many products including plants, shrubs, and trees grown on Morgan's 10-acre nursery as well as equipment for the home gardener. It also has a thriving cut flower business. The garden center not only sells to retail consumers but also to wholesale distributors. Roger has handled every phase of the business and has been taught everything he knows by Morgan. For years Morgan has referred to Roger as his "right arm." Roger earns $20,000 per year salary plus an annual bonus of approximately $5,000.

Over the years Roger has made several excellent recommendations to increase the company's profit centers, including adding a complete line of Christmas products during the holiday season. As a result of this expansion into the Christmas line, including everything from trees to ornaments, Morgan's profits have increased substantially. They have applied the same concept to Valentine's Day, Thanksgiving, and other special days. As a result of their relationship, Morgan has promised Roger that if he ever decides to sell the business he will give Roger the first opportunity to purchase it.

One day Morgan told Roger that he wanted to sell the business and retire. He was 67 years old and felt it was time to take it easy and spend more time with his grandchildren. Morgan wanted $250,000 for the business. The company was a corporation, but Morgan was only selling assets. The price included the 10-acre nursery, five acres of additional land with facilities that included two well-structured greenhouses, a small house, a flower shop and office, a small warehouse for storage of various implements and other items, and two wooden structures that resembled a typical vegetable stand but with a roof and doors which could be closed when not in use. Morgan wanted cash for the business and would not consider financing any portion of the sales price.

Roger went home and talked to his wife Crissy about the possibility of buying Morgan's business, and she was thrilled with the idea. Crissy at one time was a buyer for a large local department store, but had given up her position after she had children. She realizes that this is a dream come true for Roger, since he did not go to college and he has wanted to get into some type of business to prove himself and give his family all the material things not possible on his weekly salary. Roger and Crissy have $50,000 savings, and after checking with his local bank Roger finds that he does not have sufficient equity in his new home to warrant a second mortgage. As for the new venture, the bank's officers felt that it did represent a genuine opportunity, but they wanted a business plan and statements from Morgan for the last three years as well as his tax statements. In addition, they specifically recommended that Roger get a reputable accountant and work up a projected sales forecast, cash flow projections and the other data needed to present an acceptable package to the bank.

Roger went back to Morgan to request the data, and Morgan flatly refused to give any of his tax statements to the bank or anyone else. He went on to say that he did not have financial statements prepared by an outside accountant, but that he prepared his own records, and that because it was a cash business he just could not give Roger the information he needed. However, he did finally agree to prepare some figures for Roger to work with so he could raise the money. However, he wanted an agreement of purchase signed and a deposit received from Roger before he would give him any confidential data. Roger agreed, and the agreement was prepared by Morgan *exactly* as follows.

AGREEMENT TO PURCHASE MORGAN'S GARDEN CENTER

I, Frank Morgan, hereby agree to sell my business to Roger Davis for $250,000, but he has to buy the business in 30 days. If he does not buy the business during this time, then he will forever lose the right to buy the business and I can sell it to someone else.

Roger will give me $7,500 as a deposit on the business, which I will keep as good faith money for the transaction. Roger understands that I will not sell the business for less than $250,000 and I will not finance any part of the sales price. I want the entire amount in full when I sell the business.

> As soon as Roger gets the money then I will have my lawyer make up an agreement containing all the proper clauses that will make the sale true and valid.
>
> I agree to sell the business as outlined above and, I, Roger Davis agree to buy the business.
>
> Signatures
>
> _____   _____   _____
>
> Frank Morgan—Owner   Roger Davis—Buyer   Cathy Links—Witness

After Roger gave him a deposit, Morgan gave Roger the following figures for the previous three years.

	1986	*1985*	*1984*
Sales (estimated)	450,000	425,000	400,000
Net profit after taxes	18,000	15,000	13,750
Salary taken out—owner	40,000	40,000	40,000

When Roger received the figures, he went to a local C.P.A. accounting firm and discussed the situation with them. Roger was disappointed with the figures because he was familiar with the business and knew that the sales were much higher even though he did not handle the books. There were many weeks when sales exceeded $20,000 and during Christmas season sales per week were as high as $35,000. The explanation the accountant, Agnes MacDonald, gave him was that since at least 50 percent of his sales are for cash, no doubt Morgan was pocketing some of the cash sales and not declaring the total amount to the Internal Revenue Service to avoid paying taxes. She told Roger that it was good that he was not buying the corporation because he could be responsible for back taxes and other contingencies if there were an audit by the IRS. MacDonald spent quite a bit of time with Roger and together they came up with a conservative sales projection and estimated profits for the next three years. The projections were as follows:

	1987	*1988*	*1989*
Estimated sales	750,000	825,000	907,500
Estimated profits after taxes	30,000	33,000	36,300
Salary—Roger Davis	40,000	40,000	40,000

Roger and the accountant studied all the financial data they could get from Morgan and felt that these figures were extremely conservative. However, while Roger was enthusiastic, MacDonald had some doubts and suggested that together they contact a bank with whom she had had much success and see what kind of a mortgage they would grant for the entire property. She thought no bank would give funds on a straight-loan basis because it would want statements from Morgan, which he would not submit. Roger and his accountant went to the bank and the bank officers expressed interest in granting a first mortgage; however, it would take at least two weeks before they could give an answer.

At the end of two weeks the bank officers told Roger that the property was worth $150,000 and they would give him $120,000 as a first mortgage on the property. So Roger would have $120,000 plus the $50,000 he has saved for a total of $170,000. He would still be short $80,000 plus working capital, which MacDonald estimated would have to be no less than $60,000. According to MacDonald, the working capital would normally be higher, but since he is taking over a good-size inventory, his requirements would be less. Yet, Roger was now looking at $140,000 which still would have to be raised to take over the business and operate it properly.

Roger was frustrated and upset, but he was determined to buy this company. He even contacted all his friends and relatives, but he could not raise the money he needed. Finally, he went back to Morgan and told him that he could come up with $170,000, but he would need financing from him if he were to take over the business. Morgan was very understanding but said that he had to have cash and he was sorry that Roger could not buy the business. However, Morgan gave Roger still another possibility—a partnership or perhaps some other arrangement with Alan Stanton who had expressed an interest in the business. Roger had only heard of Stanton vaguely and knew that he was wealthy. Morgan told Roger that he had not talked seriously with Stanton about the business because of his 30-day arrangement with Roger, but if Roger would be interested in some form of partnership he would contact Stanton to see if he would be willing to accept a partner.

A week later Morgan told Roger that Stanton would like to meet Roger and that it was possible an arrangement could be worked out. Roger was excited that his dream might still become a reality. He asked Morgan about Stanton because he did not know much about him. Morgan said they had gone to school together and he was a self-made man. He said he thought Stanton was a fair man, but tight with a dollar—he has a reputation for living up to his agreements, but that everything he touches turns to gold. Morgan told Roger that dealing with Stanton would be different than dealing with him, but if he ever expected to have his own business, this might represent an opportunity for him to work with a winner and accumulate wealth.

After several meetings Roger and Stanton were getting along quite well. Stanton told Roger that at this time he did not know anything about the business except that it was profitable, and because of his lack of knowledge he was considering working out a partnership arrangement with Roger. Stanton allowed that he usually does not have partners in a business, but in this case he would be willing to set up a corporation and sell stock to Roger, permitting him to gradually increase the percentage of ownership to 49 percent of the business over a period of time. Roger was excited about the prospects and promised that he would do everything in his power to make the business a big success. Stanton agreed that at the next meeting he would have a formal proposal for Roger to sign which would cover their future business relationship after he purchased the business from Morgan.

The next week was hectic for Roger. According to his wife Crissy, Roger had been walking on air the entire week, just thinking about owning his own business. Several times he told her, "I am going to work harder than I ever worked in my life, Crissy, and you'll see, we will soon be living like royalty." Crissy was happy for Roger, and was hopeful that everything would work out as he expected.

Finally, the day came for the meeting with Mr. Stanton. Stanton's lawyer presented Roger with two agreements to sign. The first was a management contract that covered Roger's employment with the firm. Stanton felt that it was necessary because he wanted to make sure Roger was going to be the general manager. He knew that without Roger the business was a greater investment risk. Roger accepted this and read the terms of the management contract, which were as follows.

1. Roger Davis will serve as the general manager of Morgan's Garden Center at a salary of $30,000 per year plus approved expenses.

2. The term of the contract will be indefinite, but if either party should wish to cancel the contract for any reason whatsoever either party must give at least 90 days' notice in writing informing the other of the termination.

3. Roger Davis will operate the company in accordance with the operating plan approved by both Davis and Stanton. If Roger Davis wants to deviate from this plan in any manner, he must obtain written permission from Mr. Stanton.

4. The accounting and financial matters will be handled by Mr. Stanton through his accounting C.P.A. firm of Harding, Kapers, and Duper. It will set up a voucher system of accounting wherein all bills, expenses, and other items which have to be paid will be submitted in voucher form for approval. Mr. Stanton will sign all checks. In the event that Mr. Stanton is on vacation or unavailable to sign checks, arrangements will be made by Mr. Stanton to see that all invoices and debts are paid in full when due. Mr. Davis will have a petty cash fund available to him of $500 from which he can draw as needed to handle daily items. Said account will be replenished as needed.

5. Mr. Davis will report to Mr. Stanton weekly at a mutually agreed upon time to discuss the progress of the business and submit the reports required by Mr. Stanton.

6. Mr. Davis will be permitted to take a vacation of one week per year with full pay, but said vacation will be at a time when the business is normally slow.

7. Mr. Davis will be bonded for the sum of $100,000 and said insurance will be paid by the company. If Mr. Davis' application for bonding is turned down by the insurance company, then this management contract will be declared null and void and Mr. Davis' services will be immediately terminated.

8. Mr. Davis will obtain a $200,000 term life insurance from one of the major life insurance companies with Morgan's Garden Center named as the sole beneficiary. Premiums will be paid by the company.

9. The company will provide a health policy for Mr. Davis and his family under a plan selected by Mr. Stanton.

10. Mr. Davis will receive a 5 percent annual bonus on profits of the company. The 5 percent will be calculated by taking 5 percent of net profits before taxes and then subtracting any bad debt losses arising out of sales made on credit. Said bonus will be paid by no later than 30 days after the completion of the annual audit.

Roger was disappointed with the agreement because he felt that as a future stockholder such an agreement was not needed. He asked if the salary could be higher, but Stanton said he felt the company could not afford a higher amount at this time. However, he did promise that when the company was stronger he would definitely consider giving him a raise. Roger was also concerned about the overall operations of the business and the fact that he had to report to Stanton weekly and adhere strictly to the business plan that was drawn up and mutually approved. He did not understand why any deviation would need Stanton's approval. Stanton replied that since he was putting up most of the money, he felt that there had to be some controls. He went on to say that while he certainly had every confidence in Roger's ability and integrity, he felt that weekly meetings and reports were an obvious part of any partnership arrangement, and that after they got to know one another and their thinking started to mesh, he felt certain that there would be fewer meetings and Roger would be given more responsibility in areas such as signing checks, new line acquisitions, and expansion. Stanton made it quite clear that Roger had his confidence and that he felt a management contract was the proper instrument to protect each partner. After Stanton's explanation Roger felt better and signed the agreement.

The next agreement was for the purchase of stock in the new corporation. The company would be an S Corporation as a result of the Tax Reform Act of 1986 and Roger would be permitted to purchase stock on the following conditions.

1. The new corporation would be capitalized at $250,000. The company would issue 25,000 shares of common voting stock at $10 par value and Alan Stanton would purchase 20,000 shares of stock at $10 par for a total sum of $200,000. It would not be necessary to obtain a mortgage on the facilities.

2. Roger Davis would be permitted to purchase 5,000 shares of stock in the new corporation at $10 par value for a total of $50,000.
(Note: As a result of the purchase Stanton would own 80 percent of and Davis 20 percent of the company.)

3. Roger Davis also would be permitted to increase his ownership in the corporation up to 49 percent of the common stock issued. However, said purchases could only be made by Davis from profits earned by the company. Outside sources of funds could not be used to purchase the additional stock from Stanton.

4. The stock purchases could only be made in those years when the net profits after taxes are at least 20 percent of the stockholders' equity of the previous year. For example if the stockholders' equity last year was $375,000 ($250,000 paid in capital plus $125,000 in retained earnings) and if the profits after taxes were at least $75,000 (which represents 20 percent of stockholders' equity), then Roger Davis could purchase stock at the book value as of last year, which in this case would be $375,000 divided by 25,000 shares or $15 per share. Davis, who would already own 20 percent of the stock of the company, would be entitled to 20 percent of the $75,000 profit this year or $15,000, which could be applied toward the purchase of the stock of Alan Stanton.

   Further, it was agreed that Stanton would sell his stock to Davis at book value plus 100 percent. In the above example, Mr. Davis would pay Stanton $30 per share (book value $15 plus 100 percent) and could purchase 500 shares of stock in the company ($15,000 divided by $30 per share). Thus Davis' position in the company would increase from 20 percent to 22 percent.

   In years when the company did not earn at least 20 percent of last year's stockholders' equity, Davis would not be permitted to purchase stock.

5. With respect to dividends, since one of the objectives of the company was to build a strong corporation, dividends would only be declared when the board of directors felt that the company was strong enough to distribute them.

6. Since the company is an S Corporation and taxes must be paid personally by the stockholders even if the profits are not distributed, Stanton would lend, if necessary, whatever additional tax money was needed by Davis personally if he did not have sufficient funds to pay the taxes due on the undistributed profits. However, if loans were necessary, then in those years when dividends were distributed the loans would be paid in full. Said loans would carry an annual interest rate based on the prime rate at the time of the loan plus two percentage points.

7. Roger Davis would agree not to sell or transfer his shares of stock, or pledge said stock for any loans or for any other purposes whatsoever. They would

continue to remain free and unencumbered unless the company found it necessary for all stock to be pledged for a corporate loan if it was requested by a financial institution.

8. If either Davis or Stanton should die, their stock could be purchased by the remaining partner for the book value of the stock at the time of death. Payment for said stock would be made in full and should be paid in no more than ninety days from the date the book value of the stock had been determined by the company's auditing firm. The price to be paid for the stock for either shareholder would be book value plus 100%.

9. If Stanton should receive an offer from an outside party for his stock and wanted to sell his stock, he would first offer it to Davis on the same terms and conditions he had received from the interested purchaser and Davis would convey his decision in one week. If, on the other hand, Stanton wanted to terminate his relationship with the company for any other reason whatsoever and wanted to sell his stock to Davis and Davis was interested, then Stanton would sell his stock to Davis at stockholders' equity or any price and on any terms which Stanton and Davis agreed upon. If Davis received an outside offer to buy his stock, he would first offer it to Stanton as outlined above. If Davis wanted to leave the company for any reason whatsoever and sell his stock to Stanton and if Stanton was interested, then the price to be paid for Davis's stock would be as agreed between Stanton and Davis.

10. Roger Davis will be appointed vice-president of the corporation and also be made a director of the corporation. Stanton will be on the board of directors and serve as president of the company and Claude Brown will be secretary/treasurer and be the third director.

11. Further, if either Stanton or Davis terminates their relationship with the corporation each party agrees not to compete either directly or indirectly in the same type of business activity for a period of five years within a 50-mile radius.

The above constituted the entire agreement. After Roger read the agreement he was somewhat bewildered. He told Stanton that he appreciated being given the opportunity to purchase additional stock of the company, but he did not like the idea of having to produce a 20 percent return on stockholders' equity before he could purchase stock. Stanton replied that every investor, including Roger, was entitled to a return on his or her investment and that he would not permit Roger or anyone else to buy his stock without some return on his investment. In addition, if there were a few bad years he did not want to see his stock purchased for what could be less than original paid-in capital. Also, he felt that since he was giving up an additional 29 percent of his stock, which was not his custom, he felt he was entitled to a proper return on his investment. Roger said he could see Stanton's position and agreed to accept the terms and conditions of this agreement on the stock purchase.

Stanton pointed out to Roger that because of his (Stanton's) financial capacity the business could expand much faster than with Morgan's and that the profits could be tremendous over a short period of time. He assured Roger that he was not trying to put stumbling blocks in his way but merely taking proper steps to make the business successful. Stanton assured Roger that if he would just follow his methodology of doing business, he would become a wealthy man in a short time.

As for dividends, Roger felt the agreement was unfair. Again Stanton assured him that businesses must be prepared for bad days as well as good ones and that the way to build and make money is to invest earnings and make the business grow.

Roger asked for a day to think about the agreements. Stanton agreed, telling him that if he did not want to increase his percentage or purchase any stock, he would still offer him the management contract.

Roger talked it over with his wife and finally made up his mind to follow Stanton's lead. He felt that since Stanton was a self-made millionaire, he must know his business, and he hoped it would rub off on him. The next day Roger signed all the papers and became vice-president, general manager, and director of the company. Most importantly, he owned 20 percent of a business making it partially his.

QUESTIONS

1. What was wrong with the agreement between Morgan and Roger when Morgan gave him the first right to purchase the business with a 30-day time limit?

2. Do you think that Roger should have purchased Morgan's business or started a smaller business of his own? Do you feel Roger explored all the financial resources open to him?

3. What do you think of the management contract that Roger accepted? Would you have made any changes?

4. What do you think of Roger's part ownership in the company? If Roger and Stanton do not get along, what are the possible courses of action open to Roger and Stanton? How do you predict the disagreement will be resolved?

5. Should Roger have insisted on Stanton's getting a mortgage of $120,000 on the property instead of Stanton putting up the money?

6. How long do you think it will take Roger to increase his ownership to 49 percent assuming that annual sales grow at the rate of 10 percent? Assuming that Stanton is not as fair as depicted, what actions could Stanton take to thwart Roger from getting 49 percent and receiving any dividends?

7. If Stanton should die and Roger cannot purchase the business because of lack of funds and the stock passes on to Mr. Claude Brown, what could happen to Roger?

8. What do you think of the bonus plan given to Roger with the deduction of all the bad debts from accounts receivable? Do you think it was fair?

9. Could Stanton sell the entire business, including Roger's stock, without Roger's approval? What could Roger do if Stanton informed Roger that he was selling the business and Roger could not get the funds to make the purchase?

10. Do you think that Roger made the right decision?

Balanese Furniture Discount Store

Fred Townsend has worked for Andrew Wilson for the last eight years. During that period, Fred advanced from salesperson to general manager of the entire firm. Andrew relied a great deal on Fred, and since Andrew has a great deal of money, the store has not been the most important thing in his life. It was not always that way with Andrew, who was given the business as a wedding gift 40 years ago when he married Linda Ellen from Galveston, Texas. At that time, the annual sales of the business only averaged $75,000. Andrew was extremely aggressive and eventually built the business to the point where he was selling around $3 million per year and making $120,000 per year after taxes, or 4 percent of net sales. Over the years Andrew made good investments, and is now one of the wealthiest men in Galveston.

Andrew now comes to the business once a day or calls in and checks with Fred about what is happening and asks if he needs anything. While Andrew has given Fred complete power to do almost anything he wants, he is still tight with money. Fred has had to fight for every penny he ever received from Andrew in salary and bonuses and, despite Andrew's wealth, has even had to wait four months before he was paid his annual bonus. Fred presently makes $30,000 per year plus approved expenses with a bonus of 10 percent of the net profits after taxes.

Fred has problems with the compensation program, for sales have been declining because Andrew does not want to expand the business. Andrew has pointed out that he has no children so sees no reason to expand. He just keeps the business to give him something to do. He says that his wife cannot tolerate him more than a few hours a day at home, so he just has to occupy his time. Because Andrew has not been willing to expand, the inventory has been gradually decreasing to the point where it is sufficient to reach only the $1,200,000 level in sales for last year. Based on that figure net profits were $48,000 and Fred earned only $4,800. He has politely told Andrew he is not satisfied with his compensation as it now stands.

Fred can understand Andrew's position, but he would like to remain in the business because he feels comfortable in Andrew's store, and he has developed friends and clients over the years. However, he and his wife have been trying to save money to open up their own store. Their total capital at this time is $60,000, assuming he gets a second mortgage on his home, sells his stock, and adds up his liquid assets. This amount is certainly not adequate to open his own business and he knows it will be years before he gets the opportunity to have his own store. To complicate matters Fred has been offered a position as sales manager for a large furniture store in Houston at an annual salary of $40,000 plus a bonus that would give him about $15,000 to $25,000 in additional compensation. The firm is established and reliable.

Fred has decided to have a showdown with Andrew and make his final move. Unless he gets what he feels is adequate compensation, changes in the present method of store operation, and an adequate bonus plan—preferably a stock option program—he will quit the company.

Fred has a meeting with Andrew to discuss his future with the company. He informs Andrew that he is not satisfied with his compensation package and that under the present operating philosophy of the company he cannot expect his bonus to increase to more than the $4,800 he earned last year. Fred tells him that he wants a better program and an option to purchase stock in the company with the eventual option of purchasing the entire stock of the company if Andrew dies or decides to sell the business.

Andrew is quite shaken with Fred's ultimatum, for he feels that he and Fred get along well. He would not like to see Fred leave the company and asks Fred for a few days to think the matter over and then come back with either a proposal or good wishes for Fred in his new position.

After a few days Andrew decides to come up with an offer for Fred. It was time to consider what he was going to do with the business and since he liked the arrangement he had with Fred and Fred was impeccably honest, he would like to give Fred what he wants within reason. The proposal he presents to Fred is a draft, to be formally prepared after Fred and Andrew have an opportunity to discuss the conditions. The proposal is as follows.

1. Fred may purchase up to 25 percent of the business for book value. The estimated book value of the business, according to the last audited statement, was around $400,000. Fred would not be charged any goodwill for the stock even though Andrew feels that the stock is worth considerably more than book value.

2. Fred may purchase the stock from his own savings or from profits earned in the business up to the 25 percent limit. However, the amount that Fred will pay for the stock will vary each year depending on the book value of the stock. For example, if this year the book value of the stock is $200 a share, Fred will pay that amount and next year, if because of profits the stock is worth $300 a share, then Fred will have to pay $300 for each share.

3. Fred will give up the 10 percent bonus he is now receiving from the company.

4. Fred cannot use the stock of the company as collateral for a loan or for any other financial purpose. Furthermore, the stock cannot be sold or transferred to anyone before offering the stock to Andrew or his heirs. Said purchase price will in no case be greater than the audited book value of the stock at the time of the request, as determined by the company's auditors. If

Andrew's family does decide to purchase Fred's stock then it will have a minimum of ninety days to pay for the stock in full.

5. Fred will be elevated to the position of Director of the company and have a permanent seat on the Board of Directors as long as he remains a stockholder. Further, Fred will be promoted to Vice-President of the company.

6. Fred will have a base salary of $40,000 per year plus approved expenses.

7. Fred will obtain a life insurance policy for $250,000 with the company named as beneficiary. The premiums for said policy will be paid by the company. The reason for this policy is that the loss of Fred could hurt the company severely. (Fred's family would not receive nor participate in the proceeds.)

8. Andrew will still have the right to terminate Fred's employment even if he becomes a stockholder for the following reasons: Fred cannot be dismissed for incompetence, moral turpitude, insubordination, insanity, or for just cause. In the event that Fred is terminated he will sell back to the company his entire stock at book value to be determined by an audit as of the termination date, with said cost of the audit to be paid by both parties on an equal basis. When the price for the stock is determined the total amount will be paid within ninety days from the date the audit is complete. Further, upon termination Fred will be paid his salary up to the date of termination plus any approved expenses as of that date.

9. In the event of Fred's death, the book value of Fred's stock will be determined by an audit at the time of Fred's death, and the amount owing to Fred's estate will be paid within ninety days from the date of the audit. Any other compensation owing as of that date will also be paid to Fred's estate.

10. In the event that Andrew dies, Fred will have the first right of refusal to purchase the balance of the stock of the corporation. The amount to be paid will be based on the following:
    a. the best offer the heirs receive for Andrew's 75 percent of stock interest and on the same terms and conditions received by the heirs.
    b. the audited book value at the time of Andrew's death plus 100 percent goodwill.
    c. any other basis and whatever terms and conditions the heirs want to sell the stock to Fred.
    In the event that Fred elects to purchase the stock of the company, then he will pay off the balance within an agreed time frame to be determined by Fred and the representative of Andrew's estate. Thus, if the heirs want to give Fred more time and better conditions than they can receive from others who are interested in purchase, then the heirs reserve the right to offer Fred better terms and credit conditions to facilitate the purchase of the stock.

11. If Fred should decide to terminate his employment, he will give the company at least six months notice. He must offer the stock he owns to the company which they may purchase at their option at book value to be determined by the auditors at the time of his termination. Costs for the audit will be paid in full by Fred. Payment for said stock, if Andrew or his heirs decide to purchase, will be made ninety days after the completion of the audit. If Fred terminates his employment with the company, Fred agrees not to compete or engage directly or indirectly in the same type of business activities as the Balanese Furniture Discount Store for a period of five years and within one hundred miles.

12. Finally, with respect to the increase in inventory, it is clearly understood that Andrew will not invest any new capital in the company to increase the inventory. However, Andrew will permit Fred to make arrangements with suppliers for consignment arrangements or long-term credit arrangements with established suppliers to provide additional stock, but it is clearly understood that when any item is sold from stock that said item will be paid for in the credit period stipulated by the supplier. Failure by Fred to pay invoices for inventory when sold or within the credit period allowed by the supplier will be grounds for incompetence or just cause, and reason for Fred's termination.

The above constitutes the entire agreement between Fred and Andrew, and if Fred is agreeable then a formal proposal will be prepared by Andrew's lawyers and be submitted to Fred for his approval.

Fred reviews the agreement and is very interested in making the deal. He is grateful that Andrew is willing to sell him the 25 percent interest in the company with no goodwill charge, and he likes the prospect of getting $40,000 per year. Actually the $40,000 comes to more than he would be earning at the present time with salary and bonus, based on present sales.

QUESTIONS

1. Would you sign the agreement as it now stands? Why or why not? What is wrong with the proposal from Fred's viewpoint?

2. Discuss whether you think Fred should enter into any agreement with Andrew?

3. What would be your counter-proposal? Outline in detail.

4. With the capital Fred now has and the relationships he has developed with the suppliers, do you think the suppliers might be more interested in Fred than Andrew as a distributor for their products? Do you think Fred should approach them to see if he could get their approval to sell their products and to arrange some form of financing?

5. Do you think Fred could get the financing to set up his own business? Assume Fred needs a total of $250,000 to get started.

6. If Fred should sign the agreement, what problems do you foresee if Andrew should die?

7. How can Fred protect himself as a minority stockholder?

Marketing Problems

C&K Office Supply Company

C&K Office Supply Company has been one of the leaders in the office supply business in Los Angeles for many years. Bob Carpenter and Jerry Klein started the business in 1946 selling reconditioned surplus office equipment purchased from the Armed Forces. Over the years they struggled, but eventually developed the business into a $20 million company. Klein was the inside person, handling administrative, financial, and credit matters. Bob Carpenter was in complete charge of the marketing area. He was known to be a dynamic salesman. C&K was a genuine success story until Carpenter passed away two years ago, at which time Klein purchased all the stock from Carpenter's wife, and Klein assumed full control of the business.

At first Klein appointed his nephew to take over sales, but his nephew was inexperienced, unaggressive and unable to cope with the marketing problems that arose daily. Sales dropped and several staff members left the company for greener pastures. Klein did his best to cut expenses but still kept losing money. He even tried to sell the business, but because the company had lost $400,000 in the last year, $210,000 the year before, and sales had declined to $15 million, he could not find anyone who was willing to pay a decent price for it. Clearly, Klein had to find someone to come in and take over the marketing function so that he could build the business to the point where someone might be willing to purchase it.

Klein was now 72 years old and, although still active, wanted to leave the company. After searching for several months for a candidate, his local bank recommended Bill Elkins, who was president of a California printing firm. Elkins was an extremely aggressive 32-year-old divorced college graduate in Marketing. He had started in the printing company as a salesperson and within a short period became sales manager and then vice-president of sales. After five years with the company he developed a franchise system and within a few years had positioned the company as a major printing firm throughout the country. He finally became the president of the firm and was earning a great deal of money in salary and incentives. However, the owner would not sell Elkins stock in the company, and so Elkins decided to look for an opportunity to either buy his own company or buy into a larger company that would give him the option to buy out the entire company over a period of time.

Elkins and Klein met several times. Klein told his granddaughter he felt Bill had that "Old Carpenter Spark" and if he could get him into the business he felt that he could sell the company in a few years. When Klein asked Elkins how he achieved so much at such a young age, he replied: "I feel a lot of it is luck, but I am determined, aggressive and willing to work long and hard for success. I will not let anything stand in the way of success and I am willing to make any sacrifice to get ahead." Klein asked Elkins about his personal life. Elkins told him that he was divorced and had two children, who lived with his former wife. He told Klein that his marriage failed, almost from the start, because he was a workaholic who devoted more time to his job than his family.

Elkins examined all of the company's records and knew that making this company profitable again would not be easy. He was aware that he would have to become very proficient with the company's products, but felt he could acquire the knowledge in a short time. He finally made a deal with Klein. He was to be paid an annual salary of $75,000 plus expenses, and be given a car and apartment to use. He would purchase 25 percent of the business with the option to purchase the balance of Klein's stock from profits based on the book value of the stock at the end of the preceding year. In addition, he was to be given an additional 10 percent bonus on profits once the company made up the deficits it had experienced for the last two years. As soon as the losses were covered by profits, he could earn as much as 35 percent of profits which he could use to purchase stock from Klein. Klein stated that as soon as Elkins had purchased 50 percent of the company he could use outside capital or funds from investors to buy out Klein's interest at book value at the time of the sale. Klein only made two requests: that his granddaughter Betty, who was vice-president of administration, be given an opportunity to prove herself and that his nephew be given a chance as a salesperson. Finally, Klein stated that he and Elkins would operate as co-owners and that Bill would make all marketing decisions. He did state that until Elkins finally bought him out completely that he would have the final say when it came to money. Elkins liked Klein and felt that with some luck and a solid marketing plan he could accomplish his goals with this company.

Elkins asked Klein to set up a meeting of all marketing personnel at 7 A.M. Monday morning. Elkins felt that if he came in as a democratic leader the salespeople would continue to function as they had been. So, on Monday morning Klein introduced Elkins as his new partner and after a few comments about his background left the meeting. Elkins immediately informed them that during the last two years the company had lost money and sales were declining. He blamed the sales and profit slump on the sales force, and told them that he would not stand for anything less than making a profit. He said that anyone who did not produce would be out of a job, but that those who did would receive an incentive program that would eventually include generous bonuses and perhaps stock options. Finally, he told them, "I do not like meetings like this one, and I hope that future meetings will be more congenial. However, I purchased this business to make money, and I will not let anything stand in my way of success. I have experienced nothing but success and will not settle for anything less."

Bill told them that he believed in an open door policy so that if anyone had any recommendations that would help the company he would be glad to talk to them but he would not have time for trivial conversations. He insisted that all the salespeople report to work on time at 7:30 A.M. sharp each day for either meetings or conferences. Further, he expected salespeople to work on Saturdays, which they had not done for years. He also stated that the practice of preparing reports on Saturday would cease and that all salespeople would be expected to make up reports and other company forms at the end of their work days. Finally, he stated that he wanted all salespeople to call him each day from the field and inform him what they had sold and accomplished. Needless to say, at the end of the meeting there was complete silence. There were no questions, and no one remained at the end of the meeting to talk to Elkins.

As expected, several of the people who attended the meeting went to Klein and complained, but he merely informed them that Elkins was his partner and that he had full confidence in him. The sales force, which usually hung around until about 10 A.M. each morning, was gone a little after 8 A.M. Some met at Duggin's Coffee Shop, but most went directly into the field to start working. Those at Duggin's talked about how Elkins was in for a surprise and threatened to look for other jobs and take their clients with them. Eventually, they left the coffee shop and went into the field to try to make some sales. Klein was a little shaken by the harshness of the meeting but told his granddaughter that perhaps Bill's tough style was just what the doctor ordered. In any case, he was determined to let Bill have his way and defend his policies for the time being.

Bill spent the next two months pushing and driving the sales force. He now felt more comfortable with the product lines. He knew which salespeople were productive and which were dragging their feet. He also was aware of the problems that existed within the company and felt that it was time to start putting together a plan that would get the company moving. Betty, the vice-president of administration, informed him that sales and profits were up for the first two months. While he found this gratifying, he informed Betty that the only reason sales and profits were up was because of "push and shove" and some of the most productive people were waiting for positive changes. He told Betty he knew that if the company were to become a consistent winner, he would have to develop a good solid marketing strategy. Bill decided it was time to review his two-month tenure and make some decisions.

ORGANIZATIONAL CHART

The organizational breakdown of the company is presently as shown in the figure.

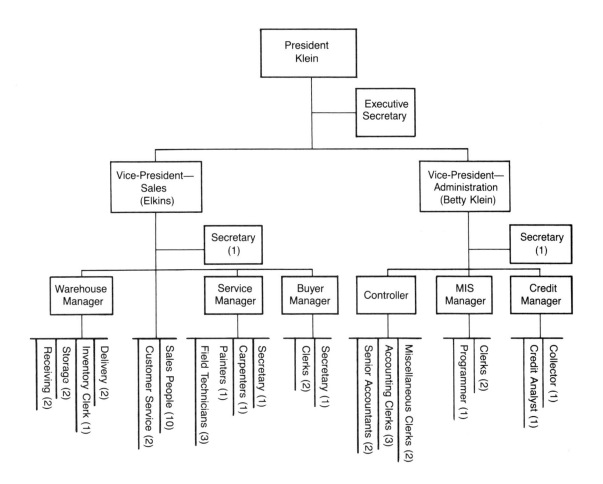

BREAKDOWN OF SALES BY MAJOR CATEGORIES

	No. of Accounts	% Total Sales	Sales per Category	Actual Gross %	Total Gross Profit	Category Profit Contribution
Government/Municipal	60	23.3%	$ 3,500,000	4.29%	$ 150,000	7.7
Educational Institutions	40	7.7	1,150,000	6.1	70,000	3.5
Old Accounts (Regular)	2,500	33.3	5,000,000	20.0	1,000,000	51.3
Old Accounts (Large Buyers)	20	6.0	900,000	15.0	135,000	6.9
Miscellaneous Sales (Floor)	—	6.7	1,000,000	25.0	250,000	12.8
New Accounts	125	23.0	3,450,000	10.0	345,000	17.8
Totals		100.0%	$15,000,000		$1,950,000	100.0%

BREAKDOWN OF COMPANY PRODUCT DIVISIONS AND
MAXIMUM GROSS PROFIT PER AREA

	Maximum Gross Profit Possible
New furniture (including office furniture, cabinets, etc.)	40%
Office equipment (calculators, typewriters, safes, etc.)	28
Office supplies (routine purchases)	30
Computers (all brands, large)	25
Computers (all brands, small)	25
Office automation including word processing	25
Software	65
Customized systems/printed forms	60
Office plants (non-living) and other office decorations	80
Used furniture and equipment	100
Service sales (including warranty claims paid by manufacturer)	45
Parts sales (including warranty claims paid by manufacturer)	50
Turn-key operations (just starting)	?

COMPENSATION OF MARKETING PERSONNEL

			Last Year Total Sales
John Baker	$55,000	(handles government accounts)	$ 3,000,000
Bill Collins	50,000	(handles educational institutions)	1,150,000
Mark Dodson	50,000	(handles large buyers)	900,000
Gloria Hunt	26,000	(sells at large)	1,450,000
Peggy Rossen	23,000	(sells at large)	1,950,000
Marty Rozak	28,000	(sells at large)	600,000
Paul Stern	26,000	(sells at large)	1,000,000
Marv Turner	29,000	(sells at large)	900,000
Ernie Klein	39,000	(formerly VP Sales, now sells at large)	750,000
Elly Zerter	28,000	(sells at large)	2,300,000
Total sales by personnel (excluding store sales)			$14,000,000

Note: With respect to Baker, Collins and Dodson, they are getting credit for sales called in to the office. In the case of Dodson, Bill Elkins also visits those accounts and Dodson's job is to follow up and see that they are satisfied with the service.

APPRAISAL OF SALES FORCE

Baker—Thirty-five years with the company and a close friend of Klein's. Very difficult to handle and causes a great many problems at meetings. Interrupts when suggestions are made and thinks he is the entire sales force.

Collins—Thirty-three years with the company. Close friend of Baker's and goes along with just about everything Baker proposes. Constantly telling Elkins that he is still a young executive with lots to learn.

Dodson—Eighteen years with the company. Works together with Elkins following up large accounts. Considers himself an errand boy and is not satisfied with his role. Feels insecure and wants to get into the field and develop his own accounts. Receptive to recommendations.

Hunt—Three years with the company. One of the best salespeople in the organization. Plans and organizes each day. Needs more direction, but is aggressive. Wants to become a branch manager some day and is still waiting for the new compensation plan that was promised when Klein's nephew was in charge.

Rossen—Four years with the company. Very unhappy with her compensation and does not intend to remain unless something is done soon. An excellent salesperson and will improve even more in time. College graduate and, before coming to work with C&K, was an assistant interior decorator for a large department store. She is using her interior design skills to sell complete office equipment systems. She has also suggested that the company market "turn-key" operations where the company designs a complete office operation, handling the layout, office furniture and fixtures, and the customized systems, forms and office automation. She feels that this is a very profitable area and at the present time is working with several new companies who are opening in the area on a complete "turn-key" operation.

Note: A complete turn-key operation is when the client permits the company to study completely the entire operation including design and layout of the office, the internal systems and automation systems. The company would work together with client personnel and then make a detailed proposal for the company to consider. After getting the order, the company then proceeds to perform the entire function, turning over the operation in final form when completed.

Rozak—Six years with the company. Strictly a price salesperson. Needs constant supervision and has to be pushed out of the office to get him started in the field. Does not follow up on his clients and does not take criticism well. Always promises to do better, but shows no improvement.

Stern—Five years with the company. Also unhappy with the compensation. Aggressive, nice personality, and willing to work long and hard. Interested in upward mobility. A college graduate with a major in computer science. Prefers to sell computers and feels that this year he will break the $2 million barrier because of the deals he has pending. Has also helped some of the salespeople who have asked him questions about the various computers and other equipment the company sells.

Turner—Four years with the company. Presently he is in a slump. Gets very little return business because he promises too much when he makes a sale, which has caused the company some embarrassment. Promised not to continue that practice but sales have not improved. Runs from store to store and has no system for prospecting accounts. Wastes time with clients who have little buying potential. Often forgets literature and his own personal cards when visiting a client.

Klein—Two years with the company. Nice person but not really interested in the business. Does not report on time and frequently neglects to turn in his reports. Constantly trying to become personally involved with some of the staff and has caused at least one good clerical staff member to lose her job. The sales he has generated have come from his uncle.

Zerter—Two years with the company. She is the best salesperson the company has and is furious with the compensation she receives. States that if she does not get an appropriate raise and a bonus plan she will quit and take her clients with her. She is very aggressive and operates systematically.

She concentrates only on clients that have potential. She never tries to grab all the business but tries to get her clients to give her some business and then lets her persistence and follow-up do the rest. She also tries to sell her large prospects on a complete in-depth Internal Systems and Automation Audit free of charge to enable them to know exactly what their strengths and weaknesses are. Because of her excellent background in business she has been quite successful this year and, if things go as planned, her sales could reach $4 million.

PROFIT ANALYSIS

Last year the firm sold $15 million in merchandise and gave away $3 million, or 22 percent in discounts. The sales force, according to Elkins, seems to think discounts are the only way to capture sales. While he has discussed the matter with them, he has not taken a definite stand because he has not yet studied all the facts. He realizes that a firm must give discounts, but the question is how much? Elkins checked Carpenter's records and found that discounts were not used as much when he was vice-president. Elkins realizes there is much more competition today than there was two years ago and that his firm is competing with small firms that give the greatest discounts because of their low overhead. However, none of those firms has the expertise or reputation that every firm needs today in hi-tech equipment and systems. When Elkins analyzed the figures further, he found that even a slight change in overall attitude and policy could make a difference. His analysis is as follows.

Discount	0%	*(in thousands)* 22%	19%	18%	17%
Gross sales	$15,000	$15,000	$15,000	$15,000	$15,000
Discounts	—	3,300	2,850	2,700	2,550
Net sales	$15,000	$11,700	$12,150	$12,300	$12,450
Cost of sales	9,750	9,750	9,750	9,750	9,750
Gross profit	$ 5,250	$ 1,950	$ 2,400	$ 2,550	$ 2,700
Expenses	2,350	2,350	2,350	2,350	2,350
Net before taxes	$ 2,900	$(400)	$ 50	$ 200	$ 350

Thus, it was obvious that if the salespeople gave fewer discounts the company could make money on the same volume of business. If the sales people gave only 19 percent discount or held back 3 percent, the firm would make $50,000 more. In addition, for every 1 percent that they held back or did not give away, the firm could make an additional $150,000 net profit.

Bill wanted to ascertain exactly what would happen if he could get the salespeople to maintain a 19 percent sales discount and increase volume back to the $20 million level. The following estimates are based on a sales discount of 19 percent and incremental increases of $1 million up to the former sales level of $20 million. Elkins is not considering any increases over present expenses although he fully realizes that increased volume will mean increased expenses for the company.

(in thousands)

Gross sales	$16,000	$17,000	$18,000	$19,000	$20,000
Discount (19%)	3,040	3,230	3,420	3,610	3,800
Net sales	$12,960	$13,770	$14,580	$15,390	$16,200
Cost of sales	10,400	11,050	11,700	12,350	13,000
Gross profit	$ 2,560	$ 2,720	$ 2,880	$ 3,040	$ 3,200
Expenses	2,350	2,350	2,350	2,350	2,350
Net before taxes	$ 210	$ 370	$ 530	$ 690	$ 850

These figures clearly point out that if the firm increased sales and maintained a 19 percent sales discount, profits would improve enormously.

BUSINESS AREA

Ninety percent of all the company's business is in the Los Angeles area, with the balance coming from San Diego, San Jose, San Francisco, and Sacramento. Most of this business originates from large clients in Los Angeles who handle the purchasing for their branches in the outlying areas. Elkins is very much aware businesses are growing dramatically throughout California and would increase his area outside Los Angeles. However, he does not see how it would be possible since the Los Angeles business is still in need of reorganization, and opening up branches would cost a great deal of money. However, Elkins feels that perhaps some other channel of distribution might be possible and even feasible to get representation in the outlying areas.

COMPETITIVE NICHE

Many firms are offering the same products that C&K is selling and somehow Elkins must establish a niche that will make firms want to pay a little more to do business with C&K. When he examined the entire client database he discovered that at one time the firm had more than 10,000 regular accounts. However, confusion over changes in personnel, new lines, the lack of supervision, and Mr. Carpenter's death, have cost the company a large chunk of its business in the past few years. Elkins also found that when the company acquires a new account, because of the fierce bidding to get the account, the initial profit is averaging 10 percent; however, when the client becomes a regular account the profit increases to 20 percent. He concluded that this indicated that when the client develops confidence in the company, while price is still important, their emphasis shifts to service and having their needs satisfied in an efficient manner.

PRICE STRUCTURE

Bill noticed that while their sales to government and educational institutions do contribute a significant volume of business, the gross profits from these sales are inadequate. When Elkins pointed this out to Klein, Klein stated that he agreed with Bill but there was another side to the story. Klein told Elkins that because of the large sales and the subsequent large purchases from suppliers, the company picks up large cumulative discounts that make the company more competitive. For example, if they eliminated the government and educational institutions accounts they would be purchasing about $4 million less and this would decrease the discounts the firm is now getting. However, because the firm is buying in volume from most of the suppliers, the company enjoys greater discounts, which makes it possible to compete and get clients they might otherwise lose.

ADVERTISING

Klein cut down on all advertising expense. All advertisements in the trade magazines were eliminated. The only items now being purchased are catalogs, which cost the company $7.50 each, and Klein has limited the quantity to 1,000. The salespeople do have literature from all the suppliers which they usually hand out when they visit their clients.

SALES SUPERVISION

Presently, Elkins does not have time to work with the salespeople to discuss their clients and what problems they are facing in the field. Salespeople are not engaged in target marketing. They use the "shotgun" method where they all go out on their own and do what they can. It is not uncommon for two salespeople to visit the same client. There are no territories, routing plans, scheduling, or client visit frequency policies. The clients are not graded or classified and no one has given any thought to using the State Industrial Guide, which can be found in most libraries. When Carpenter died, Klein told the sales personnel to assume that everyone is a client and the sales force just followed that policy.

PRODUCT LINE SALES

Everyone in the sales force does not sell the entire product line. Some are more comfortable with certain products, such as furniture or computers, and neglect the balance of the products unless the client makes a special request. The salespeople need a lot of work in this area and no training programs have been established.

SALES QUOTAS

Sales quotas do not exist. Salespeople are just told to get sales.

PERSONAL ASSISTANT TO THE VICE-PRESIDENT

Elkins feels that under the present organizational structure he cannot handle all the daily marketing problems efficiently, develop a marketing plan, train and work with the sales force, and perform a host of other tasks. He feels that he needs a personal assistant or someone who can follow his orders and take care of details that he does not have the time to handle. Elkins feels that his time should be spent productively and not in time-consuming tasks that someone else is capable of doing. He would like to appoint someone from the sales organization, but the job would only pay $30,000 to $35,000 per year.

COMPENSATION PROGRAM

Elkins knows that unless he comes up with a compensation program he is going to lose his top people. He also would like to attract new people to the firm. The present plan arbitrarily sets salary scales. Elkins would like to establish a plan that would pay a higher salary to people like Hunt and Rossen, while at the same time provide incentives that would be tied to sales, discounts, and profits. Klein agrees that something must be done, but warns against incentives based on profits because it could mean opening company books to prove to the sales-people exactly how much profit was actually earned from their sales.

COMPETITION

Elkins has analyzed competition and feels there is plenty of business out there for all firms. C&K enjoys a good reputation, although it has lost a lot of accounts. The smaller firms do not have the people power to cover the area or do the technical job that is being demanded more each day by firms and organizations. Elkins' competitors advertise heavily in trade magazines and have more salespeople than he does at this time. One of the largest firms has more than 35 salespeople working for it full time and has branches in San Diego and San Francisco.

TECHNICAL PERSONNEL

The company has a strong technical staff. The people in the service department are experienced in working on high-tech equipment. This has been a big plus with the firm's clients. Elkins feels the company should promote this advantage.

USED FURNITURE & EQUIPMENT

The firm has neglected the used furniture and equipment market. The company has longstanding personnel who can do an excellent job reconditioning used equipment. Elkins found that the sales force does not even attack this profit center. He feels that since many firms are going out of business, his company could pick up the equipment and furniture as low as $0.10 on the dollar. However, Klein has been reluctant to set up a fund to take advantage of investing in such opportunities as they crop up. Elkins feels that a $50,000 initial investment would pay for itself over and over. He also feels that advertising used furniture in trade magazines for firms who are starting out in business with inadequate capital could attract much business.

PURCHASING

Elkins would like to see the firm expand into more stylish furniture and equipment and take advantage of importing some office equipment at cheaper prices. Elkins is satisfied with the present group of suppliers but thinks they could be pushed for better discounts and perhaps consignment deals. In addition, he would like to see better credit terms where possible. Although Klein disagrees with him on this point, Elkins feels that the firm should explore the possibility of importing some additional products to give them more diversification and better prices.

CONCLUSION

Elkins has taken his concerns to Klein and both agree that they must take action immediately. Klein agrees to go along with everything Elkins wants, but he made the following points clear:

1. He will not invest any more money into the firm, although he will explore new credit lines for used furniture purchases.

2. He does not want to see advertising exceed $50,000 the first year exclusive of the catalogs unless there is a dramatic increase in profits.

3. He does not want to open up branches at this time.

4. He will not sanction a wholesale hiring of personnel. As long as the personnel are productive and contribute profits to the firm, they have his approval. Any hirings would have to be justified.

5. He will permit an assistant for Elkins, but would like to know what the assistant would be doing.

6. He will approve a new compensation program as long as it will lead to more profits.

Elkins now knows what has to be done, but must come up with a marketing strategy.

QUESTIONS

1. Do you approve of the way Elkins threatened the marketing personnel? Would you have handled it differently? How?

2. Outline the first priorities that Elkins must deal with at this time.

3. What type of competitive edge or niche should Elkins establish for the firm? How would you go about developing such a niche?

4. How should Elkins handle the present attitude problem he has with the sales force regarding discounts?

5. What type of target marketing program would you establish? Do you approve of the present "shotgun" method, or do you feel that the firm should direct their attention to various target groups? Do you think that the State Industrial Guide would be of assistance in target marketing?

6. What would you do about the 7,500 clients who are no longer doing business with the firm?

7. What type of supervision would you establish for the sales force and how would you carry out such a plan? Where would the assistant to Elkins fit into the plan you establish?

8. Although you do not have all the financial data you need, devise a plan for the present and future sales personnel, including basic salary plus incentives. (When you develop your incentive program, consider $700,000 as breakeven sales. Therefore any bonuses and incentives would have to be based on volume over $700,000 annual sales.)

9. Do you think Elkins should try to open up in the areas of San Diego, San Jose, San Francisco and Sacramento at this time? If you do, indicate what type of channel of distribution you would use and what type of arrangement you would try to establish. Your plan could include all or part of the entire product lines.

10. Summarize your marketing strategy for the company.

CASE 19

Schuler Manufacturing Company

Three years ago, Rupert Schuler purchased an electrical machinery equipment manufacturing firm, and now he is interested in entering the international field. Although Schuler worked for a year in the international department of his former employer, he does not think he knows enough about the international scene. He thinks there should be a good international market for his equipment because his products are well built, he uses hi-tech equipment to manufacture his products, and his quality control is excellent. He has appointed Henri Villard to investigate the possibilities. Henri speaks and writes in French, Spanish, and German. He has traveled to all the countries in Latin America and the Far East. Although Villard is not familiar with the entire product line, Schuler feels he can quickly learn about it.

Schuler's venture into the international field has the backing of the Department of Commerce and other international agencies. Henri has been working with them to gather information. He decides to make a trip to the Caribbean, Mexico, Central and South America to access the market. Henri's first stop was Caracas, Venezuela. He checked in with the correspondent bank in Caracas and was immediately welcomed with open arms. The bank representative, Joaquin Betancourt, gave Henri a complete analysis of the Venezuelan market and offered his assistance. Henri asked to meet with some interested and reliable firms. Betancourt contacted several companies and made appointments with four firms. Henri was elated and made plans to visit each of them.

After two days of conferences and meetings, Henri found that there was genuine interest in many of the products Schuler manufactured, partly in the domestic market but mainly to compete in government bids. Each applicant wanted an exclusive agreement with Schuler in Venezuela, and each expressed interest in a long-term contract. Henri agreed to get back to them soon regarding the contract and conditions. Henri went back to Betancourt and asked for credit checks on all the firms. One company, Productos Electricos, S.A. turned out to be especially attractive. The company had substantial assets and the management team was good and aggressive. Henri began negotiations with the company agent, Don Ulloa, for a representation agreement. Ulloa was very businesslike and stated clearly what he wanted:

a. exclusive representation for five years

b. credit conditions including 30 days' sight draft against documents and longer terms, if necessary, for sales to large companies or the government

c. engineering assistance when necessary for special projects and installations

d. all catalogs, price lists, brochures, and bulletins available in Spanish

Henri was willing to do the following:

a. grant a one-year exclusive representation agreement for Ulloa in Venezuela; if the arrangement proved to be satisfactory after one year he would be glad to entertain a five-year exclusive contract.

b. grant the exclusive agreement if the distributor would stock at least $350,000 of equipment for himself and his dealers; the first order must be opened by a letter of credit.

c. give credit terms for 30 days, but extensions would be on a case-by-case basis.

Ulloa agreed to the one-year contract and accepted the credit terms, but he did not want to invest $350,000 in stock at this time. He would first like to assume the line and then select particular inventory based on perceived needs. After much discussion with Henri, Ulloa agreed to purchase the beginning inventory within six months. He signed a contract prepared by Henri in Spanish, which made Ulloa the exclusive distributor in Venezuela.

After this visit Henri proceeded to Guyana, where he appointed another distributor, Emil Sangar, a highly-respected Moslem. The terms of the agreement were similar to those with Ulloa, except Sangar agreed to purchase a beginning inventory of $50,000 with a 30 day sight draft.

Henri went next to Colombia, but found the market closed for economic and political reasons. However, the representative did suggest he talk to some possible distributors who might be interested if an opportunity arose. Henri met with Jose Marin who sold products similar to Schuler's. Marin explained that because of the present economic condition, only essential products could enter the country and then only under special conditions. If particular items were needed for a government job, or an essential industry, the government would permit products to be imported, but they normally only paid in coffee beans. Henri would have to make bartering arrangements, a practice with which he was unfamiliar. Marin told him that other countries had barter brokers throughout Europe to facilitate these sales. Henri indicated that he would be glad to work with Marin, although he did not sign any agreement. He told Marin that if an order did come up to contact him.

Henri proceeded to several other countries and found the following type of conditions.

1. Distributors were interested in handling the products, but they wanted consignment inventory.

2. In some countries the distributors wanted the sales price quoted to them increased by as much as 50 percent, with the difference between the invoice price and the actual cost to be deposited in a New York bank account. The statement would be forwarded to an address they designated.

3. On future visits the distributor would take care of all expenses and make money available to them in the local currency; when they traveled to America Schuler would do the same for them. By doing this, they would be able to accumulate U.S. currency.

4. Distributors asked Schuler to set up a plant in their country under some arrangement. Because of the anticipated explosion in some economies it would be beneficial if components or products were produced within the country. Government support could be in the form of a factory, personnel, and other costs. Schuler would supply the manufacturing equipment, provide working capital and be willing to accept a 49 percent stock interest. This was to avoid having foreign investors controlling businesses.

5. In many countries Henri was told that to be successful you had to pay out cash bonuses to certain government officials who would favor the company in bids. The commission would be paid to a legitimate intermediary who would act as a selling agent or consultant for the government official. It was perfectly legal to pay for that assistance. Purchases of other products used by the government, even those not being handled by Schuler, could be diverted to Schuler who would proceed to buy them and charge a fee for his services.

All in all, Henri had a good trip when you consider that it was his first made for the company. On his return, he immediately met with Schuler, who was pleased with the sales and made arrangements for the products to be shipped. He did not quite understand the 30 day sight draft so Henri explained that the goods would be shipped and 30 days after document presentation by the bank to the client and acceptance of the draft, the total amount would be paid by the distributor. All shipments would have to be invoiced on a CIF basis—this is with the price broken down to indicate the factory F.O.B. cost, insurance, freight, and handling costs to the destination.

Henri said that he would attend to the details of invoicing and shipping. He admitted he had a problem with some of the other conditions demanded by a few new distributors. He was reluctant to pay bribes to intermediaries to get business. He was also unwilling to inflate the sales prices and make deposits in foreign accounts. Schuler did not like this method of business either, and was opposed to doing anything that was even slightly unethical. Henri explained that they were selling overseas and the company might have to play by local rules. Schuler replied that he would have to think about this for quite a while.

Henri hired an engineer from Spain to translate catalogs, brochures, price lists, bulletins and service manuals into Spanish. Henri contacted the Department of Commerce and discussed handling barter or countertrades with foreign countries. The people at the Department of Commerce were cooperative though they were reluctant to offset exports with imports. They would help find firms to render quotations for coffee or other products.

Soon after the trip, orders started flowing into the company, and Schuler was very pleased. However, many difficulties began to emerge. One problem developed soon after the first shipment was sent abroad. Customs would not accept the goods because they were not packed and marked as required. Henri called the distributor, who was getting the matter resolved through his political connections, but all shipments would have to be forwarded correctly in the future. Shipping overseas involved a tremendous amount of paper work: commercial invoices; packing lists; shipper's Export Declaration; export licenses; insurance certificates; consular invoices; and certificates of origin. The paper work, as well as the packing, was too much for Henri and he wondered if some firm could handle this function for him. Another problem was that transportation costs were quite high, but Henri learned that if he used non-conference boats instead of conference lines he could save a great deal of money on the freight costs and make himself more competitive.

One incident illustrated a third area for concern. A distributor did not pay a $15,000 sight draft when it was presented to him at the end of the 30-day period. Bank officials cabled that they were filing a protest within 24 hours and would have a local attorney handle the collection, but it was not guaranteed. When Henri called, the distributor reported that the client who ordered the goods would not pay as agreed, and he needed more time, specifically 90 days. Henri felt that there was no other alternative and agreed to the terms. He cabled the bank officials and told them he had made other arrangements. Finally, Henri faced the problem of one of the countries in Latin America refusing the brochures and catalogs because they felt some of the wording was "obscene." It seems that the Spanish words have other connotations in some Latin American countries. These written materials would have to be changed.

Four months later Henri was asked if he wished to bid on a $5 million project for the government of one of his overseas distributors. Henri was to give the distributor his best initial estimate, and then visit them to work out other arrangements concerning payments to the intermediaries. Henri spoke to Schuler, who thought the matter was worth investigating. Henri took a sales engineer with him to help determine the exact price. The bid, based on the government specifications, included Schuler's F.O.B. factory costs of $5,450,000, a 20 percent profit of $1,090,000 for Schuler. This would mean the F.O.B. factory price for the products the government wanted would cost the distributor $6,540,000. The distributor felt the prices were too high and said that for him to make any money he would have to sell the products 10 percent higher than the figure Henri gave him. This would mean the selling price based on F.O.B. factory would be $7,194,000 plus about $545,000 for freight and insurance, making the government price approximately $7,739,000. Henri and the distributor met with the intermediary, Pedro Jimenez, who judged the price too high when compared with other bids. Jimenez suggested a reduction of $800,000 and a personal consulting fee of $100,000. The price quoted to the government would then be $6,839,000, which was calculated as follows:

Original price as calculated (F.O.B. factory)		$7,194,000
less:		
Price reduction	$800,000	
Commission	100,000	
		900,000
Adjusted selling price		$6,294,000
Plus: estimated freight costs		545,000
Estimated sales price to government		$6,839,000
CIF landed at their port of entry		

Henri could see that based on these figures the distributor would not make a profit, which would not be acceptable. So he and the distributor agreed that Henri would grant a 5 percent commission on the adjusted selling price, which would allow $314,700 profit for him, and Schuler would still make $529,300 profit. Henri told the selling agent that this was acceptable to him but he had to get approval from Schuler. The distributor told Henri that the bid would likely be accepted since he was related by marriage to the Minister of Finance, who is directly involved with all government transactions. Henri returned home and presented these figures to Schuler. Schuler was concerned about the legality of the fee to Jimencz, but he did find the profit potential attractive. Since they had already reached their breakeven point in the factory, profits would increase because they would only have to consider variable costs.

Schuler's bid was accepted and the government order was forwarded. However, the financial terms requested were different from those indicated in the bid. The government proposed that 50 percent of the equipment be covered by a letter of credit with the balance financed over the next year with interest. The government asked for this change because several of the other bidding firms offered to grant these terms, and government officials felt they had to replicate these terms. Henri knew that Schuler could not carry these costs and that no bank would finance Latin America projects even in a fairly stable country. Henri had to find a solution to this problem fast.

In addition to these financial difficulties, engineering problems were developing in the field. Equipment was breaking down at a pace he could not understand. When Henri sent out engineers, they discovered that the equipment was not being properly maintained and inadequate parts were being used to repair the equipment. The engineers suggested that spare parts and proper tools be supplied with each piece of equipment sold. They also suggested that field training programs be available for those who purchase and use the equipment. To do this Henri would have to assign some of his engineers just for field service visits to the area the company now serviced. However, many of his engineers were unfamiliar with languages and customs other than their own. Henri knew he would have to find a way to solve this problem quickly.

Schuler decided to re-examine his involvement with international business. Sales had reached $10 million, but more than $1 million in receivables were outstanding. Collection was likely, but the timing of receipt was uncertain. It was difficult for him to carry the accounts, and he wondered if he should continue in this business.

QUESTIONS

1. Do you think it was a good idea for Schuler to enter the international market?

2. Would you have made the contractual arrangements with a distributor if he refused to carry your suggested stock of products? What other conditions would you want included in the agreement?

3. Do you approve of the payment of commissions to selling agents who really are a go-between for the officials in the government? Do you think that Schuler was operating unethically and should stop doing business with countries that request such transactions?

4. What can Henri do about the nonpayment of invoices? How is he going to handle shipments to foreign countries that demand terms of up to one year or more? Is there any way Henri can protect the company from bad debt losses?

5. How should Henri handle the service problem that is quickly developing in the foreign markets?

6. How can Henri handle the problem of the tremendous number of documents which must be processed? How could Henri relieve the company of this burden?

7. Would you make a sale to a foreign country that demanded that you exchange your products for beans, coffee, or sugar?

8. How would you handle the problem of vocabulary for brochures and other publications that have to be translated from English to Spanish?

9. Would you agree to conditions of sale where you had to increase the actual sales price by 50 or 100 percent and then when paid, deposit the money into a New York bank account for the person designated by the distributor? Do you think that is illegal or unethical?

CASE 20

Arthur Sandburg Self-Development Center

Arthur Sandburg had been Vice-President of Marketing for Opt-Tech, Inc. for 25 years, and was earning a substantial salary. He owned his own home, worth at least $200,000, and he had a summer home in Ocean City, worth approximately $450,000. Arthur and his wife Eleanor were highly respected in the city of Baltimore, Maryland. They and their family traveled extensively. In general, Arthur's life was ideal. Then his company merged with a giant multinational firm that overwhelmed his organization and combined marketing into one consolidated division. The company's new officials asked Arthur to remain with the organization, but he declined, feeling it was time to go out on his own and see if he could be successful in his own venture.

Arthur was not only a natural salesperson, but he had a unique capacity for taking "burnt-out" salespeople or employees and rejuvenating them. He had conducted countless seminars in the various departments of his former organization in all the branches throughout the United States. Because of his tremendous success with seminars, Arthur felt that someday he could go public with these talents. Now that the opportunity had arisen, perhaps he could build a series of seminars based on successful selling and developing self-confidence. He also thought he could have seminars dealing with other topics, such as the following:

1. How to deal with management successfully, and increasing chances of upward mobility.
2. Managing difficult people and developing loyal workers.
3. How women can increase their chances of success when interviewing for an executive position.
4. Effective public speaking.

Arthur knew he would have to refine his topics to make them attractive to diverse audiences, but he felt that with his background, experience, and distinguished appearance, his chances of success were excellent.

Arthur decided to try his idea in Baltimore to see if there was a market for such self-development seminars. He decided to offer three seminars:

1. How to Speak Effectively in Public
2. How to Be a Sensational Salesperson
3. How to Develop Confidence in Yourself

He would charge $45 per seminar or $100 if the person attended all three. Arthur rented a 100-seat conference room in one of the local hotels. He placed advertisements in the local newspapers promoting the benefits of each seminar. He appeared on local television, promising that his seminars would help people learn the ten keys to self-confidence and be at ease under any conditions, skills which would lead to a happy life.

The seminars were planned for two weeks from the date of the first advertisement. At first very few people responded, but then Arthur was bombarded with people who wanted to take a seminar. It seemed that nearly 300 people wanted to take the confidence-building seminar, and only 35 people were interested in the others. So Arthur decided to cancel the other seminars because of lack of interest. To handle the 300 people he asked the hotel to give him a larger room. This room cost $2,500, but included the seating arrangement Arthur needed, screens for slides and a short movie, and a long table for serving refreshments.

Arthur rented a temporary office and hired a secretary to answer the phone and register clients. More than 300 clients enrolled and Arthur made the necessary adjustments with the hotel.

On the night of the seminar Arthur greeted everyone, welcoming them with a pleasant smile and a few comments about how pleased he was that they could come. Finally, Arthur took the stage, introduced himself, and asked each person to examine the folder they found on each chair. Arthur began his presentation, sprinkling his comments with a little humor and asking the audience for questions. Some did have questions but, as he expected, most merely sat and listened to him talk. He could see that some audience members were yawning, others were daydreaming, and some had confused expressions on their faces. A few were very interested, but silent. During the break Arthur circulated throughout the crowd to get feedback. Many were pleased and liked what he said, but some were disappointed because they expected him to teach them individually how to be more confident. Arthur could see that there had to be some adjustments, but he could not make them on the spot because he had a carefully outlined program. However, during the second half he started giving lots of examples and tried hard to pinpoint typical problems, as he transmitted the keys to instant confidence. It seemed to work, but Arthur was not completely satisfied with the outcome. After the break about 90 people had left, and those vacant chairs did not do much for his own confidence. During the last part of the program Arthur asked each participant to name other topics they would like covered in future seminars. The applicants came up with the following.

1. How does one deal with an irritable spouse who brings work home and upsets the entire family?

2. How can experienced workers over 50 convince their bosses they are still as productive as they were when they were younger? How can one compete with students coming out of college?

3. How does a person handle sexual harassment on the job without jeopardizing his or her position?

4. How do you successfully apply for a position when you are over 40 years old? Should you alter your appearance by using wigs, make-up, and dress to get a positive reaction?

5. How can you lose weight without gaining it back?

6. How can you prepare for retirement? When should you retire? How much money do you need to retire? What kinds of jobs are open to the retired to supplement their income? How should you approach an employer after retirement?

7. How to handle one's sex life after 25 years of marriage.

8. How can you make people like you? How can you keep friends? Do's and don'ts with friends.

Arthur thanked everyone for coming and said he would let them know of additional seminars. Arthur received a scorecard from the participants on their opinion of the seminar. Twenty percent said it was excellent, 25 percent that it was good, 40 percent that it was fair, and 15 percent said they did not learn anything and it was a waste of money.

Arthur reviewed the entire seminar and felt that while it was a success financially (he cleared around $4,000 after deducting for the hotel room, refreshments, advertising and office expenses), he felt something was missing, and that he was not headed in the right direction. The topics proposed for future seminars would have to be refined, and he might even have to call in experts from different fields to work with him. He also judged that groups of 300 kept him from close contact with the participants. If he had about 25 people maximum at a time he could do a terrific job. However, for that he would have to charge much more than $45 per seminar. He could cut down on the hotel space, refreshments, and visual aids, but he would have to charge about $250 per seminar to make money and that figure was too much for the average person. Another possibility was that he could still handle 300 people but break them down into smaller groups after a basic presentation. However, this would mean hiring other people to work with him. In any case Arthur thought that the concept of selling seminars needed more refinement. Perhaps a different methodology would make them more successful, not only financially, but from the participant point of view. Perhaps a series of topics could be repeated in different places for different audiences.

To assess his needs, Arthur decided to send a form letter to all the participants thanking them for coming and asking them for suggestions. The response was interesting. Of the 100 responses, many suggested there be some type of entertainment to go along with the seminar. Many said they started getting bored after about 45 minutes, and some entertainment would have made the seminar hold their interest. Arthur was grateful for the comments, but confused. In his former organization people were always interested. He had acted seriously with the poise a serious subject should demand. Apparently the public was different. They wanted to learn, but they also wanted to have some fun while they were learning. He was not a comedian and he did not know what type of entertainment he could use to make it more interesting. However, he decided to make another attempt and give the public what they wanted.

A few months later Arthur again announced on television and in the newspapers that he was offering the same seminar on building confidence. This time the television commercials included paid actors who appeared with him to give testimonials. After Arthur made his statements about the wonders of the seminar, he referred the audience to two of his success stories. One professional-looking woman gave the impression of a successful business executive. She claimed that before she had met Mr. Sandburg she was shy and afraid, but after his seminar she got on the confidence track that eventually spelled success. The other person was a man who also clearly conveyed an impression of dignity, poise, and confidence. He stated: "Would you believe that six months ago I was so afraid of my boss that I used to hide from him in fear? Now, that same boss appreciates me and has given me more important assignments. I owe it all to Arthur Sandburg who taught me how to develop confidence in myself and more importantly hold on to it."

Arthur rented the same hotel facilities and 310 people enrolled for the second seminar. This time Arthur gave a brief presentation and then introduced the paid actors to the group. They each told stories which Arthur had meticulously conceived, and they were received with warmth and enthusiasm. There were many questions and the actors were so schooled by Arthur that they fielded these with ease. Arthur returned to his presentation. Soon after, someone rushed up on the stage and took the microphone away from Arthur. Of course, this was all planned and the paid comedian told a few jokes about confidence and what it did for him, then collapsed on the floor. There was much laughter and within 10 minutes the comedian left the stage. After the little interruption, Arthur went on with his presentation until break-time.

This time the comments were good. However, several people recognized that the people he presented as proof that his technique worked were actors from the local playhouse, and they asked him to verify that fact. Arthur vehemently denied anything underhanded and said that it could be they performed for the local playhouse theater, but when they came to him they were in need of help and help them he did. When the break was over Arthur went back to the center of the stage and proceeded with the last segment of his program. Then one of the people who confronted him during the break asked if she could question the people he presented as living proof that his methods and techniques were successful. Sensing that this could be trouble, Arthur asked her to be specific. The participant said she felt they were frauds, for they were actors she had seen perform in the local playhouse. Arthur maintained his poise and called the two people to the stage. Each of them was smart enough to see what was happening and neither denied that they were actors. One of them, Sally Clements, affirmed that while she did act, she had problems with confidence and might have to leave the stage. Arthur Sandburg made it possible for her to tackle the theater again. The other actor, Richard Dean, said that he had been acting for nearly five years but could never get a meaningful part. He usually ended up holding a long spear or uttering three words as a waiter. He was never given a larger role because he did not have that sense of presence or confidence needed for success. He had been so despondent that he was thinking about giving up his career and going into another field. He turned his head and looked straight at Mr. Sandburg with obvious gratitude and sincerity, claiming that without his guidance and help he would never have achieved the new success he was now having in his career. He had asked Mr. Sandburg to permit him to speak before this group, for he wanted them to know that even an actor, whom everyone expects to have built-in confidence, can become desperate and need help. After these comments, the questioning participant demanded to know if they were getting paid. Both of them vehemently denied it. The participant sat down apparently satisfied, but the entire episode had upset the group.

The seminar ended after the small group sessions, and Arthur asked them to evaluate his performance and the seminar in general. The questions and responses were as follows.

1. Did you get anything worthwhile out of this seminar? Thirty percent indicated it was excellent, 20 percent good, 15 percent fair, and 35 percent poor.

2. Did you find the seminar interesting and entertaining? Fifty percent of the group stated the comedian was ridiculous and encroached on their time, 30 percent said he was funny and was a delightful surprise, and 20 percent had no opinion.

3. What did you think of the two testimonials presented to the group who had been successful? Sixty percent said in the beginning they were an inspiration, but after the question was raised about the fact that they were actors, they were confused and doubted their sincerity. Thirty percent stated they felt the testimonials helped a great deal and 10 percent had no opinion.

4. Should there be a follow-up seminar? A large segment felt there should be follow-ups and others indicated they would like to attend different seminars covering other topics, including the following.
   a. How to become a millionaire without investing in real estate.
   b. How to become a successful female business executive and be accepted.
   c. How to write a successful resume.
   d. Straight talk about marriage with workaholics and alcoholics.
   e. Safe exercise programs for people over 40 years of age.
   f. Nutritional information for middle and later years of life.
   g. How to prepare for death.
   h. How to achieve peace of mind.

When Arthur evaluated these responses he realized he could be identified as a fraud and liar if the two actors had not come through as they had. He made only $2,000 on this seminar, for he had to pay the actors and give them a bonus. Arthur was careful to pay them in cash because he did not want any fall-out later.

The seminars were not what he had expected. Arthur had hoped that they would be wildly successful and he could eventually make videos and cassettes to distribute all over the country. However, he never got to that stage. At this point he does not feel he should go further because adjustments have to be made if he wants to deal with the public. Arthur has called upon you, a marketing expert, to get advice.

QUESTIONS

1. Do you think that Arthur researched his market in depth? What approach would you have used and what would have been your objectives?

2. After the first seminar, do you think Arthur should have quit or should he have continued? Do you feel the results of the first seminar were en-

couraging? Do you think that Arthur should have paid the two actors to testify about his system? Do you think it was unethical? What other methods could he have used to convince his audience? Do you think the comedian was appropriate? What type of entertainment, if any, would you have come up with?

3. Do you think that Arthur should hold seminars on some of the other topics? On what basis would you make the decision to conduct other seminars covering the topics requested?

4. Do you feel Arthur should be directing his efforts toward other segments? Name those segments and outline a marketing plan that would be successful.

5. What other advice would you give Arthur if he intends to continue in business? How could such an obviously intelligent and experienced business executive who was very successful working for someone else not make this venture successful? Why did Arthur fail?

CASE 21

Belcher and Huntly Printing Company

Jack Belcher and Elmar Huntly sat back and looked at one another, each trying to figure out what went wrong. They had entered the printing business 10 years ago with great enthusiasm and energy, and even had dreams of building their own empire. Today the business is not breaking even. Both are taking about $100 a week out of the business, and even this makes them feel guilty. How different this was from when they started the business when they faced no competition, and could afford to drive luxury cars, pay their mortgages, and have everything their families could ever want. However, today it seems that everybody is selling business cards and stationery. Even as they bemoaned their troubles, they still retained their sense of humor. Jack suggested they burn the business down and collect the insurance. Elmar retorted that they were both worth more dead than alive and should both let their wives collect on the insurance. Finally, Jack said, "You know Elmar, we could write a book about this business and it would be a best seller." Elmar replied, "Jack, if you printed that book the churches would ban it."

Suddenly Jack jumped out of his chair. "Elmar," he said, "you just gave me an idea. I think we will publish books." Elmar thought he was kidding. However, he listened as Jack went on, "Look, Elmar, everybody wants to write a book. They all want to write the great American novel and be famous. Let's help them accomplish that dream by putting their novels or whatever they want published in print." Elmar replied, "We do not have the capability and where are we going to get the money?" but Jack just told him to forget that point for a moment, and to think about the concept. All they had to do is advertise in the right papers and magazines and then help the people write their books. He pointed out to Elmar that although most of them couldn't write well, they would help them if they wanted or print it just as written. Then they would put it in hard copy and print as many copies as the client wanted. They could even help the client market the books. Elmar thought it sounded great, and might be a way out of their difficulties. However, he wondered how they were going to get the start-up money and how they were going to market the books.

Elmar had another idea that could work. He felt they were spending too much time selling forms, which left them competing with many cut-throat firms. He thought they needed a marketing differential that would set them apart and give them a new niche in the field. If they could sell accounting systems for small firms, both profit and nonprofit, as well as other business systems, they could make a great deal of money. They should approach a prospective client and request that they be permitted to construct a Business Systems Audit without requiring a fee. They could look at all their forms and make recommendations for an entire package. This would increase their printing business. The only problems Elmar could foresee were finding a designer for the systems and actually conducting the Business System Audits.

Jack listened intently while Elmar was talking. He could see that in a few minutes the two of them had come up with concepts that could revolutionize their business. Both of them liked the concepts, and they decided to think about them and confer again the next day. Jack called Elmar at about 3 A.M. and asked if he was awake. Elmar said, "Of course, I am. What do you think I have been working on all night?"

The next day they met, and Jack calculated the amount of money they would need in order to first get into the book publishing business. He could get good used equipment from a friend whom he had already contacted, and he could have six months to pay for it. Jack estimated they would need $85,000 to purchase the equipment and make the concept a reality. However, he still did not know how to market a book once it was published.

Elmar reported that he had contacted a friend who was a Certified Public Accountant. He had agreed to design accounting systems for small business firms as well as nonprofit organizations. He could design a procedure that the salespeople could follow when they made their audits. After they completed the audit, he would offer his services to evaluate the results. He promised to charge a reasonable fee. However, Elmar was faced with the problem of finding salespeople. They would have to be trained with the new concept of selling business systems. Because it was a new approach there would be no restrictions on territory; they would not be restricted to Reno, Nevada, but could cover Utah, Arizona, Idaho, and other nearby states. The training would have to be intensive and the salespeople would have to be compensated, for it would take some time before they would be productive. Elmar estimated that they would need at least four salespeople, and he wanted to hire only women. Jack asked him if there were any special reasons for this, and Elmar said, "No, it's just that I think women are better administrators than men and based on my experience I find them to be more determined and aggressive than men." Jack did not especially agree with Elmar, but felt since it was his concept, he could do what he wanted.

Elmar felt they would need to pay each salesperson at least $300 per week plus a bonus. He felt that incentives based on sales volume would be the best approach to get them to reach their assigned quota, after which they would be paid 5 percent of sales. Thus the salespeople could each make $50,000 or more a year if they worked hard. Elmar estimated that their gross profit on the forms would be at least 40 percent because there could be standard forms within the customized design for a firm.

The discussion returned to the four salespeople. Elmar estimated that it would take six months before they would be producing much profit. That meant an investment of at least $50,000 considering payroll costs and traveling expenses. When salespeople were in place the company could begin to earn a handsome return on their investment. So the question boiled down to money. For the business systems, they needed a salary for their accountant and $50,000 to get the salespeople on the job. For book publishing, they needed $85,000 for equipment and supplies and fee for a consultant to edit their books and make corrections. In all, they needed $150,000 to $200,000 in cash.

Jack and Elmar went to the bank and learned they could get a total of $100,000 on second mortgages on their homes. Jack and Elmar were not able to raise the balance of the money locally. They had heard about a loan broker in Reno who had many sources of money and so they went to talk to him. He examined their package and in a few days came back with a proposal to pay off the first mortgages on their homes, take a first position on all of the properties, including the building where the business was now located, and lend them the money they wanted plus $25,000 for working capital. Jack and Elmar would have to pay a fee of 4 percent of the money they borrowed in addition to the lender fee and closing costs. In addition, the loan company would factor all their receivables and establish a credit line on sales made on credit, thus helping the company grow. The rate for the factoring was 6 percent over New York prime. While Jack and Elmar felt this was somewhat high, it was the best deal available and the loan broker promised to work fast. Within three weeks they were ready for the closing.

With the money Jack purchased the equipment for book publishing and was ready for business. He advertised in the local papers and was surprised to receive more than 10 calls from people who wanted to have their manuscripts printed in hardback. He contacted and made separate deals with each of them. Some of the titles were *Nuts with Computers, How to Meditate and Be at Peace on Your Job, The Banana Split Diet, Philosophy and Meeting the Opposite Sex, How to Avoid Paying Your Bills, Advertising in the Soviet Union, How to Spy for Your Country and Make a Million, Hunting with Your Own Blow Gun, Tweety Yao Pang and the Loves of Her Life*. Each person was willing to pay anywhere from $2,500 to $20,000 to have a hundred books published. The only problem was promoting their books. After the books were published the authors were pleased. However, they wondered what to do to make themselves famous. Jack told them to give the books to their friends as presents, and soon word of mouth would sell them. He also suggested that they donate the books to libraries and send one to the major newspaper publishers to review. However, none of them ever sold a book and the authors felt cheated.

Jack and Elmar wondered what to do for these authors. In some cases, Jack could have an English professor edit their books and correct the grammatical mistakes being careful not to alter the content. Jack had two problems—how to promote this area of the business and how to hook them up with some distributor for their books. Elmar was having more success with his venture. He was pleasantly surprised when Gloria and Tammy, two of his younger salespeople, went sharply out in front in sales. Each took to the business like naturals and managed to get into places the company never dreamed possible, selling the idea of a Business Systems Audit and getting orders for forms used by the company. The accountant, David Garrick, was running up some large bills, but he was good and they decided to ask him if he would be interested in participating in profits of the company instead of getting a fee. David initially resisted and threatened to stop reviewing the systems unless he was paid. (At the moment they owed him more than $12,000.) Because sales in the systems area had already exceeded $500,000, David finally offered to accept an interest in a percentage of ownership if they offered him at least one-third of the business. Neither Jack nor Elmar liked that idea but after some consideration decided to accept him as a part-owner.

Elmar now suggested that they start to franchise their systems program. All their standard forms were copyrighted and they could handle custom designed forms for others. The idea appealed to Jack, and Tammy and Gloria felt the franchise concept could be sold. The franchisee would not need to be a printer, but could make a small investment in a store, or even operate from home, get a sales kit from the company, receive at least three weeks training, and then would own his own business. Elmar thought that if each franchisee were really aggressive, sales in excess of $1 million annually could be generated in the individual states. If the franchisees paid them 10 percent of sales they could earn $100,000 a year. In addition they could increase the percentage up to 20 percent if they reached certain sales goals. They needed to determine how much to charge for the franchise fee, which would have to include training, lodging, and a kit.

QUESTIONS

1. Do you think it was a good idea to go into the book publishing business? Do you really think a lot of people want to get their own book published, even though they do not sell? Consider the fact that the average client would be spending a minimum of $10,000 for 100 books to get their name on a book.

2. Do you think they should have gone into both directions or gone into the area Elmar suggested first?

3. How would you suggest that Jack advertise the fact that his company will publish books for individuals? Who are his target markets? What methods should he employ to reach them? What methods could he use to promote their books once they are published to get them out of his hands into a promoter's?

4. Do you think he should publish obviously stupid books or only those that make sense? Does Jack have any obligations to tell those clients who think they have a potential Nobel Prize winner that their books don't stand a chance of success? Do you think all books should be checked for gram-

mar, punctuation, spelling and other errors first or should Jack just publish their manuscripts as he receives them? Does Jack have any legal liability in publishing books?

5. With respect to Elmar's business, do you think he should sell franchises? If you feel he should not pursue franchises at this time, indicate why. If you feel he should start the franchise network, what should the franchise fee be and what kind of royalty should he add, if any? What type of contract should he use? Do you think he was wrong to hire only women on his sales force? Do you think he should opt for an all-female franchise organization? Do you feel there is a market for such a service?

Yukon Hearing Aid Company

Calvin Books worked part time for an optometrist selling eyeglass frames. Although he had a full-time job at night working as a dispatcher for a trucking company, he enjoyed his part time job more. This job had helped him develop confidence in himself. He discovered in himself a great ability to sell, usually selling clients the most expensive frames in the store. The optometrist was happy with Calvin's performance, and asked him to work full time. Calvin was grateful, but declined the offer. He was really using the job to gain sufficient selling experience to sell hearing aids. His uncle, Dan Endicott, was in the hearing aid business, and he wanted Calvin to work for him in Anchorage, Alaska. Calvin had resisted in the past because he did not feel he could be successful selling, but now he liked dealing with people, and he felt he had the ability to succeed. Calvin finally joined his uncle, and after working with him for the required period of time, received his state credentials as a certified hearing aid salesperson.

Calvin still had much to learn. Calvin was surprised to discover that nearly 20 million people in the United States have hearing problems, so he felt he was in the right field. There were many hearing aid manufacturers, which created much competition in the field. Calvin found that hearing aids cost from $300 to $1,000. His uncle made at least 200 percent profit on each hearing aid and he would give Calvin $100 for each he sold. The life cycle of a hearing aid is from three to five years, and the clients come in regularly to purchase batteries which cost $3.75 a package. The batteries are good for up to six weeks.

Uncle Dan advertised in various papers and had direct response advertisement inserts placed in newspapers. When people send these response cards in, he contacts them and tries to sell them hearing aids. He also places an advertisement in the Yellow Pages, which brings many leads.

Uncle Dan is 60 years old and he is aware of the fact that the greatest source of business is with senior citizens. Calvin was now fully trained and went out with Uncle Dan to make some calls. He was amazed at how well Uncle Dan related to the senior citizens. He treated them as if he knew them all their lives, handling them with the care of a surgeon operating with the exact precision needed to be successful.

Finally, Calvin began to make calls by himself. He tried to emulate his uncle, but it backfired. The people, many of whom were senior citizens, did not have the confidence in him that they had in his uncle. Calvin tried hard to take care of their needs, but he just could not make a sale no matter what he did. It seemed to Calvin that they were afraid to make a decision based on Calvin's recommendations. He talked to his uncle who told him to be patient and not to try so hard. During the next two months the confidence Calvin had developed previously began to evaporate. His uncle did not know what to do. Calvin's wife also was concerned, because she could see Calvin's distress. She tried to encourage him, but he told her he was doing everything he could to get a sale. He showed the client the unit, tried it on him, and fitted it perfectly. Although the client would say it was fine, he would find some reason not to buy it, often blaming his prices. Calvin felt the clients were still skeptical about his ability. As Calvin was approaching his twenty-fourth birthday, he decided he was not cut out for selling.

Uncle Dan decided to take Calvin out again so Calvin could watch him make a sale. Again, Calvin was amazed at how easy it was for his uncle. Uncle Dan told him he should talk to people just like he would hold a conversation with a friend. To show that he had confidence in Calvin, he told Calvin that he had bought an established business in Fairbanks, and that he wanted Calvin to operate it for him. Calvin could not understand this because he felt he was an abysmal failure and was sure he could not manage the office successfully. Uncle Dan told him that the new business had a base of more than 1,000 clients, so he would not need to acquire clients, but just be there to make contact and sell the hearing aids.

So, Calvin agreed to this arrangement and moved to Fairbanks to take over the office. A clerk, Shelly, handled all the records, equipment, and supplies. Soon after Calvin arrived, calls started coming in and Calvin went out determined to make sales. Much to his surprise, he started to click. He was making sales even to senior citizens. He could not understand why, but nonetheless he was happy. His uncle was pleased and told him to hire another certified salesperson as soon as possible. Shelly applied for the job. She was 25 years old, intelligent, and knew a great deal about the business. After she had been certified, Calvin encouraged her to start selling. He took her out in the field with him so she could watch his sales techniques. Shelly worked with Calvin for several weeks and then went out on her own. She tried to make sales but was not successful, just as it had been with Calvin. This situation continued for several months until finally Calvin asked her to return to her old job. Shelly agreed and returned to her position as clerk.

Calvin immediately began looking for another salesperson. More aggressive competition was developing in the area and it was becoming important to find new clients. Calvin was not experienced in prospecting new clients and had been working only with the current client base. He wanted to expand the business but did not know where to start. He went to a school for the deaf to see if the officials there could assist him, but they were of no help. He knew that his big market was senior citizens, but he did not know how to penetrate that market and increase his sales.

QUESTIONS

1. Why was Calvin not successful with his uncle?

2. What training would you have given Calvin if he had come to work for you? Do you think that Calvin was well prepared to sell hearing aids to clients?

3. Why was he successful in Fairbanks?

4. Why was Shelly not a success? Should Calvin have worked with her longer? Do you think that Calvin will be successful with another salesperson who comes to work for him who does not have experience selling? What qualities or characteristics does he lack to be a successful sales manager?

5. What advice would you give Calvin to develop his sales? How can he penetrate the senior citizen market more than he has? What other possible sources of clients should he explore?

CASE 23

Lyons New Car Agency Inc.

Kitty Lyons was the only child of Gary Lyons, an established new car dealer in Little Rock, Arkansas. Even though Gary did not want Kitty working in the agency, she spent all her time there. Gary felt that automobile sales was a "man's business" and a woman would get crucified if she tried to succeed in it. However, Kitty insisted that she could be a success in anything she wanted to do and the automobile business suited her just fine.

Gary represented both a major American automobile manufacturer and a popular foreign car manufacturer. He sold approximately 500 new cars and 800 used cars annually. He had a fair service department and an average parts department. The sales force was adequate, but according to Kitty, they should all be replaced since all they ever did was stay in the office and wait for customers to come into the showroom. Gary did not think that she was right, and was content with the money he was making.

Kitty graduated from college, earning a degree in business administration. Kitty asked her father to appoint her as general manager because she knew the business inside and out. Her father was reluctant, for he continued to hold the opinion that a woman did not belong in the automobile business. Some of the male salespeople in the firm reinforced this opinion with oblique remarks that "Kitty was a nice kid and would make some man a good wife." Her father denied Kitty the position, and she quit the business. Naturally, he was upset, but he felt she would eventually see that he was right. Kitty took odd jobs working as a salesperson for other companies, but automobile dealers would not give her a genuine opportunity in management. One dealer gave her a chance but then sexually harassed her. She ended up working for a car rental agency handling sales and so learned something about that business.

In the meantime, her father had made arrangements to sell the business to a person from Pine Bluff. Kitty was heartbroken, for she had hopes of someday returning and taking over the business. After her father retired, he soon died, and Kitty received $250,000 from her father's estate. She decided to establish her own agency with the money. She contacted the American manufacturer her father represented and spoke to one of her father's old friends there. When she explained that she wanted her own agency, he was very interested. Hank Slocum, the vice-president of marketing, was confident that she had the necessary skills and he promised to look for the right agency for her, although he did not guarantee that he could find one in Little Rock. Kitty was pleased with his response and waited for him to call her back. Within a week Hank had located a small agency in Tucson, Arizona, that had a great deal of potential. The area was booming and he felt that if she handled the business right she could make it a success. Kitty met Hank in Tucson, and they looked at the agency. The location was poor, not in the main shopping area. However, the dealership did own land on the main street, Broadway Avenue, which was being used as an outlet for the used cars they took in trade. The new car division was located in a building in the old district in town, and the rent was extremely reasonable. The building would have to be renovated, because it was run down. When Kitty looked at the books, she was astonished to find that for the last two years the company had been losing an average of $2,500 a month. When she asked why, she was told that the present owner, Rich Muller, had not paid much attention to the business. Under her good management, it could be profitable because the product line was attractive. The agency handled top-of-the-line luxury models as well as trucks.

Kitty was impressed and talked with the personnel. The treasurer was conservative and a stickler for details—just the kind of person she wanted in that position. The new car department did not have a manager, but there were seven salespeople in the division who handled all the lines. The used car division had a good man, Gene Barker, who impressed her very much. He had three sales-people working for him. The used car stock was lopsided and not what she thought was desirable. In the office, which was operated by the treasurer, James "El Paso" Wilson, there were three people who seemed to know what they were doing. When Kitty asked for the records, she found the general ledger and journals right up to date. She was impressed.

Wilson griped that the salespeople were administratively incapable of turn-ing in a sale with all the documents, and he had to run them down to get every-thing in order. She knew from experience that all salespeople were like that, and she sympathized with him. He also complained about credit approvals. He could not keep the accounts receivable current because Muller would override him on check approval and on service credit. He felt he should be the only one in charge of credit approval.

The parts manager, Howard Hill, was not particularly courteous when Kitty was introduced. He avoided all her questions and she felt he would be a prob-lem. The service manager, John Kirney, was a character, and while he was warm and charming, he did not especially impress her at the meeting. However, Wilson said he was good, except when he and the parts manager fought about inter-company profits on work performed on company vehicles.

Kitty left and thought over the prospect of buying the business. Two things that bothered Kitty were the location in the old section of town, and the fact that the business was losing money. She knew she could make money, but this place was not like her father's. It would be a challenge and was a risky venture. Hank found that the business could be purchased for $100,000. The building was owned by another auto dealer from Phoenix and his rental was $1,000 a month for the building with yearly lease renewals. Kitty had hoped to offer an import line, but all the major ones were already franchised in town. Yet she thought maybe she could get a European manufacturer to give her a line.

After much consideration Kitty decided to buy the agency. The agreement was signed, and Hank sent her the franchise agreements, giving her the rights for life. She told Hank that she would buy the dealership, but that she wanted the factory to give her new car support. She wanted to begin with the most popular models, even though they were hard to get. Hank agreed to supply them. Al-though Muller had been selling 200 new cars a year, Hank estimated that Kitty could sell about 100 of the top-of-the-line products, 300 of the mid-size prod-ucts, and about 50 of the trucks. Kitty shared his optimism.

Kitty began to make changes in each department. She took a tough stance with the salespeople. She told Wilson not to pay out any commission if the salesperson did not turn in all the paperwork as requested. Also, she suggested he make up a checklist for new and used cars for salespeople to follow when they sold a car. She gave Wilson complete authority to approve credit and he could even override her. However, she told him that if he lost one dime of credit it would be taken out of his bonus at the end of the year.

When Kitty asked the used car manager what would help him make money in his department, he told her that the new car department was allowing too much money for trade-ins. He went on to say that when the first trade-in was sold, another trade-in was taken in, which resulted in a lot of junky cars on the lot. So Kitty gave him permission to buy 20 cars of better quality. She urged him to have his salespeople cut down on coffee time and become more aggressive in seeking customers. Although he seemed reluctant at first to "take orders from a woman," he agreed to get control of his staff.

Back at the showroom Kitty decided to become the new car manager as well as the general manager. She changed the compensation program immediately. She decided salespeople would get paid a fixed sum per car regardless of how much profit was made. They could offer discounts up to a maximum amount, but she asked to be consulted if that amount were exceeded.

In the service department she recommended that more attention be paid to customer cars than those on the lots. She told the manager, John Kirney, to develop service sales. She also told him not to repair very old cars because they usually continued to break down, which made the customer dissatisfied with the service department. Rather, she wanted more attention paid to dealer prep on cars sold. The customary "sun-bath" treatment of simply cleaning the cars was to be replaced with a thorough inspection as recommended by the manufacturer. Kirney agreed with these recommendations.

With these changes in place, the business started improving. The first month the company made $1,800 instead of losing $2,500. Kitty took out $1,500 as salary. She was living in a local hotel which kept her close to the business.

One day the used car manager called her to inspect the cars she had authorized him to purchase. After Kitty looked at them, she told him he had paid $7,000 too much for them. Barker took this criticism personally and quit. He immediately began working for another dealer as general manager. Even though Kitty thought he had paid too much the cars sold quickly and the company made more than $15,000 on the sales as well as some income on the financing and insurance. Thus, Kitty knew that she had to find a constant source of good used cars to supplement the ones she took in on trade.

Kitty learned from a friend who worked for the manufacturer about a dealer who needed $10,000 cash quickly to pay an overdue bank note. The dealer had 50 cars on the lot, some between one and five years old. Kitty offered him $10,000 for the entire lot. The dealer, Lester Hampton, was confused and told her he wanted to sell the entire 50 cars, not just a few of them. Kitty replied, "Lester, I am offering you $10,000 cash right now for those 50 cars and not one cent more. If you can sell them for more right now, then you have every right to do it." She then put the $10,000 on the table. The cars were easily worth $150,000. Lester was slowly burning, but he knew he needed the money now. So after what seemed like a lifetime, he picked up the money, counted it, and went to the safe. He came back and threw the 50 titles on the table, obviously upset.

Kitty asked him to sign the titles and then called her employees to pick up all the cars and tow them to the lot.

Kitty took the cars back to her agency and advertised them, which put the entire group of dealers in the area into shock. But they just could not compete with her. In retaliation, one of the new car dealers purchased one of the luxury cars she sold and displayed it on his used car lot, which was also on Broadway Avenue. He advertised it in the local newspaper at the same price she was asking, which temporarily drew some of her customers away. However, business for her was still brisk.

Kitty called the manufacturer again and found another new car dealer up north who was smothered with snow and going bankrupt. He had 40 new cars (which incidentally were the same brand that the local dealer in her area sold). Kitty was able to buy the entire stock of new cars at $500 to $1,000 under the dealer cost. She also purchased 60 used cars for very little. She then made arrangements to have them shipped to her agency. Kitty was able to do this because she purchased the cars for cash. She even had a line of credit with the local bank, but she turned them down. When the local bankers came around to her when she opened, they all felt she would be needing money. When they informed her they would be willing to offer her financial arrangements if she needed them, she told them, "I want to thank you, boys, but I really don't need any money at this time." This statement shocked them and as a consequence they were always asking her if she needed anything. Actually what Kitty was doing was setting them up not for anything devious but for future lines of credit down the road if she ever needed it. When she purchased all those cars up north, she called the president of the local bank and told him she might need about $350,000. The banker was only too glad to give her anything she wanted and told her to write out a check for the amount she needed and they could sign the papers for the short-term loan when she came back. When she did return, she signed the papers and the loan was subsequently paid off within 90 days.

When Kitty received the new vehicles she placed a large advertisement in the newspapers offering them at $100 under the local new car dealer's cost (the same dealer who tried to destroy her market for luxury cars). As soon as the ad appeared, he approached her and demanded to know what she was doing. She told him "Selling cars, Mr. Sutter, just like you do." Then she added, "How does it feel to have the shoe on your foot for a change?" Sutter was speechless and asked if he could make a deal. Kitty ended up selling him all the 40 cars, which she had purchased from $500 to $1,000 under dealer cost, to him for $300 over dealer cost. So, Kitty made $30,000 clear profit. Each promised to avoid further destructive competitive practices. However, Kitty knew she had the advantage since now he had a lopsided inventory. So, Kitty's entire operation was going along fine, and she was making plenty of money. The old facility was renovated, and she had finally replaced the used car manager, as well as the parts manager. Except for the fact that she could not get a foreign line, Kitty was pleased with her business. Then, not more than 10 miles from her agency, the new car manufacturer she represented opened up another dealership that sold the same products she did and so would be in direct competition with her. However, the owner had a small office and an inadequate shop and was selling cars at $100 over cost. Kitty complained to the factory, but since Hank had left to take over his own agency, she had no one to support her. Legally they had every right to allow this, but Kitty could not understand why the manufacturer would do this to her. The factory representatives told her they had considered the marketing area and felt it would not harm her. Then they pressured her to increase her parts inventory, complaining that she purchased too many parts from outside sources. She replied that she could avoid the manufacturer's excessive mark-up by buying the same parts under a different brand name.

As a consequence of her statements, when the new models came out Kitty received only 10 cars instead of the 50 she had ordered. The 10 units were loaded with options not appropriate for her clients. She complained bitterly, but the manufacturer representatives stated that they were doing the best they could. They added pressure by complaining that she was buying too many used cars and should depend on getting used cars from the sales of new cars. Kitty pointed out that she felt she had to complement her used car inventory to achieve the balance of stock needed to bring people into the lot. They agreed with her in some respects, but felt that she was a maverick and should depend more upon the manufacturer to run her business.

Kitty had been making plans to build a new facility, but because of the pressures from the factory, she decided to wait. She felt a visit to the factory might clarify the situation.

After she spent a week at the factory, the manufacturers agreed that if she would erect the building and start buying more parts from them they would give her the cars she needed. She won their approval on purchasing used cars on the open market to balance her inventory and proved to them that it actually helped her move more new cars.

Kitty did as they asked and they did send her new cars. In fact, it seemed to Kitty that every time she turned around there was another truck pulling up to unload cars. Now her problem was how to move the new cars and trucks. She faced increasing competition from the foreign car market. She had an inventory of more than 200 new cars and trucks and more were coming.

A television station salesperson suggested that she make a ridiculous commercial with her dressed up as a queen. Kitty absolutely refused. Kitty concentrated on the newspapers and radio spots, but sales did not increase. The new sales compensation program she initiated with extra bonuses was not working. The only areas doing well were the used cars division, and service and parts. However, the Floor plan costs were consuming her profits because her stock was swollen and not selling.

Kitty has been contacted by someone who wants to buy the business. She is seriously considering the offer because of the increased foreign competition and pressure from the American manufacturer. If she sells the business she will get the money back that she has invested plus retained earnings of $600,000. There would be no goodwill.

1. Do you think that Kitty should have remained with her father's business? Do you think that working for parents can be successful? Do they demand too much and present too many problems? Do you think that most parents who own businesses don't take their children seriously?

2. Do you think that Kitty acted too quickly in buying the dealership? Do you think she should have waited and checked around for one with a better record and with an imported car franchise?

3. Would you buy a business that had a loss record each month for two years? Under what set of circumstances would you purchase such a business?

4. Why do you think the factory pressured Kitty? Do you think it was fair for the manufacturer to appoint a dealer to sell the same product line she was selling just 10 miles from her?

5. Do you think Kitty was unethical when she purchased the cars for $10,000 from a dealer whose inventory was worth $150,000 wholesale? Is this like buying stock with inside information?

Was the factory right in giving her that information?

6. Was it ethical for the new car dealer in her area to offer one of the luxury cars she sold at cost? Was it ethical when Kitty sold him 40 cars of the same make he sold in his agency and made $30,000?

7. Why do you think the factory was putting the "squeeze" on her when she was such a profitable dealer and had actually done a better job than her predecessor?

8. Why did the car manufacturer dump new cars and trucks on Kitty when she was having difficulty selling them?

9. Do you think she should appear on television and make a fool out of herself? Do you think it would sell cars?

10. What recommendations would you make to Kitty to sell new vehicles?

11. If you were Kitty, would you sell the business for $600,000 just to get out?

CASE 24

Harper's Appliance Store

A year ago Bob Adams purchased the Harper's Appliance Store for $375,000. The price included the building, equipment, fixtures, inventory, and some goodwill. At the time of the purchase, the business was selling about $2,500,000 annually and earning about 5 percent before taxes. Although the parking facilities were inadequate, people still bought more from Harper's than from any other appliance store in town because of the Harper reputation for service and the brands carried. Adams started a major advertising campaign to attract new clients. After several months of intense advertising, sales and profits were higher than ever before. Adams was quite satisfied, as it seemed that everything he planned turned out well.

Just when everything seemed to be going successfully Murdock's Appliance Discount Center opened directly across the street. Murdock carried the same brands as Adams, but he was not an appointed appliance dealer. He purchased his stock from out-of-state dealers who were carrying excess inventory and were all too glad to dump the excess stock for under cost. Murdock's strategy was to let Adams advertise to attract customers. The customers would notice the signs in his windows advertising discounts far below what Adams could offer. He could thus attract clients without cost. Murdock also cut overhead by offering no services or part replacements. Murdock did not deliver appliances, but instead used a local trucker who charged the client a small fee for delivery.

As a result of the competition from Murdock's, Adam's sales and profits suffered. Adams did not know what to do. The manufacturers would not give him better prices because it would be a violation of the Robinson-Patman Act. They did promise to find out which dealers were selling to Murdock from out of state and try to make those dealers desist. But Adams knew that this action was useless because the dealers would claim that they thought they were selling to builders or contractors, and that they did not know that the products were going to be used as inventory for an illegitimate appliance dealer.

Adams tried to teach his sales force how to overcome the competition from Murdock, but many already had a mental block about price and had difficulty telling potential clients that Murdock was not a legitimate dealer. Adams tried advertising, warning customers to beware of dealers who were not authorized to sell the brands he was selling. He also emphasized his large inventory of spare parts and emergency service. He even reduced his prices somewhat to promote sales. However, people still came to his store, talked to his salespeople, noticed the ads at Murdock's, and left without buying. The client would cross the street and purchase the appliance at Murdock's. Murdock would also follow the lead of Adams' advertising. If Adams offered a particular brand at a special price, Murdock would offer the same brand at a lower price.

After doing all he could in marketing, Adams decided to find out about Murdock's background and financial status. Adams discovered that Murdock was operating on a one-year lease at $2,500 per month. The building Murdock occupied had been vacant for nearly 18 months before Murdock came along. The owner had been trying to sell the building for $175,000, but resorted to leasing it on an annual basis. Adams found out that the building had an appraised value of $150,000, and that he could get a mortgage on the building for $100,000 if he purchased it at that price. Thus, one avenue open to Adams was to buy the building and throw out Murdock at the end of the lease.

However, if Adams decided to buy the building he would have to come up with $50,000 in cash plus closing costs. If he did buy it he didn't know what to do with it. At this stage he could not use it himself and leasing it would be difficult. Another alternative was to try to pick up the lease when Murdock's expired, even if he had to pay more than the $2,500 a month. But if Adams was willing to pay $3,000 per month and Murdock offered the same amount, they could get into a battle leaving the owner of the building the winner.

A third alternative was to match Murdock's prices. He could also seek out dealers in Ohio who were interested in dumping excess stock and then advertise dramatic discounts to drive Murdock out of business. Adams made a short trip to various cities in Ohio. He talked to some of the dealers he met at the convention last year, and some of them were willing to sell him excess stock. Adams thought this was a great idea until one of the manufacturer's representatives informed him that if he purchased from other sources than the manufacturer it would be a clear violation of his franchise agreement. He would risk losing some of his lines that were the backbone of his business. Adams understood the manufacturers' position and yet he needed their assistance. He called the vice-presidents of each manufacturer and asked them to give him 90 days to make purchases in Ohio. He was making this urgent request so he could drive Murdock out of business and get back the profitable position he once enjoyed. The manufacturers finally agreed to the proposition, for they felt that Adams would deplete their Ohio dealers' stock and they would be able to make further sales in those areas. They also hated to lose a good dealer like Adams.

The manufacturers made it clear that Adams could not use their floor plan and he would have to make arrangements with a local bank to handle the financing. After the arrangements were made, Adams went on a buying spree in Ohio and came back with more than $250,000 of new stock. He then put a full page advertisement in all the local papers as follows:

GREATEST APPLIANCE SALE IN NEWFIELD
HISTORY
NONE, AND WE MEAN NONE, CAN MATCH
HARPER'S APPLIANCE PRICES
ALL APPLIANCES WILL BE SOLD AT
DEALER COST PLUS
5%
AND YOU STILL GET THE FAMOUS
HARPER SERVICE AND PARTS WARRANTY
PLUS
24 HOUR EMERGENCY SERVICE
IF YOU CAN GET A LOWER PRICE WE WILL
MEET IT EVEN IF WE LOSE MONEY ON THE SALE

HARPER'S APPLIANCE STORE
52 MAIN STREET
277-5555

People started coming back to Harper and sales were brisk. Murdock's sales appeared to halt, yet he still remained in business after 65 days. Adams' sales were higher than ever, but his profits were next to zero. He was just giving too much away and expenses were cutting into the profits. At this point Adams was quite worried because his 90 days were running out.

One day Mr. Murdock called Adams and asked him out to lunch. Adams agreed and they met (for the first time) at the local country club. Murdock was very direct and said that he knew he was a thorn in Adams' side. He said that he knew Adams was buying from Ohio dealers just as he was, but he also knew that Adams could not survive in the long run because his expenses would consume him and he would eventually go out of business. Adams protested, but Murdock held his ground. Finally, Adams asked, "What is it you want, Murdock, because I am a very busy man?" Murdock said that he would leave if Adams gave him $50,000 in cash. In addition he wanted Adams to pay off the balance of the lease (which had five months to go), amounting to another $12,500. Adams was shocked at the proposal and said he would never consider it under any circumstances. Murdock told Adams, "Look, Adams, think about it for a few days and then get back to me. But remember one thing—if you do not take my offer I will stick around a little longer and drive you out of business."

Adams was upset and confused. He was still the largest dealer in town, but he had destroyed his price structure by offering large discounts to compete with Murdock. If he did get rid of Murdock, it would take months before he would be able to get his pricing back in line. Adams also knew that the manufacturers were not going to stand for his purchasing from other dealers again when he was the appointed dealer for his area. After 90 days were up, they would expect Adams to resume his purchasing as before.

So Adams was in a difficult position. All his money was tied up in this business. It was a good business until Murdock entered the picture. He did not know which direction to turn—should he hang in there for the balance of the 90 days and then make an offer to Murdock or should he call Murdock and make him an outright offer? If he did get rid of Murdock, the building would be vacant and someone else like Murdock might do the same thing. Adams wondered if he should purchase the building and use the $50,000 as the down payment and mortgage the rest. Should he attempt to lease the building when Murdock's lease expires? He is confused and wants your advice.

QUESTIONS

1. Has Adams handled Murdock correctly? Should he have maintained his position and not undercut prices?

2. Should Adams purchase the building?

3. Should Adams buy off Murdock? How would you have handled Murdock? Do you think Murdock would have lasted? Do you think Murdock was bluffing?

4. Do you think the manufacturers gave Adams all the assistance they could?

5. What other advice would you give to Adams to get his company back into its former position?

Velazquez Art Gallery

Barbara Velazquez was an accomplished portrait painter and sculptor. She had studied in New York, Florence, Rome, Amsterdam, Madrid, and Paris. She had numerous exhibits and was highly acclaimed as a promising artist. While she appreciated abstract art, she preferred realistic art, and she stayed with that area. Barbara did not attempt to imitate anyone, developing her own unique style. She would paint anyone with an interesting face, and several times she chased people down the street to ask them if they would sit for a portrait. Her fame was growing in Europe, but she wanted to return home to New York where her career had begun.

While some of Barbara's acclaim had reached America, she had to work hard to establish herself as she had in Europe. She managed to get a few exhibitions, but sold very little. Even one of her prized paintings, which was acclaimed all over Europe, did not bring a substantial offer. She suspected that her lack of clients was due to the fact she was a woman. Barbara decided to give up on New York and move to another state. She wanted to find a place where she could settle and have interesting people to paint. If she could not sell her paintings, she would set up her own gallery, bringing in works from other painters and sculptors who were having similar problems getting started. Barbara finally decided to go to Maui, Hawaii. She had never been there, but she had been told it was a paradise. After she moved, she did not know anyone, so she decided to take her time and study the land, people, and tourists and basically assess the possibilities that existed there for artists. To make ends meet while she got acquainted with the area, she took a job as an in-house portrait artist with one of the largest hotels on Maui. She would do pastel portraits of guests in the hotel for $35 to $50. This was a real compromise for Barbara, but she wanted to be prepared before she opened her own gallery. She kept this position for more than 15 months, during which time she became familiar with an artist colony, which consisted of some excellent artists who were barely surviving and waiting for miracles to happen.

Finally, Barbara decided to open her gallery and found an excellent location. She arranged to feature each artist in the colony at a different time of the year. She would exhibit the paintings and other art work at no charge, but she would split the sales price with the artist. She would compose a program outlining the artists' backgrounds. The program would also list each artist's works of art and prices for each. Barbara promised the artists that the program would make them appear famous. She would serve champagne, wines, tea and hors d'oeuvres during the exhibitions. She asked the artists to help her get the gallery started and to help her make changes from time to time.

The gallery finally opened and clients started to come in to look around. Paintings of local natives sold well, but others, including her own, did not. Some of the artists were disappointed and many of them started looking for subjects that would appeal to tourists. Paintings of Hawaiians with sarongs around them or standing under a palm tree near the beach would sell for up to $500. The artists began producing these paintings in great numbers, and the gallery became more like a straight commercial enterprise directed toward the tourist market. Business was brisk and profitable, but from Barbara's viewpoint, the gallery was a failure. She felt she was selling her soul down the river for a buck and forsaking her art.

Barbara talked with the other artists, and some thought she should continue operating the gallery as it was. They felt that they were at least getting their names into the public forum and making money, whereas before they were starving. However, Barbara decided to sell out and return to New York where there was still some appreciation for art, even if it was not for hers. She made a quick deal with the local artists and left the island with some regrets, for she had grown to love it.

When Barbara got back to New York, she decided to get involved once again with painting. She eventually hoped to open her own gallery even though there was a great deal of competition from very prestigious houses. She first found architects who would allow her to supply the paintings for the building they were constructing. Then she got in touch with friends in the local artists' colony and offered them a financial arrangement similar to the one in Maui. She made up a catalog with a complete range of art work, including paintings and sculptures. She also included porcelain, papier mâché, oils, pastels, and water colors. She also decided to offer expensive frames in the catalog.

With her profits she made an arrangement with a direct mailing firm in New York to supply her a list of households with incomes over $100,000 a year. She sent to all those homes a catalog indicating that they could buy original works from promising artists. This proved to be a successful venture and she accumulated a substantial sum of cash. The artists in the colony increasingly looked to her for an avenue to market their art.

She was finally able to open her gallery in New York. It was in a prestigious location. It presented paintings not only from a few well-known artists, but also from unknown but promising artists. She also was selling her own works of art, which she attributed to the fact that she was signing them with B. Velazquez. So, Barbara was now on target, but some problems were developing. She had to reject some artists' works because in her opinion, they were terrible. One day when she was working in the back of the gallery, one of the rejected artists came in and started cutting up canvases. He also overturned and broke some sculptures. He shouted at her before he left, "The next time I come back you had better take my work seriously." Barbara immediately called the police, and then surveyed the damage. She was heartsick, and when the artists found out, they were enraged at her for letting it happen. She paid each the expected sales price for their works, but they refused to forgive her. The whole affair left Barbara confused, but she vowed to forge ahead.

Eventually, Barbara's gallery became well known and she found her works being exhibited alongside those of established American artists. She still continued to work with promising young artists, but she became more discriminating, committing herself to the ones with whom she had the greatest success. Barbara built up a nice clientele and dedicated herself to working to satisfy their needs. She developed relationships with other galleries and they worked together in many ways.

When Barbara reflected on her climb to success, she had to admit she was not a complete success as an artist. She was not able to sell her works in New York when she came back from Europe, nor was she successful in Hawaii with her own art work, and now in her own gallery she felt she had to use the initial "B" in front of her surname in order to sell her paintings. She was able to sell others' works, but somewhere along the way she had lost what she valued most. Now she was an entrepreneur and a part-time artist who was afraid to use her own name.

QUESTIONS

1. Do you think that Barbara is the failure she views herself?

2. Should she have left Europe where she was gaining recognition? Should she have gone back to Europe?

3. Was it a mistake to to go Hawaii? Should she have worked as a pastel portrait painter just to make money?

4. Did she do the right thing when she opened up the gallery in Maui? Was the gallery a success? Was she right in thinking it was a failure? Did she do the right thing when she decided to quit and go back to New York? What would you have done?

5. Do you think her New York gallery was a success? Do you feel she should have kept signing her name as Barbara Velazquez instead of B. Velazquez? Does Barbara appear to be as good an artist as she claimed to be?

6. Do you think she was correct in departing from the basic concept of exhibiting the works of unknown artists? How could she have prevented the destruction the one rejected artist inflicted in the gallery?

7. How would you rate Barbara as an entrepreneur?

8. If Barbara wants to establish herself as an artist only, what advice would you give her? Do you feel it is too late?

CASE 26

Cecilia's Old-Fashioned Soups

In 1930 when the Great Depression hit, Cecilia Cromley had three children and was in desperate need of money. Before the depression she and her husband, Kenneth, were wealthy and material things were never discussed. Then when the depression hit, Kenneth lost everything and committed suicide. Cecilia worked odd jobs to try to make ends meet. One day she struck upon the idea of selling her homemade soup to earn money. People who used to come to dinner at her home had always raved about her unique soups. Several of her guests had even suggested to Kenneth that he buy a soup company to market her soups, but he never took the suggestions seriously.

Cecilia decided to make soup in her kitchen and sell it. However, she did not have sufficient funds to purchase Mason jars for preserving the soup once it was prepared. Cecilia was a proud woman, but she did get up enough nerve to ask an old friend, Claude Rouget, for a $1,000 loan. Claude agreed to loan her the money and asked if he could do more for her. She assured him that she would be all right. She wanted to succeed on her own and felt that if her children got to know hard times they could face even more difficult times in the future. Claude said he would check in on her from time to time to see how she was doing.

So, Cecilia started making soups. In the beginning she concentrated on just four kinds: New England clam chowder, chicken noodle, tomato, and vegetable. She went to all the stores in the neighborhood and asked them to sell her products. Most of the stores refused, but Cecilia was determined and kept trying. Eventually, a few stores stocked the soup and they sold well. At the end of the first year Cecilia's sales reached $3,000, which was a lot of money in those days. She did not make much of a profit, probably not more than $300 after all the expenses. However, Cecilia felt that she was going to make it. She continued to work as a part-time maid and seamstress. Somehow she was able to manage, and she even was able to send her son, Robert, to the prep school in Duluth, Minnesota, where her husband had gone years ago. The costs were high, but Robert managed to get a scholarship that paid for 50 percent of the tuition. He was an excellent student who delivered newspapers every morning to earn extra money. He had 200 people on his route and brought in $2 per week.

As the years went by, Cecilia's business grew rapidly. Stores that had once rejected her products were begging for them, and she was producing soup as fast as she could. However, she was running out of space. She wanted to pack her soup in cans and get herself a nice label so people could identify her products more easily. Her sales had exceeded the $200,000 mark, and she estimated she was earning about $20,000 a year.

Claude had come around often during the years and was always very helpful. He understood her dilemma, and found a plant that could be converted to a canning factory for a small sum. Cecilia was excited, but she told Claude she "wanted no hand-outs." He laughed and told her he intended to become her business partner. On that basis she agreed to work with him. Cecilia took over the plant and Claude hired the employees needed to put the operation into working order. When they finally discussed costs, Claude had stated that he felt one-third of the ownership would take care of his cash outlays. He offered to provide her the rest of the working capital on a loan basis. Cecilia shook hands with him and the new plant was under way.

As time rolled on, Cecilia's son, Robert, graduated from the university and her two daughters, Mary and JoAnn, soon followed. All of them majored in business and were very intelligent. Cecilia managed the production line, and she turned over the marketing end of the business to Robert. He originally kept things as they were, but gradually made some minor adjustments. He did not want to upset the business' success.

It was obvious that no other brand in the region could compete with Cecilia's soups. Cecilia had added 11 other kinds, and they were all successful. She had plans for adding more to the line when suddenly she suffered a stroke. She fought hard to overcome its effects, but she was paralyzed on the right side. Although she was mobile to a small degree, she was of little use to the business.

So it fell to Cecilia's children to keep the business running. JoAnn took over Cecilia's production management position. Mary, who had majored in finance and management, eventually took over the general management of the company. At the time of the stroke the company had reached sales of $25 million and future prospects still looked bright.

Robert proposed they think about expansion to other areas of the country. There were people interested in handling their products outside the region, but transportation and handling costs put the price of the soups out of reach for the average consumer. Robert wanted to expand, but needed some advice on how to proceed.

Mary, however, was investigating the possibility of expanding into additional product lines to complement their present line. She felt that since they would be going into the same stores and selling to the same wholesalers, it would cost nothing more to offer additional products to each outlet. However, she didn't know whether to pack the additional products on the premises under the present brand name or to buy a company with a name that might be a target for a takeover.

The siblings were faced with another possibility for expansion. Presently, the plant was not being utilized 24 hours a day, operating only about 10 hours a day with at least 12 hours of free time available for use. Robert had been approached by other companies who wanted Cecilia's to pack for them under their own private label using any soup left after completing packaging of the soup. Robert had not accepted these offers because he did not want to have his mother's soups end up in competitors' cans to be sold at a cheaper price. Yet, he knew he could make money on that type of business.

The company continued to grow. JoAnn was doing an excellent job and had not only increased the line, but also increased sales. Mary had hired two nutritionists, who were giving advice on how to make the soups more attractive to a health-conscious public. JoAnn kept strict controls over quality and maintained impeccable records. She traced every can of soup produced to make certain that the products didn't exceed their shelf life and pinpointed the location of all products sold. JoAnn developed other soups which were less distinctive than her mother's, but that could be packaged for those firms who wanted soups under their own private label. Robert liked that approach better because they would not be selling out quality to make money.

Claude, who was now 75 years old, had become like a father to all the kids. He had found a small successful operation for sale that packaged fruit juices, vegetables, and ketchup. The name of the company was Hayes Food Products and the owner was Orville Hayes. Hayes wanted $7 million for the entire operation. He knew that the facilities would have to be improved, but since the Hayes label was respected he felt the investment would be worth it. Hayes was also a regional company. The idea of buying this business made a great deal of sense because the Hayes products would complement their present line. However, if they did purchase the business, they didn't know whether to keep the Hayes brand name or to have the same products packed under the name of Cecilia's. Claude had made Cecilia go public with the stock on the over-the-counter market ten years ago. So he proposed that they sell the treasury stock to purchase the firm. Though Mary understood what he meant, Robert and JoAnn were unclear, so Claude explained.

Ten years ago Claude had suggested to Cecilia that they sell 40 percent of the business to the public. Then occasionally they would buy the stock back at bargain prices. When the stock first came out it sold for $25 a share. Over the years the stock sometimes would drop to $5 or less, and Claude and Cecilia would rush in and buy up the stock silently. Consequently, the company had nearly 400,000 shares of stock repurchased over the years (treasury stock). The average price of that treasury stock was approximately $10 per share, and the present market value of the stock was $28 per share.

Claude offered to handle the purchase of Hayes Food Products, and the siblings gratefully accepted. Claude managed to get the price reduced from $7 million to $6,188,000. He then offered to exchange 221,000 shares of stock at the present market value for Hayes business. Claude pointed out to Hayes that Cecilia's was a respected progressive firm, and that it had not missed a dividend payment of $0.25 per share per quarter for the last 10 years. Hayes agreed to the exchange. So the treasury stock that was purchased for approximately $2,210,000 bought the company worth easily the $6,188,000 that Claude agreed to buy it for. Thus, they saved a total of $3,978,000. The siblings were all pleased, and grateful to Claude for his constant attention.

Then, sadly, after the new company was purchased, Cecilia passed away and the entire family felt a great loss. Claude was greatly saddened, for he admired and loved Cecilia very much over the years. He was always astonished at how she bounced back and never lost that special warmth and charm she possessed in by-gone days. So Claude decided to hand over all his stock to the kids. He was now 75, and did not need the money. He had never really wanted to take the stock or own any part of the business right from the beginning. He only took a one-third interest in the company to help Cecilia because he knew she would never accept his financial help in any other way. Claude asked them to call him if he could ever help them, although he felt they could certainly handle anything that came along. He asked that they take a portion of the profits earned on the stock he gave them to help organizations who house and feed needy people. He asked that a foundation be set up to help those agencies from all religious groups that take care of retired pastors, ministers, priests, and others who could no longer make their way. Cecilia always had gone out of her way to help them because they had given her faith and hope when she needed it the most. Claude offered to put $500,000 in the trust in honor of their mother. Mary, Robert, and JoAnn agreed and the procedure was undertaken to handle the trust in the future.

The new business was under way. Robert kept the Hayes name, but found some resistance when he started to expand. He discovered that freight costs were exorbitant and while he knew he could expand nationally, he didn't know how to do it without eating up profits. Also supermarket chains wanted the company to package their own brands, and he was not certain whether he should even be engaged in that line of work. Robert felt they should expand their own product lines and was pushing in that direction.

While the siblings were wrestling with these difficulties, a complaint about botulism came up suddenly. Some people claimed they were sick after eating Hayes vegetables. On television they mentioned that Hayes was a subsidiary of Cecilia's. The siblings called an immediate conference to decide how to respond before too much damage occurred.

In the meantime, the company had been approached by Jacob "Tiny" Ramsey, who wanted to discuss a possible merger or a sell out to his firm. Ramsey had been accumulating stock in Cecilia's for some time now and owned 15 percent of the total shares outstanding. The stock was now selling for $35 a share and he was prepared to offer $55 per share to take over the business. When Mary told him the company was not interested in a merger or sale, Ramsey threatened to get the company one way or another.

By this time Claude had also passed away, so there was no one to give the siblings advice. However, they felt they could handle things by themselves. Sales of the company had swelled to more than $100 million a year and the company was still growing. However, the botulism problem had to be resolved without delay.

QUESTIONS

1. What characteristics did Cecilia display that made her a success after being thrown into poverty?

2. Do you think it is still possible to start a business in a little kitchen and develop it into a large empire? Why is it that Cecilia was able to take an ordinary product and make it a special and saleable product?

3. Do you think that Claude was crucial to Cecilia's success?

4. How can Robert market their products to other areas? Can you think of any possible arrange-

ments which would make it possible? How do companies on the West Coast sell their products on the East Coast without having freight costs ruin their price structure?

5. Do you think that they should pack more products for other firms who want their product under their own label? Could this develop into a profitable business?

6. Does this company have a forward-looking organization that will be able to keep up with changes in diets and other medical bulletins? Do you think that every organization should concern itself with the long term as well as the short term? Why don't more companies look at the long-term picture?

7. What are the siblings going to do about the botulism problem? What advice would you give them? Do you think that after the botulism prob-

lem, the Hayes product line should be dropped? Do you think that Jacob "Tiny" Ramsey might be behind the botulism situation in order to drive the price of the company down?

8. Do you think the request for the foundation made by Claude was out of order? Do you think that companies have social responsibility to spend some of their profits on charity? Would you do this if you were in this position? How much would you have to make before you would think about donating some portion of it to charity?

9. Would you sell the company if you were one of the siblings? Would you continue to buy back stock of the company when it dropped and expand by buying other companies with the treasury stock?

10. Finally, how would you get Ramsey out of the picture?

CASE 27

Detweiller Marketing/Research Company

Otto Detweiller graduated with honors from a major university in Kansas with a degree in marketing research. He remained at the university to earn his M.B.A. and take additional courses in computer science, mathematics, and marketing. He felt prepared to enter the field of marketing research with a solid foundation in business. After graduation Otto was offered several attractive positions, but he decided to start his own business instead. He hoped to challenge the giants in the field by using the most modern marketing techniques known.

Otto opened his firm and circulated a brochure among all businesses in Kansas outlining the marketing research capabilities of his firm. Otto received a few calls, but when he went to visit the prospects his lack of experience and uncertainty about charges discouraged the potential clients. Otto continued to advertise in the newspaper and the Yellow Pages. In the meantime, Otto called marketing research firms all over the state to try to obtain their prices for various services.

Finally, it occurred to Otto that if he did several research projects at no charge for a few established companies he would gain experience and make connections which might lead to future business. He visited several firms, talked to them about his background, and offered to tackle research projects to prove his worth. A couple of firms accepted Otto's offer, and he started on the projects. When they were completed, the firms were very satisfied and offered to use him in the future and let him use them for a reference. Otto asked that they not tell anyone he did not charge them a fee.

Sure enough, a few assignments did come in. Otto managed to make enough to keep his head above water. However, Otto knew that his savings would only hold out for a few more months, and then he would have to reassess the situation. Then he remembered something that was mentioned in one of his classes. It was now getting close to election time in the state, and there were several candidates running for election for the first time. Otto decided to again offer his services free of charge to the people he felt were going to win. He had made a quick telephone poll and decided to offer his services to four candidates who looked like potential winners. He managed to meet each of them. He came prepared with some specific research information data. He designed his questionnaire items making the candidates appear as knights in shining armor, and as though they were terrific. He offered his services to them free of charge with the provision that they help him when they were elected. He also requested that when they referred to the poll they mention that "According to a recent poll taken by Detweiller Marketing Research Company, Candidate Nugent was ahead by 20 points," before the poll broke down the findings. Otto won recognition from the newspapers and television and his name became well known. He was still sending out brochures, and now he was beginning to get business from numerous companies. His sales rose to the point where he could hire office personnel, including an assistant, who was also a graduate of his alma mater.

The company was beginning to take shape. Although each of the "freebies" took time, Otto thought they were enhancing his business. Otto wanted to get involved with a national election so his name would be mentioned all over the country on the major networks. Each of the people he backed in the political campaign in Kansas won their elections, and when they could, they did give him valuable recommendations. Otto asked them to assist him when the national election came along and they promised to do everything they could for him.

All of this success did not come without problems. The people who worked in the field gave him trouble from time to time. While he and his assistant knew their business, every once in a while they would get some interviewer who would distort the information. However, Otto had tried to build in corrective measures. He also was very selective when he hired interviewers.

As business expanded so did the number of employees, and soon he had many managers and specialists in certain types of research. While Otto was an expert in research, he was not too experienced in office procedures or security. One of his managers used to remain late supposedly to learn as much as he could so he could excel in the business. However, he was actually getting the names of all the clients, the prices they were charged, and copies of the research reports they paid for as clients. He then left the firm and went into business for himself.

He did not harm the company much, but Otto was quite shaken because all the information was very confidential.

Otto was still satisfied with his business and sales were increasing, but he wanted to do more. He decided that there was potential in the international field, but he was not knowledgeable about marketing research overseas. He thought that many companies in the United States would pay to get a good analysis of certain foreign markets, so he began to research this area. Finally, he did get an assignment from one of the *Fortune* 500 companies to conduct a research investigation overseas. He was to obtain demographic data on the consumers and other information that would be helpful in the overall evaluation of market potential. The company wanted his recommendations as to whether they should enter the market. Otto sent his assistant to the country in question and after a month he came back with a large bill for expenses, but nothing in the way of facts to substantiate the investment in that country. He told Otto that when the country's officials found out who he was, the government stepped in and gave him all the facts he asked for. The assistant could not confirm facts as they were presented because he was not able to confirm the data he received since he was not permitted to gather primary data. Otto went to the client and explained the situation. During the meeting Otto suggested that he go back to that same country and try another approach.

Otto knew this represented his greatest challenge ever and that if he could handle it he would really have his foot in the door. He comes to you, an expert in the international market, for advice.

QUESTIONS

1. What characteristics did Otto display that made him a success from the beginning? Examine his approach and comment.

2. Do you think he was right offering his services free of charge? Would you, assuming you did not know what the outcome was, offer your services and perform these tasks free of charge?

3. Do you think that Otto should get involved in a national campaign? If the political party that wants him to make a poll loses, won't it hurt his credibility? Will it ally him with a particular party?

4. How do you think Otto should approach the international market in the country that apparently conveyed questionable information to his assistant? What would you do if the officials of the country in question threw stumbling blocks in your way of getting to the root facts? How would you overcome them?

The Old Bavarian Village

Frances Wright inherited 100 acres of prime land just outside Houston, Texas. She decided to convert the land into a unique shopping center, The Old Bavarian Village. It would have shops with authentic German features and products. She asked her uncle, a construction contractor, to build her shopping center so she could go forth with her concept. He suggested she hire a well-known Houston architect to design the shops, which she did. Together they traveled to Germany to get that "special feel" needed to design the village concept.

The architect came back and designed a center containing 100 stores. Frances felt there should be more, but the designer felt that there was ample space for expansion if necessary. The designer also pointed out that she might want to use another concept, such as a Far Eastern group of stores, which would be set apart from the Bavarian Village. Her uncle agreed with the architect, and they proceeded to build the village.

In the meantime, at the suggestion of her uncle, Frances contacted a marketing expert to prepare a marketing plan for the village. About four months before the project was to open, he started teaser advertising and announcements in the papers and on billboards in German. He had actors appear on television dressed in typical Bavarian costume and talk about the center using the High German dialect of Bavaria. Of course nobody knew what the advertisement was about, and few knew what the actors were saying. However, the ads created quite a stir in Houston. The local papers got into the act and found someone who could explain the matter. Then on television, about two weeks before the center was to open, the same actor came on television, began talking in German, and then switched to English. For a moment people thought they understood German, because he had switched so fast. The actor turned out to be a "good old Texas Country Boy" whose parents were from the old country. When he switched to English with his Texan accent, he told about the Old Bavarian Village and suggested that people go on opening day because everyone would receive prizes and get to see some of the most expensive merchandise ever in Texas.

When the shops opened, the parking lots were jammed. The decor was so skillfully done that those people who had visited Germany were stunned to find that such a place could exist just outside Houston. There were stores selling antiques, clocks, toys, jewelry, furniture, and countless other products you would not find in the local department stores. The prices were high, but the people didn't mind, and business was brisk. Frances had brought some musicians over from Germany, who played Bavarian music and danced on a stage. There seemed to be something for everyone, and, of course, German beer was being served in all the restaurants. All in all, the opening was a fantastic success and

Frances, her uncle, the architect, and the marketing promoter were happy. However, they wondered how to sustain this interest.

After a few months the novelty started to wear off and the sales were down. Frances went to the promoter and asked him to get things moving. He replied that they would always get business, but they could never expect it to equal opening day sales. Frances could not understand this and informed him that it was his job to find a way to keep things moving.

Several of the store owners decided to pull out, citing lack of sales. Although sales were great in the beginning, they were now sagging and they could not go on paying the high rental Frances demanded. Frances lowered the rent in these stores and the other store owners found out about it. They also demanded rental adjustments. Finally the clock maker and the antique dealer left the center. She tried to find some other tenants to fill the space, but she was not successful.

She then had an offer from a supermarket chain to move into the location and give her the rent she demanded on a long-term contract. She also received similar offers for a pizza parlor and a Chinese restaurant. The space was available, and expenses were creeping up to the point where she was now losing money on the entire operation. She went to her uncle, and he told her that the concept for the Bavarian Village was great, but she had to face reality. He felt she should accept the three tenants who wanted to come in on a long-term lease and pay the rental she needed. He thought that as long as she has some stores that were related to the Bavarian concept she shouldn't be concerned. Frances signed the leases, and business started picking up again.

However, a few more tenants left, including the German furniture store, the art gallery, the toy store, and the German variety store. They felt that she had betrayed the original concept and that they were now no longer in the type of environment they had expected. They each indicated they would find their own location in Houston and create a lasting Bavarian image which would attract clients. In their place Frances signed up a drug store, a dry cleaner, a book store, and a shoe store. Not much remained except the German restaurants, which were booming.

The marketing promoter tried to get the stores to advertise as a group, but they declined. After one year Frances looked back and saw that her basic concept was destroyed. The tenants that remained were not balanced. In some cases the drug store sold products the supermarket sold, and there were other stores who competed with one another. The Chinese restaurant, which had served great food, went out of business and its space was vacant. As soon as she signed up one tenant, another would close up or go bankrupt and the store would have court notices plastered on the doors. Finally, the supermarket announced it was closing its doors because business was not as good as expected. Frances reminded the store owners that the lease had 10 years remaining at $10,000 a month. They stated that they would continue to pay it, but would use the location as a storage center for their Houston stores. When they boarded up the store, the entire complexion of the center changed. People thought that the center was closing up. The owners of the German restaurant told her that she had to do something or they were going to close. The village had lost its image, and people were not calling for reservations so their sales were down.

At this time, the center has the supermarket closed down and 24 stores vacant. Frances is losing money and does not know what to do. She is not afraid of going bankrupt because she had inherited a fortune from her father's estate. However, she wants to be a success. Frances decided to go back to the architect and talk to him about the entire matter. He suggested that maybe it was time to renovate the entire center with a new concept. He suggested she erect reproductions of some famous landmarks, such as the Alamo, or maybe a small version of Disney World. These would attract year around attention from tourists, who also would shop at the stores in the shopping center. He also suggested that it might be possible to attract stores from all over Europe to come to Texas to open up a branch in the center. Having a complete European touch would broaden the scope.

At this point Frances does not know what to do. She has just received an offer from a donut shop to open in the center on a one year lease. In addition, a flower shop, a computer store, a video rental, an adult bookstore, a small loan company, a firm selling used clothing, and a surplus store selling discarded surplus Army and Navy goods have also indicated interest. Frances has heard that you are an expert in business and is willing to pay you a large fee if you can solve all her problems.

QUESTIONS

1. Was Frances too fast in her decision to build a Bavarian shopping center? Do you think she should have researched the concept further?

2. Was Frances prepared to enter a business venture of this scale? Why or why not?

3. Do you think that the types of stores Frances selected for the center had anything to do with its failure? What types of stores should she have looked for?

4. What did you think of the initial promotion before she opened the Village? After the Village was open?

5. When she was informed by the first two tenants that they wanted to leave what should she have done? Did she do the right thing by lowering the rents for all tenants?

6. What type of activities could have been offered that would have kept traffic high in the center?

7. Should she have rented the space out to a supermarket, pizza parlor, and Chinese restaurant? Did that doom her concept?

8. What type of marketing plan should have been in operation from the beginning to keep this center successful?

9. When the supermarket decided to board up the doors, what should she have done?

10. Do you think she should have taken over the operation of some of those stores?

11. Do you think that renovating in the manner suggested by the architect will solve the problems?

12. Do you think she should visit Europe and try to get some of those firms to come to Texas? If they will not come, what could she do?

13. Do you think she should take on the new rentals in the center?

14. What other suggestions do you have for Frances? What lessons did you learn from this problem?

CASE 29

Perkins Employment Agency

Esther Briggs graduated from college at the age of 39 with a degree in Human Resources. Esther attended school at night and worked during the day in the personnel office of a local manufacturing company. In her position she handled grievances and performance appraisals. Esther also had a part-time position working for Les Perkins, who owned an employment agency. When she filled a position for him, he paid her 20 percent of the fee. She liked employment work because when she found a good position for someone, it made her feel that she was accomplishing something important besides earning a fee.

After her graduation Les asked if she would like to work for him or buy into the firm. Esther decided she would like to come in to work full time with the option to buy into the company when she was ready. Les was happy with this and said when she was ready, he would sell her 50 percent of the business for $25,000. Actually the business did not have much in the way of assets except for a few desks, two separate offices, a conference room for interviewing, and a small waiting room for applicants. It also had equipment for copying résumés and other documents. But Les did have an established name because he had been in business since 1969.

Soon after her employment started with Les, she received her state certification and was ready to work. Les had begun to teach her the business when suddenly he was in an automobile accident and died. Esther could not find anyone who was related to Les and at the funeral no one appeared, so Esther paid for all the funeral expenses. After Les was laid to rest, she tackled the business and decided to make it a success. At first she was somewhat confused because she was not familiar with all the clients and they were uncertain about her abilities. Those with contracts did not all stay. Esther hired someone with experience to work with her so she could visit all the companies. By this time she had studied the files and knew who the regular clients were and those who had contracts. Les did not keep many records, apparently keeping everything to himself when it came to money. He did have an accounts receivable list of those employers and employees who owed fees, and she attempted to collect that money.

The agency did not specialize in any particular type of jobs, and Les had operated on a shotgun basis. He advertised mainly in the Yellow Pages where his ad stated the company placed secretaries, word processing operators, data processing operators, engineers, executives, sales accountants, clerks, and other personnel at all levels. His advertisement concluded by indicating that no job was too small nor too large for them to handle.

The major problem that Esther faced was locating personnel for the jobs. She had lots of orders for positions, but not enough candidates to fill them. She found herself pushing people who were not really qualified for the job. As a result some of the employers stopped using her services. For example, she needed two accountants and could not find them. She called the local colleges and universities, but when they found out that the student had to pay a fee they did not give her much cooperation. It was difficult for some employers to pay the 15 percent fee of the estimated annual salary, and some only did if the employee lasted six months. Even then some employers were slow in paying. To make matters worse her own employee, Dave Stubbee, took one of the jobs they were asked to fill. She was upset at his leaving, but when they refused to pay the fee she was really upset.

Thus, it was up to her to handle all phases of the business. She was at the office day and night, never taking a break and staying until the early hours of the morning. She tried to reconstruct the operation and learn more. Esther did not have much experience interviewing applicants, but had learned a great deal from her instructors in college. She was not yet proficient, but she was getting better each day at identifying applicants' qualifications.

Esther was often asked by companies to supply temporary help and decided that maybe she could come up with additional income if she entered that business. However, she was not familiar with temporary employment, and had no applicants ready to work on a part-time basis. Esther advertised in the papers and did get some people, but they were also working for two of the largest temporary agencies in town. However, she managed to offer comparable rates, and she did get into that business on a small scale. The new venture gave her headaches because she would get involved with a client who was looking for someone for typing or word processing at the last moment, and clients always complained at the rates. Sometimes the person handling the job would inform Esther they worked with the client for only a few hours when in fact they worked longer. The temporary employee then billed the same client for the extra hours at a lower rate. She also was obliged to pay the part-time worker immediately and had to wait to receive the money from the client. It was taking up a lot of her time and she was not making much money in that area.

Esther kept up with the business, and it was developing more revenue, but the volume was not at the level she needed to generate much profit. She continued to have problems filling positions, such as a recent order for a $50,000 a year position where she could have earned a fee of $7,500. She would advertise when she got the order, but she seldom got the right person to respond. As the matter now stands, she is stuck in the office and cannot visit clients, and she does not have the applicants to review and send to fill orders. She has to find a way to solve these problems and she has come to you to see if you can help her.

QUESTIONS

1. What suggestions would you give Esther to find applicants for job orders?

2. What can you do to prevent employees you hire from leaving your firm to accept positions that go through your office?

3. Does Esther have the characteristics needed to be an entrepreneur?

4. What would Esther do if one of Les' distant relatives claims the business?

5. What is she to do when tax time comes around at the end of the year and she has to report income? Does she report the sales of Les as well?

6. If no one comes into the business in a year to claim it as their own can Esther change the name? If the lease is up and the landlord wants a new lease, under whose name should the lease be recorded?

7. Was the idea to get into temporary help good?

8. What recommendations do you have for Esther to make her business more viable? Do you think she should quit the business and look for another position?

CASE 30

SBLG Center: A Private Small Business Lending Group

Leon Bellamy and five of his friends decided to go into the private lending business in San Jose, California. Together they have approximately $2 million, and they can borrow $3 million to $4 million at very favorable rates from the bank if needed. Leon feels there is a definite need in small business for a company that grants short-term loans. His own experience suggests there are well-established firms that cannot borrow money from banks. He believes that they would pay him 15 percent interest on an unsecured 90-day Promissory note. A short time ago he loaned money to a friend and was promptly paid back. Since that time, others have approached him, and he has accepted notes averaging $5,000 for 90 days at 15 percent interest per annum. One firm even offered him the opportunity to purchase some of its stock if he would lend it $15,000 for six months at 15 percent interest, but he declined. The firm now is very successful and Leon is sorry he did not take the owner up on the offer. Although Leon was apprehensive in the beginning to go any further because he did not want to "become a bank" or compete with them, he now is convinced that the opportunities are limitless in the small business lending field.

　　The others in his group share his enthusiasm, and since they all have money and are not dependent on this revenue for their principal income, they feel that they would like to give it a chance. However, they should establish criteria for the type of firms they are willing to lend money to privately and the amounts of loans they will extend. They also discussed whether the group should take a stock interest in a firm or stick to cash lending only. They finally decided to consider requests on a case-by-case basis.

The basic rules the group agreed on were as follows.

a. No friends or relatives would be considered for loans.

b. Any firm that is insolvent would not be considered for a loan.

c. Any firm that wants to borrow money must submit financial statements to their accountants for evaluation. If the accountants approve the loan, then the group will lend the money.

d. Notes will not exceed 90 days, but can be renewed at the option of the group.

After this agreement was approved, the operation was set in motion. The group did not actively promote their services, but rather let it be known by word of mouth that they would consider lending money on a 90-day basis. The applications were heavy for the first few months, and the group members were surprised at how many firms had been turned down by banks, but which they found worthy of a small loan. They did not lose any money on any of the loans they gave. All were either paid in 90 days or renewed by the group. The 15 percent interest rate was a handsome figure to earn these days because of the low interest rates prevailing in the market.

Some small companies were offering the group members stock in exchange for loans larger than those offered. As a matter of fact, some companies offered up to 40 percent of their stock for far below its actual value. One company even offered them $50,000 of preferred stock at 15 percent interest per year with options to convert each share of preferred stock into five shares of common stock. However, the group members weren't sure they wanted to become minority stockholders in firms, which would mean a long-term commitment as well as loss of control of their assets.

At this time the group has more than $1,750,000 loaned out at 15 percent interest. While this interest rate was good considering present low interest rates, Leon and one of the other partners felt they should explore a few special situations to see how they could earn more on their investments. They decided to explore the possibilities with one company.

Charles Delaney had a fast growing importing company that was doing business with Japan and Korea. Delaney was importing hi-tech parts and materials. Delaney could not obtain another loan from his bank and asked Leon if his group would be interested in lending him money for expansion. The net worth of Delaney's business was $1 million and he thought he needed about $3 million in additional financing to handle additional purchases. The manufacturers he dealt with would not extend credit to him. He had to pay for the merchandise before it was shipped to customers who had already ordered it. He kept in storage the excess inventory until requested. Delaney had to order months in advance to have sufficient stock because if he experienced a stock-out he would lose many customers.

The estimated financial profits from such an investment were as follows:

Present company:

Sales to date	$2,000,000
Cost of sales	1,200,000
Gross profit	$800,000
Expenses	575,000
Profit before taxes (Subchapter S)	$ 225,000

If $3,000,000 injected into the business:

Estimated sales	$12,000,000
Cost of sales	7,200,000
Gross profit	4,800,000
Estimated expenses	3,000,000
Profit before taxes (Subchapter S)	$ 1,800,000

Leon liked the business because the companies Delaney represented were top quality manufacturers. Each was very aggressive about the U.S. market and had excellent research divisions so they could be expected to maintain leadership in the field. Leon found that the products Delaney imported would be competitive for some time because American companies could not match the production and technical knowledge of these Japanese and Korean firms.

What would they get for their money? After all, the difference between $1 million and $3 million was great and nothing Delaney could generate seemed fair to the group. Delaney proposed the group lend him $3 million in the form of a bond, or preferred stock, and that the group purchase 40 percent of the company stock for $400,000 (40 percent of $1 million original capital stock). The group would not accept this agreement, because it presented too many problems. They counter-proposed the following:

a. They would purchase 60 percent of the common stock on the company for $600,000 ($1,000,000 × 60%). Delaney would have complete authority to operate the company as long as he met corporate goals. They stressed they were only lenders.

b. They would lend the company $3 million in form of a 10-year debenture bond at 12 percent cumulative interest.

c. Once the bond was paid off, or they received 10 years' interest in full plus payment of the bond, then they would resell Delaney sufficient stock in the company to give him a 51 percent interest in the company and the majority vote.

d. They would also give Delaney the option of buying out their stock interests at the audited book value plus 100 percent at any time as long as the bond was paid in full plus the full ten year interest.

Delaney thought about this for some time and did not know what to do. He liked being his own boss, yet he knew he would have to be willing to give something up to realize his company's growth.

As for the group, some members felt that the money they were lending represented a major risk and they did not like the odds. They felt the business was certainly worthwhile but that if the American companies really started making better hi-tech products, their investment might be lost. One member suggested that they just buy stock in Japanese firms specializing in manufacturing hi-tech equipment. Another member wanted to remain with the original concept of making small loans, and feared they would lose a great deal of money on their investment. Another member suggested that the group lend a lower amount and they take a closer look into Delaney's organization's entire financial structure. The accountant thought a trip to Japan might convince the manufacturers to give them credit which would take the big bite out of the investment. If they increased the net worth of the company to $2 million and obtained controlling interest, they might be able to get the credit because of their combined financial net worth. At this stage both Delaney and the group are undecided.

QUESTIONS

1. Do you feel that the basic mission of this group was practical? Do you think that banks are more interested in asset backed loans and forget or overlook people's characters?

2. Do you think the group should remain in the business of handling short-term unsecured promissory notes at 15 percent interest?

3. Do you think they should deal with firms that want them to come in as common stockholders or equity lenders where they would have a minority position? If they should do this, how can they protect their position? Should they consider making deals that make them majority stockholders?

4. Do you think that they should enter the Delaney deal? Do you think that Delaney was asking too much?

5. What did you think about the position of Delaney after the group made their proposal? Do you think that Delaney would still be as enthused if he lost control of the business?

6. Do you think that Delaney should accept their offer or turn them down? Where could Delaney get money to finance his merchandise?

7. What do you think of the other suggestions made by other members of the group?

CASE 31

Kelly Toy Manufacturing Company

The Kelly Toy Manufacturing Company has been in business for nearly 30 years. During that time, it has grown from a small company which sold $25,000 worth of small fire engine trucks for small children to one with sales of $32 million annually. The truck which at first cost $3 now sold for $29. The company has added trains, dolls, wagons, educational toys and many other items to its product line. Charles Kelly, one of the partners, thinks the firm could double or even triple its earnings if he restructured the marketing department and hired more dynamic salespeople. His more conservative brother, James, points out that they make about 3 percent after taxes, or almost $900,000 a year. Charlie admits that the business is making money, but he is concerned about the future. He thinks they have missed too many new ideas and concepts which have made a fortune for their competition.

Jimmy Kelly agreed that Charlie should restructure the entire marketing department. Jimmy hoped that the established client data base, carefully developed over many years, would not be upset. However, Jimmy favored new client development. Charlie hired an outside consulting firm to conduct a marketing audit. The findings supported Charlie's thinking. The department had insufficient salespeople to cover the U.S. market, and the present sales force did not spend its time productively. Some territories were not being covered, salespeople needed more training in administration, too much time was spent on each account, and they did not look for new accounts. In general they were not aggressive enough. There were also no women or minorities on the sales force, which put the company in violation of Affirmative Action regulations.

After the auditors left, Charlie made some changes. He rearranged some of the territories, but waited to open new areas due to insufficient sales personnel. He began to hire women and minorities. He circulated a job description throughout the company for the sales positions. He was surprised to find that among 350 employees, more than 45 women and minorities had majored in marketing but were working in other jobs within the company. Charlie contacted employment agencies, advertised in local and regional newspapers, asked local colleges and universities for assistance and invited women and minorities to apply.

After a month's search, Charlie hired three men and nine women, five of whom were minorities. Four came from the organization. Each would initially earn $25,000 a year with a bonus tied to their net sales. If they each worked diligently they could easily earn the first year $35,000 or more. They would be assigned to various territories and relocation might be involved. There were opportunities for advancement.

Charlie mapped out an extensive training program that lasted 14 weeks. The program allowed each salesperson to work in production, shipping, quality control, testing, customer service, credit and administration. An outside consultant gave training in sales techniques. At the end of the 14 weeks Charlie felt that the company had 12 potentially productive people.

Each was assigned to a territory and given a quota to meet for every product in the line. The sales people submitted their weekly itinerary, including active accounts to be visited, the date of the proposed visit, the area, the nature of the call, and new accounts to be contacted. Each salesperson could give immediate credit if the firm was rated in The Dun and Bradstreet Directory. If special problems arose, each could contact Charlie.

After several months of operation, sales results were encouraging and the salespeople were making great strides in their respective areas. Charlie was pleased and felt that they would easily double their sales for the year. In spite of the success, there were some problems. Benson Hooper, the sales manager for nearly 25 years, thought Charlie was pushing him out of his job. He and others did not like having women on the sales force.

Because of his long employment with the firm, Charlie tried to pacify Benson. He pointed out to Benson that the women salespeople were doing an excellent job, in several cases outselling every man on the force. Benson replied that this was due to luck and not salesmanship. Charlie was furious about that statement. He told Benson that he could cooperate in the new marketing policies or be transferred to another department within the company.

Then sexism emerged in another way. Each month the company had a sales meeting at the home office in St. Louis, Missouri. Charlie and the entire sales force, now including 44 people, discussed new product lines, sales techniques, common problems, and other relevant issues. Whenever a woman asked a question, one of the older salesmen would try to make her look ridiculous. The women refused to get angry and continued with their questions. One woman reported that she was getting misleading calls from clients. Another reported that in Logan's former territory, which she now handled, some clients insisted that they do business with Logan or they would look for another manufacturer. When that comment was made, several other women reported similar situations.

After Charlie had heard all the comments and complaints, he knew the salesmen were trying to sabotage the women. He made it clear that the women were staying as long as they produced and that if the men did not stop causing trouble, they would be dismissed. He wanted the salespeople to work as a team. He emphasized that everybody deserved an equal opportunity, and if anyone tried to deny another of one, he would be fired. The situation settled down for a while after this. Business continued to increase, especially in the territories handled by women. Maria Santiago was the top salesperson and Gloria Sanford was a clear second. The women seemed to handle administrative matters well. The men tended to be sloppy and incomplete. In general, they did not have the determination that the women displayed. Charlie also found that the women, as instructed, sold the entire range of products, while the men sold only those toys that were popular and requested.

Finally, Charlie decided to change the management of the marketing department. He transferred Benson to the "New Toy Concepts Division," and Benson promptly resigned. Five other salesmen submitted their resignations as well. Charlie kept control and posted bids for more salespeople and for a general sales manager. He also decided to hire four regional sales managers who would report directly to the general sales manager. Charlie followed the same recruiting procedures as before and hired 10 additional salespeople, two men and eight women. Six women came from within the company. The two women who came from outside sources consisted of a Korean American and a black. Charlie received over 400 applications for the positions of general sales manager and regional sales managers. Many were from the outside, but Charlie preferred to hire from within the organization. After sifting through the applications, Charlie chose Maria Santiago for general sales manager. She was a college graduate, majored in marketing, and was the top salesperson in the organization. She had an excellent administrative background, for in her last position she was administrative assistant to the marketing vice-president in a computer company, and she was aggressive. Charlie was concerned that she might be too assertive, yet he felt that she would handle that properly in time.

Immediately after her appointment, protests arose from the marketing department as well as some of the other departments. Some protests were absurd and others were slanderous. One rumor stated that the "Hot Tamale" was going to rename all the toys in Spanish so she could understand them. Another rumor purported that Maria and Charlie were having an affair. Instead of responding to the rumors, Charlie kept going and worked together with Maria to select the regional sales managers for the department. They finally decided on four women from the company, one of whom was black. Charlie felt that this would clearly indicate to everyone in the organization that upward mobility was possible regardless of sex, race, or creed. Charlie felt that each person selected was the best person for the job, and he was not just window dressing for the E.E.O.C. He fully expected this group to increase sales and profits for the company.

After the appointments Charlie vacated the department and gave Maria a free hand to organize the regional sales managers and to supervise the entire sales force, which now consisted of 49 salespeople, 35 percent of whom were women. Maria first met with the sales force. She located the meeting in a nice hotel with conference rooms. Maria came well prepared for the meeting and made a speech asking the salespeople for their cooperation and assuring them of hers. Abruptly, Micky Dyer asked her if it was now going to be necessary to learn Spanish. Maria smiled and replied sarcastically, "Micky, if it will sell our products then learn Spanish and if it requires Russian or German I would suggest you learn those languages also." She then asked if there were any other questions before proceeding with the rest of the program. It soon became obvious to everyone that Maria was well organized. She presented her program, the company sales position, new products in the process of adoption, and what the company was doing in various areas. Maria made it clear that attention to administrative details was crucial. She expected reports promptly, fashioned in the manner stipulated by the company. She expected to be called for big sales and promised to fly anywhere to assist in making a sale. As the meeting adjourned, it was evident to the salesmen who had been with the company before the women came that she had been directing her comments to them.

After a few weeks Maria could see that some of the salesmen were not following her instructions regarding administrative details. One of the best salespeople in the organization, Thomas Ferguson, was especially lazy. Another top salesman, Mark Schwab, also was not performing up to par. Each handled some of the firm's largest accounts, and while Maria did not want to lose them, she felt they had to be taught a lesson. She wrote to them, as well as a few others, regarding their administrative responsibilities. Ferguson sent back the envelope containing the letter torn into shreds. He did not make any other response. Ferguson and Schwab joined together and flew into the office one day to see Charlie Kelly or his brother. Charlie was in, and he was surprised by their sudden appearance. They immediately went into a rage about Maria and her lack of consideration for them and their years of service with the company. They said they could not sit down to complete all the required reports and still sustain an adequate level of sales. Charlie asked them to speak to Maria.

Maria knew by this time that Ferguson and Schwab had left the field without permission to see Charlie. She met them with reserved coolness and they proceeded to tell her what they thought of her and her memorandums. They made some vile remarks about her sex and heritage. After they finished, Maria asked why they had left their territories without permission and why they did not have the courtesy to respond to her memorandums. The two stated flatly that they needed no permission to make a trip to the home office. Maria ignored the insults and informed them that if they did not conform to the policies of the company or ever left their territory again they would be terminated on the spot. They replied that their only responsibility was to make sales and they would operate as they always had regardless of what she said or did. Further, Ferguson said he did not have time to fill out his reports for this week and would get them in when he could. Schwab repeated Ferguson's comments. At that point Maria fired them.

When Ferguson and Schwab told Charlie they had been fired, he was stunned. He felt that Maria failed to handle the matter satisfactorily. Charlie called them together and asked Maria if her decision was final. Maria answered affirmatively. It was going to be her way or theirs, and since she was responsible for sales it was going to be hers. Charlie tried to change her mind, but she was adamant. Charlie could see Maria's viewpoint and decided to support her completely. The men received their final paychecks and left the company. A few weeks later both were working for a competitor, and Kelly lost their largest accounts. When Jimmy heard about it, he conferred with Charlie who indicated there was nothing else Maria could have done and he backed her 100 percent.

Maria found two female replacements and revised the territories. She sent two experienced men to those vacated by Ferguson and Schwab and sent the two new salespersons to other areas. Sales continued to increase from new accounts, but the company was losing some of its established customers as a result of the conflict.

After the Ferguson incident, other problems arose from the old sales force. Maria tried to figure out what was wrong—why she could not get their cooperation. She wanted to adhere to her established policy since it worked well with the new personnel. The older workers continued to resist, so she eventually dismissed nine more of them. Seven immediately found positions with competitors. Maria replaced them with seven women and two men from within the company. More than 50 percent of the sales force were women now.

In the meantime Charlie and Jimmy were also thinking about why the older salesmen would not accept Maria. While she could be abrasive and a stickler for details, the new people were doing well. It seemed that the old crew wanted to "rock the boat." The conflict was becoming known in the trade and competitors were actively seeking some of the more experienced salesforce for their contacts with established clients. Eleven more of the senior force left the company, claiming Charlie was not loyal to the crew that helped build the company. Charlie defended Maria, but Jimmy was having doubts. He was concerned that the company had lost more than 60 percent of its former client base. While sales were climbing to $35 million this year, a new peak, he wasn't sure the new clients were secure. Charlie is beginning to wonder if Maria will succeed or whether he has made a terrible mistake.

QUESTIONS

1. Do you think that a marketing audit was the correct approach for Charlie to take with the marketing department?

2. Do you think Charlie was right in taking charge of the department, pushing Benson into the background away from the decision-making process? Would you have handled it differently?

3. What were Charlie's reasons for hiring women and minorities?

4. Do you think that Charlie prepared the male sales force for the entry of women into the department? Could he have done anything to eliminate the problems that developed?

5. Do you think that Charlie's training program was well planned and effective?

6. Do you think that Charlie was correct in appointing Maria as the general sales manager? Do you feel she was qualified and ready for that position with this company? Do you think that one of the older salespersons who had been with the company longer would have been a better choice?

7. What do you think Charlie should have done

when Ferguson and Schwab came to his office? Should he have persuaded Maria to retain them? Do you think Maria handled the situation properly?

8. Do you feel that in light of the fact that the company has lost 60 percent of their former client base and a majority of their male sales force that Maria should be replaced?

9. What future do you see for this company? Do you think it is possible for the company to regain some old clients? What methods would you suggest?

Autumn Leaves Pet Cemetery

Beverly Pickford and Donnel Jenkins were sisters who were widowed and living together. They had not inherited much money from their husbands, and it would be nearly 10 years before they would be eligible to receive social security. They decided to open a business which was both satisfying and meaningful to them. They wanted to make enough money to live comfortably.

After much research Beverly and Donnel decided to establish a pet cemetery. The nearest one was approximately 75 miles away. If they established one nearby outside Lincoln, Nebraska, it would have great appeal. They had a 100-acre piece of property with an abundance of beautiful trees that would make it ideal for a cemetery. Since they did not know much about the legalities of the business, they contacted their attorney and asked him to investigate the requirements. Their attorney, Kevin Pendleton, told them they would have to have the property zoned to ensure that perpetual care could always be maintained no matter who eventually owned the property. The property couldn't be used for any other purpose in the future. It took more than 10 months before he was able to get approval for the location as a pet cemetery. Meanwhile, the sisters checked to see if they satisfied all the requirements of the state and county.

The sisters hired an architect to create a design and layout for the cemetery. He would have to create a serene environment so that pet lovers would want to bury their pets there. In a month the architect came up with a design with a distinctive brick wall surrounding the facility. The wall facing the main highway was lowered so people could see how beautiful the cemetery was. The landscaping plan included separate areas ringed by shrubs and trees, small waterfalls, and statues of all types of animals. The cemetery exuded peace and harmony.

The architect designed a building to house the inventory of stones, tools and other equipment. The building also had a display room for caskets and other products for sale, plus two rooms for private viewing. He also designed a crematorium to accommodate animals up to 200 pounds. The proposed layout was simply magnificent. The architect estimated the entire project would cost $150,000 to construct. The sisters approved the design and construction began.

The sisters had to decide how much to charge for services. They checked and found that cemetery lots for people could range from $400 to $1,000 for one person. This included perpetual care, the opening and closing of the grave site, and sodding. It cost an additional $100 for weekend burials and another $75 for tent and chairs at the burial site. The sisters also guessed that certain locations were more valuable than others and did not know how to vary the charges. They also did not know how much to charge for cremation. The fee for a person was about $1,000 without the urn. Beverly and Donnel judged that $500 would be adequate, but perhaps should be varied according to the size of the animal.

Next the sisters had to decide how to advertise the cemetery. Since neither of the sisters had any marketing experience, they thought that maybe an advertisement in the papers would be sufficient, or perhaps they should advertise on television.

The sisters soon opened for business and the first clients arrived. They still were uncertain about charges. One client wanted her Persian cat buried near the waterfalls, so they quoted $100 for the lot, $50 for the casket, $15 for perpetual care, and $10 to open and close the burial site. The woman ordered a stone, and they charged her $20 plus $10 for the engraving. The woman paid the amount gladly and was very happy and pleased with the site.

One couple came in with their dog "Skeeter," who had just died. Windgate, the helper who handled the gardening and grave digging, took the dog and put him in the preparation room. Donnel and Beverly did all they could to console Skeeter's owners and then proceeded to take care of all the arrangements. The couple who owned the dog stated they wanted the best. In this case, the sisters charged the owner $250 for the lot, $75 for the casket, $50 for perpetual care, $35 for opening and closing the grave, and $95 for the stone with engraving. The couple also wanted to use one of the viewing rooms and requested music. Beverly promised to obtain appropriate music and charged $50 for the room. The couple picked out a site just under an oak tree and paid them the total sum of $555 for the burial.

Now that the sisters had had two clients they decided to assess their prices. They wanted to have established prices because it was neither fair nor ethical to charge on the basis of emotional investment, with some pet owners paying just about any price and others paying the bare minimum. Some prices could be determined by available products. For example, a casket company offered fancy models from $1,000 to $2,500. A local builder met requests for mausoleums for approximately $1,500 depending on specifications.

The two sisters also had requests for financing future burials. Some people wanted to finance the lot, casket, and other items in advance of a pet's death. Donnel stated the cemetery had no such plan at this time, but would look into it.

In summary, the sisters had invested about $150,000 into a 100-acre cemetery and there appears to be a great deal of potential. They have asked you to solve their marketing problems.

1. Do you think that Donnel and Beverly went into the right business? Did they research the business thoroughly? What factors would you have considered?

2. There are many pet segments in the pet cemetery market. Where do you think they have their greatest potential and how would you approach these segments?

3. What would you do to solve the pricing problem? Do you think the sisters should have a standard price or do you feel they should use variable pricing as they did with the first two clients? Do you think that the price they charge should be related to how much love and grief the pet owners display when they call for burial or bring their pet to the cemetery?

4. Do you think that the two sisters are playing on the sympathies of pet lovers when they have a private room for caskets and try to sell $2,500 caskets? Or do you honestly feel that they are trying to satisfy the needs of pet owners?

5. Would you enter this type of business if you were given the opportunity?

6. What other marketing advice would you give Beverly and Donnel to make their business successful?

CASE 33

Mainline Gift Shop

Carol MacDonald owns and operates the Mainline Gift Shop in suburban Houston. Carol purchased the business seven years ago, and gradually its annual sales have grown from less than $200,000 to more than $900,000. The business has an excellent reputation, is beautifully decorated, and is stocked with gifts from all parts of the world. Carol is pleased with her success and attributes her prosperity to total dedication, close contact with her clients, appropriate merchandise, and a good marketing plan. However, Carol admits to having serious problems and has talked about them to several of her friends, including her accountant, lawyer, and banker. The problems deal with location as well as some internal changes which she feels might have to be rectified.

When Carol purchased the business seven years ago, the landlord would not give her more than a one-year lease. Because the previous owner of her business had no difficulty renewing the lease each year, she felt that she would not encounter problems in this area either. Further, when Carol was starting out she was somewhat reluctant to commit herself to a lease over one year because she had doubts about her ability to successfully run the business. However, the business did succeed, and for the last seven years the lease was renewed. However, three months ago the landlord died and his widow turned over all property management to her son, Andrew. Naturally, Carol expected the lease arrangement to remain the same as it had been in the past, and, indeed, Andrew assured her that when her present lease expired she would receive a new one. But at the end of the year, Carol received a new lease for five years with a rent increase from $1,000 to $3,000 per month, or 5 percent of total annual gross receipts, whichever was higher. Needless to say, Carol was furious and contacted Andrew. He told her that there would be no adjustments and that if she did not like the new terms, she could move. Andrew insisted that based on comparable rental values throughout the community, the rental he was asking was fair. Andrew did offer "for old times' sake" to give her a six-month extension on her present lease at the new rate. Carol told him she would give him an answer in a few weeks.

Carol does not want to move because she has spent a lot of time building her business at that location and she does not want to risk $900,000 in sales and profits. On the other hand, she cannot afford either 5 percent or $45,000 a year in rent. Since her business is growing at the rate of 20 percent per year, she knows moving would set her back. She decided to contact several real estate brokers and finally located a vacant lot 10 blocks from her present location. The new location would have room for parking and future expansion and still be close enough to keep most of her present clientele. The total cost of the building would be $375,000. She could get a mortgage for $300,000, which would require payments of $3,600 monthly for 15 years. The earliest she could move into the location would be 6 to 8 months from the present. The builder did say that he could make the location reasonably presentable and functional sooner, but it would not be totally complete for about 8 months.

In the meantime, Carol heard that Andrew was thinking about opening his own gift shop in her present location. When Carol confronted Andrew about this, he did not deny it and said that his wife, Shelly May, was going to open up a shop as soon as Carol left. Carol was familiar with Shelly May because she had worked part time for Carol for several years. She was very capable, and, in fact, knew the suppliers, customers, and price structure necessary to operate the business.

Carol asked Andrew if he would be willing to sell the building. Andrew immediately told her that he would be willing to sell it for $400,000. He would take $100,000 down and hold the mortgage himself at 11½ percent fixed for 20 years. The monthly payments would be $3,200. Carol knew that the building was not worth that much and that there was little room for expansion. She did not know whether Andrew was bluffing in order to sell the building or if he really intended to open a gift shop. Since the old lease clearly indicated that all improvements she had made became part of the property of the landlord; if he opened a gift shop, Shelly May would be opening with the same type of decor that Carol had operated under for years. Carol worried about whether all her customers would shop at her new location as well as whether having two gift shops on the same street would cause her to lose business. She felt that if sales dropped she might not be able to afford the mortgage payment on the new building. Carol told Andrew she would let him know her decision. She asked for an extension of eight months on her lease, but Andrew insisted that she would have to sign a five-year lease.

Carol is considering another alternative. For some time she has been contemplating opening a second location. She had finally settled on a new growth area in another section of Houston. A new building is available there which Carol could either lease or purchase. The property is strategically located among a cluster of stores that would complement her business. There is plenty of parking space and room for future expansion. The owner is willing to lease the facility for $2,000 per month on a three-, five-, or ten-year basis, or sell the property for $250,000. The owner will accept $50,000 down and can arrange financing at 12 percent over a 20-year period. The monthly payments including principal and interest would be $2,202. Carol is tempted to call it quits at the old location and start from the beginning in this new growth area; however, when she thinks about the time and effort she has put into the original location, she is hesitant to start over again.

So Carol's alternatives are: (1) to pay an exorbitant amount of rental under a five-year lease at the present property; (2) to purchase property for $400,000 which will probably be too small within a few years and is overvalued; (3) to build a new building 10 blocks down the same street and take on a mortgage of $3,600 per month with the threat of having Andrew's wife open the same type of business and perhaps cut into her sales; and (4) to open a new location in the growth area and start over again, where Carol would be faced with uncertainty in sales and income. While she feels more confident than she did when she opened up the original store, she would still have to face it as a new business.

In the meantime, Carol is having other problems. She is not satisfied with her inventory control system. Differences constantly arise between her book inventory and actual physical inventory. At the end of each buying season (such as Easter, Christmas, or Mother's Day) there is usually an abundance of inventory that has to be stored until the following year. When the physical inventory is unpacked and counted, there is either a shortage or overage when compared to book inventory. Carol thinks that perhaps the discrepancy is due to returns, withdrawals, or exchanges. In any case, last year the physical inventory was $17,000 lower than the book inventory. Carol had given some consideration to purchasing a computer, but does not know much about them. She is afraid that if she puts all business transactions on the computer, anyone who can tap into the computer will know the details of her business, just as Shelly May does.

Carol is also having a problem with shoplifting. Now that the business is growing and she has more customers, more shoplifting is occurring. Because those she has caught are always clients who can afford to buy the merchandise, Carol has not enforced her own rules. When shoplifters are caught, she merely warns them that if they do it again she will report them to the police. At one time Carol had dummy TV cameras, in addition to mirrors, around the store, but some of her clients complained that they did not like being followed around the store by a camera when trying to shop. So, she took down the cameras and now has only mirrors.

About nine months ago Carol appointed Joyce Lamont as store manager to assist her and fill in for her when she wasn't at the store. Joyce has done an excellent job and is totally dedicated to the business. She works late and even refuses to take a vacation. Carol has become very dependent upon her. Recently, Joyce brought to her attention that daily gross cash receipts are not following typical days. For example, on some Saturdays when the store is packed with customers, the cash receipts are sometimes $300 off what they would be on a normal Saturday. Joyce thinks that some of the employees might be stealing and has asked for permission to fire people if she does discover thefts. Carol was shocked and told Joyce she should handle the matter carefully because many of her part-time employees were related to very influential people in the community. Since all the clerks are working fast to relieve the congestion on the busy weekends when the store is packed and the lines are deep, and all the clerks are dipping into any cash register that is open, it is impossible to hold any one person responsible for a particular cash register. Joyce did report that she noticed one girl stealing and quietly informed her that she was being let go because they were cutting back on staff. As Joyce pointed out, it would be difficult to prove she was stealing and it was better not to create a scene. Carol agreed with this approach and commended Joyce on her tactfulness.

Over the next few months, Carol became concerned when the same thing happened several more times. She wonders if something else has been overlooked since the same scenario keeps occurring. Carol has thought of getting fidelity insurance, but found that it would be very expensive for the gift shop business. She has also considered hiring an outside organization that specializes in investigating employees by coming in and buying items for cash and then leaving without a receipt. She has even toyed with the idea of putting a live T.V. camera near the counter where she could privately monitor activity herself. As yet she has not mentioned this to Joyce because she wants to give it more thought.

Finally, Carol is having another problem with the vendors. Carol has been dealing with them since she opened the store, and in a lot of ways if it were not for their help the business would not have survived. Lately, however, she has been having second thoughts about some of her vendors because new suppliers, who are trying continually to attract her customers, have been offering much better prices and credit terms. Some have even offered consignment arrangements. Carol feels a tremendous loyalty to her old suppliers and has talked to some of them, but they always point out how they helped her when she needed them. Some did give her better prices and terms and made other concessions. However, it seems that unless she complains, nothing happens, and when she does, they do come up with better prices and terms. Carol wonders just how long she should operate under this condition. After all, she adjusts her prices for her customers constantly, and she cannot understand why her suppliers cannot do the same. She wonders whether she should give some of the new suppliers a chance or stick with the old vendors who helped her when she started the business.

QUESTIONS

1. What alternative would you advise Carol to take concerning her location and rental arrangement? Be specific and consider all alternatives.

2. How would you handle the problems of inventory control?

3. What should Carol do about the shoplifting problem?

4. Should Carol computerize her operation?

5. Do you think there is any relationship between the shoplifting and the difference between the physical and book inventory? Explain.

6. Do you agree with the manner in which Joyce Lamont has been handling the theft problem? Should she have reported the employees to the police?

7. Should Carol use some other system to determine what is happening to cash receipts? Do you think she should install a private monitoring system? Should she inform Joyce?

CASE 34

Lincoln Motors Inc.

Benny Mill and Byron Sidney have both been working in the automobile business for 10 years in a small town outside Cheyenne, Wyoming. They recently worked in the used car department for a new car dealer in Cheyenne. Selling used cars was their specialty, and they have decided to go into business for themselves. Benny and Byron were complete opposites. Benny was devious and totally unscrupulous when pursuing a deal. Byron was more honest and would tell people the truth about cars if they asked. Benny referred to himself as the last of a dying breed called "the pure Used Car Jockey." Byron knew of Benny's practices and policies, but they had always gotten along and he felt that they could work together profitably.

Benny and Byron began their venture by buying 50 used cars. Many of the cars were not in good shape, but they would run. They found an adequate location on the main highway near a new car dealer who had a good reputation. The new car dealer's advertising stimulated a busy flow of customers, and its proximity would create an advantage.

Benny and Byron fixed up the lot and erected two small sales offices, one of which Benny insisted be "bugged" so he could listen to the customers' conversations. Byron knew this was illegal, yet he agreed. The dealership opened for business. When a customer accompanied by a spouse or friend came in to buy a car, the salesperson would leave them alone so he could go into the other office to listen to their conversations. This would help him determine how to close the sale.

Another trick Benny used was to carry a Bible. He would greet the customers and walk them solemnly by all the cars, clutching the Bible and discussing the merits of each car. He would tell them that he could not in good conscience sell them a particular car. Some customers were so impressed with Benny that they would buy the car that Benny was leading them to from the beginning. As soon as the sale was closed, Benny in front of the client would hold his head down and read a passage from the Bible. Byron could not tolerate this performance and left every time Benny did it. However, Benny thought it was funny and clever.

A small one-car shop was added to the facilities to clean up the cars for sale. Benny hired an expert "get ready" man for $50 per car. He was to work on the exterior paint, scratches, tires, wiring, upholstery, steam cleaning and painting the engine. When he was finished each looked years younger.

Initially, Benny made connections with local companies to arrange financing, but then he started his own consumer finance company and offered terms to his clients. If a customer had no down payment and could not afford high monthly payments, Benny would sell them a car and have them pay $5 per week for an indefinite number of weeks. When they complained about the car he would switch them to an $8 or $10 a week car. Benny even had a bogus guarantee printed up to offer to customers. A customer could obtain a 50–50 guarantee, where Benny would pay half of the repair costs and the client would pay the rest. He also offered a 70–30 warranty where he would pay 70 percent of the repair costs and the client would pay 30 percent. In those cases where the client received a 50–50 guarantee, the agreement would state that the client had to bring the car back to Benny for service. When the car was left Benny would rent them a "junker" for $9 a day. He would then take the car to a repair shop for repairs since his business was not equipped to handle servicing. If the bill came to $90 Benny would charge the client $180. Thus Benny made money from selling poor quality cars.

Benny also advertised cars without a down payment in the following manner:

LATE MODEL CARS AND TRUCKS AT
TREMENDOUS DISCOUNTS
NO DOWN PAYMENT
NO PAYMENT FOR 60 DAYS
FULLY GUARANTEED FOR ONE YEAR
IF WE DON'T HAVE WHAT YOU WANT WE WILL GET IT
WE WILL NOT BE UNDERSOLD AND CAN'T BE UNDERSOLD
THIS SALE GOOD FOR ONE WEEK ONLY
LINCOLN MOTORS INC.
(Where Integrity and Truthfulness Meet)
Open from 8 A.M. to 9 P.M. seven days a week.

145 WOOD STREET
666–6666

The response to the advertisement was great, and many people came to see the cars. Actually Benny had purchased taxis from auctions in other states. He removed the designation of "taxicab" from the title and altered it to show one owner. Benny purchased these cars for $2,000 each and charged $7,500. If the model had had a single owner for one year, it would have sold for $10,000. Benny had painted over the cabs' yellow paint, put on new seat covers, and installed rebuilt motors. Sales were brisk, and after a six-month period, more than 700 used cars had been sold and profits after salaries were about $50,000.

However, Benny's manipulative practices began to catch up with him. He had been setting back speedometers to reduce the mileage shown. After several complaints, the Consumer Frauds Division began an investigation. Benny denied everything and swore on his famous Bible that he was innocent. However, the state police traced the serial numbers back to former owners who indicated the mileage was much greater when they sold the cars. Benny was finally brought up on charges and managed to get off with a substantial fine as a first-time offender. However, in spite of the fine, Benny continued, and Byron left the partnership.

Finally, Benny sold a car to a customer who thought she was getting a one-year-old car with low mileage that had been owned by a local resident. Benny gave the woman a phone number which she thought was the name of the former owner, but which actually was that of one of his salespeople. When the customer called the number, the salesperson told her that the car was in excellent condition. The client then felt confident and paid $8,765 for a one-year-old cab. The new owner had trouble after she purchased the car, and Benny gave her the "treatment" on repairs. When the paint started to peel he told her it was the factory's fault. The woman bought this story until the paint kept coming off and it was clear to her that something was wrong. She finally went to the state police and they charged Benny with fraud. This time Benny was convicted and sent to jail.

Benny swore he was innocent, but to no avail. When Benny went to court, he held his Bible close to him, and the judge noticed it when Benny was being sentenced. The judge's last words were, "While you're enjoying your stay at the state's expense, Benny, I would suggest you try to get something out of that Bible, for you really need it."

QUESTIONS

1. Could Benny have been a success in the used car business without resorting to schemes?

2. Is it possible to be 100 percent ethical and still be a success?

3. Is a used car operation particularly vulnerable to dishonest practices?

4. If Benny's customers were satisfied with the transaction he made with them, what was wrong with doing business this way?

5. What is the difference between Benny's operation and some large manufacturer who will not recall vehicles even when it is aware of a major problem which might be endangering lives?

6. If you were a salesperson in Benny's business making lots of money and then found out about his techniques and methods, would you quit the job? Does the law of "caveat emptor" apply here?

7. What lessons did you learn from this case?

Financing Problems
and Methods

Herman Glass Corporation

Barbara Burke has been in the retail and wholesale glass business for nearly 20 years and is presently general manager of the Clark Glass Company. Her company specializes in auto glass, plateglass, windows, store fronts, glass tops, mirrors, and other glass products. Clark Glass caters to retail as well as industrial and commercial clients. A major part of Clark Glass' business is with insurance companies and building contractors. Barbara has an excellent reputation in the glass business, and has been looking for an opportunity that would allow her to start her own business.

A few weeks ago Barbara was contacted by her banker, who was aware of her interest. He told her that the Herman Glass Corporation was for sale. William Herman had passed away after a long illness and Alice Herman, his wife, now wants to sell and move to Hawaii. Ms. Burke knows the company well, and while it is not as big as Clark Glass Company, it has a good reputation and sells essentially the same products. Herman Glass Company is located in Riverdale, about 60 miles from Clark. The area has a good economic base and is considered a growth area. The competitors in the area are small and, in Barbara's opinion, do not present a threat to Herman Glass. Barbara feels that with a better marketing campaign Herman Glass can increase its sales dramatically.

Barbara met with Mrs. Herman and received the financial statements and tax returns for the past three years, as well as other information that she had requested. Mrs. Herman offered to either sell the stock of the corporation for $155,353 plus $100,000 goodwill or permit the buyer to purchase assets (less cash and prepaid items) plus $100,000 goodwill. In either case, Mrs. Herman wants cash and would like to sell the business within 45 days. She offered to sign a noncompetitive clause and to stay with the business for 30 to 60 days to effect a smooth transition (see exhibits I and II). She told Barbara that two other people also were interested in the company.

Mrs. Herman, who owns the building, offered to rent it to Barbara for the first two years at an annual rate of $24,000. She would give Barbara an option for five more years, but the rental per annum would be tied to the preceding year's Consumer Price Index. Barbara asked her if she would consider an option to purchase the building, and she agreed to sell the building any time during a five-year period for $360,000 cash (the market value of the building is presently $260,000).

A few days after the first meeting Mrs. Herman sent the additional material Barbara had requested, including copies of the proposed lease, aging of accounts payable and accounts receivable, payroll breakdown, and a list of all equipment, furniture and fixtures. After several conferences with her attorney and accountant, Barbara decided to make a cash offer of $148,880. Barbara decided to take her lawyer's advice and purchase only the assets of the business and assume the accounts payable. Her attorney believes that because the Herman Corporation has been around for nearly 25 years the possibility exists that some unknown contingent liability might arise, spelling disaster. Barbara also feels it is important that the accounts payable be paid because if for some reason they are not paid as expected, it could impact upon the company.

The methodology Barbara used to compute the purchase price is as follows:

Accounts receivable (gross)	$140,000	$47,775[1]	$ 92,225
Notes receivable	5,400		5,400
Inventory	134,293	40,228[2]	94,005
Equipment (book value)	31,500		31,500
Furniture & fixtures (book value)	8,500		8,500
Total asset value for each party	$319,693		$231,630
Less: accounts payable	115,600		115,600
Balance	$204,093		$116,030
Plus goodwill	100,000		32,770[3]
Price desired by each party	$304,093		$148,800

[1] Barbara's accountant feels the accounts receivable over 90 days should be excluded.
[2] Barbara estimates that 30 percent of the inventory is obsolete.
[3] Barbara based goodwill on five times 1985 earnings before taxes ($6,554 × 5 years = $32,770).

Barbara met with Mrs. Herman and offered her $231,600 for the assets less $115,600 for the accounts payable, or a total amount of $148,800. Barbara said that she wanted the name of the business, plus a lease for two years at $24,000 per annum and the option to renew for an additional five years at the same price adjusted by the Consumer Price Index. In addition, Barbara wanted an option to purchase the building for $260,000 any time during a five-year period. Further, Barbara wanted the noncompetitive agreement plus assistance for 30 days.

The following day Mrs. Herman presented her final offer to Barbara. Mrs. Herman acknowledged that the accounts receivable and inventory were overvalued, but she strongly feels that the goodwill figure of $32,770 is grossly inadequate. Since Mr. Herman had been ill for several years he could not devote full attention to the business; however, if he had been active, the profits would have been substantial. She also pointed out that the area is growing, the personnel are experienced, and the company has an excellent reputation. Mrs. Herman said that she would only sell the assets of the business and, because Mr. Herman contracted those obligations with the suppliers, she would pay them off herself and provide whatever proof Ms. Burke needed to substantiate that fact. She agreed to sell the assets to Ms. Burke for $231,630, but the goodwill figure could not be less than $64,370, thus making the selling price $296,000. Further, Mrs. Herman said she would sell the name for one year only, but she would give a rental lease for two years at $24,000 per annum and the additional five-year rental option would be tied to the Consumer Price Index. In addition, she said that she would grant an option to purchase the building for $300,000, but the option at that price would only be valid for two years. If Barbara did not pur-

Exhibit I Herman Glass Corporation, Balance Sheet, December 31, 1986.

ASSETS

Current Assets

Cash		$ 15,000
Accounts receivable	$140,000	
Less: allowance for doubtful accounts	2,800	137,200
Notes receivable		5,400
Prepaid items		5,900
Inventory		134,293
Total current assets		$297,793

Fixed Assets

Equipment	$ 70,000	
Less: allowance for depreciation	38,500	$ 31,500
Equipment, furniture & fixtures	$ 25,000	
Less: accumulated depreciation	16,500	8,500
Total fixed assets		$ 40,000
Total Assets		$337,793

LIABILITIES

Current Liabilities

Accounts payable	$115,600
Accrued state taxes payable	5,300
Accrued federal taxes payable	8,500
Accrued interest payable	1,500
Accrued sales taxes payable	1,540
Total current liabilities	$132,440

Long-Term Liabilities

Note payable	$ 50,000
Total long-term liabilities	$ 50,000
Total Liabilities	$182,440

Stockholders' Equity

Common stock	$150,000	
Retained earnings	5,353	$155,353
Total Liabilities and Stockholders' Equity		$337,793

chase the building in two years, the purchase option price in three years would be $350,000; a four-year option price $400,000; and a five-year final option price to be negotiated, but no less than $450,000. She also agreed to the noncompetitive clause and that she would remain 30 days to assist as directed. Mrs. Herman said that her offer was final and expected Barbara's answer the following day.

Exhibit II Herman Glass Corporation, Comparative Income Statements Years Ended December 31.

	1986	1985	1984
Sales	$550,950	$501,700	$476,548
Cost of sales	358,118	326,105	333,584
Gross profit	$192,832	$175,595	$142,964
Operating Expenses			
Salary expense (owner)	$ 40,000	$ 30,000	$ 25,000
Salaries (other)	70,050	69,150	47,000
Payroll taxes, 12%	13,206	11,898	8,640
Rent	24,000	24,000	18,000
Insurance	6,700	6,450	6,500
Advertising	145	275	190
Delivery, car, travel	3,260	4,105	3,750
Supplies	1,410	1,390	1,470
Accounting & legal	4,000	4,000	4,500
Telephone	3,967	3,892	3,600
Utilities	6,840	6,715	6,200
Repairs and maintenance	950	1,140	980
Depreciation—equipment	3,500	3,500	3,500
Depreciation—furniture/fixtures	1,500	1,500	1,500
Interest expense	6,000	6,000	6,000
Miscellaneous	750	871	650
Total expenses	$186,278	$174,886	$137,480
Net Before Taxes	$ 6,554	$ 709	$ 5,484
Income Tax	983	106	823
Net After Taxes	$ 5,571	$ 603	$ 4,661

Barbara thought about the terms and, while she did not like some of the conditions, she felt this was the opportunity she was looking for; she therefore decided to make the deal. After having her lawyer prepare the agreement, she met with Mrs. Herman and gave her a $25,000 deposit.

Barbara discussed the finances with her accountant and he informed her that, in addition to the $296,000, she will need $38,600 for initial working capital. Barbara analyzed her personal resources and can raise all but $100,000. She has talked to bank officers, who are willing to give her a 10-year loan at 12 percent providing the SBA is willing to guarantee the loan. If she borrows the money from the bank, the monthly payments will be $1,435. For purposes of this problem assume that $602 is for interest expense and $833 is for principal.

The second option is to sell $100,000 of stock to her sister Lilyann. Lilyann is close to Barbara and is more than willing to invest in her new business. The problem with this alternative is that her sister would be investing every cent of her resources. While Barbara is quite confident about the business, if it should fail it could have a tremendous impact on her sister.

Lilyann has offered to forgo dividends the first year, but would like to earn at least 10 percent on her investment starting with the second year. Her sister is flexible on the rate, but thinks it should be comparable to bank money market funds. When her children start going to college in a few years, Lilyann would also like to come into the business in some capacity, either full or part-time.

If Barbara does sell stock to her sister instead of borrowing from the bank, she will not have to give her personal guarantees. The latter option could be an advantage if she needed to borrow additional funds from the bank.

QUESTIONS

1. Analyze the financial statements and compute the following ratios, comparing them to the industry median.

Median

Current ratio	2.7
Quick ratio	1.1
Debt ratio	60.0
Total debt to net worth	1.50
Average inventory turnover	3.5 times/year
Receivables turnover	5.61
Average collection period	65 days
Net sales to total assets	2.0
Net profit on sales	5.6%
Net profit/Net worth	10.7%

(See exhibits I and II for financial data.)

When calculating the average inventory turnover, the inventory at the beginning of the year was $127,500. When calculating the receivables turnover, you will use 70 percent of total sales ($550,950) as credit sales for the numerator and use gross accounts receivable plus notes receivable for the denominator.

To calculate the average collection period ratio, use 365 days as the numerator and the receivables turnover as your denominator.

2. In order to arrive at your decision, prepare a monthly cash budget for this year. Assume that you are going to borrow the money from the bank. (See Cash Budget financial assumptions following the questions.)

3. Prepare a monthly income statement for this year and the first six months of next year. (See Monthly Income financial assumptions following the questions.)

4. Should Barbara borrow the money or sell stock to her sister? Do you have any other suggestions? Will Barbara have sufficient funds in the business by June of next year to put up the $60,000 which includes closing costs? (The bank is willing to finance $250,000 at 12 percent for 15 years. Monthly payments would be $3,000. If sufficient funds are not in the business at that time, where could Barbara get the $60,000? Should Barbara defer the decision to purchase the building? Explain.

5. Would you advise Barbara to file for Subchapter S status?

6. Calculate the breakeven point for this year and next year. You will consider $227,034 as your fixed expense this year and $291,000 as your fixed expenses for next year.

CASH BUDGET FINANCIAL ASSUMPTIONS

1. *Cash balance when business begins: $38,600*

2. *Sales are 30% cash and 70% credit*
   Credit sales are collected in the following manner:

   > 25% of credit sales collected in 30 days
   > 50% of credit sales collected in 60 days
   > 25% of credit sales collected in 90 days

   Note: The accounts receivable and notes receivable purchased by Barbara were $145,400. This amount will be collected as follows and must be included in the cash budget forecast for the present year:

January	$33,425
February	25,900
March	14,150 (includes $8,750 + $5,400 note receivable)
Totals	$73,475

   The attorney received a check for $50 in May of 1987 and forwarded it to Barbara. The balance of the accounts receivable is in dispute at this time and has been turned over to her lawyer for collection. All of the accounts making up this list are contractors, but there is a good possibility that about 50 percent might be collected at some time in the future.

3. *Sales forecasts are as follows:*

Sales Forecast this Year		Sales Forecast Next Year	
January	$ 60,000	January	$ 80,000
February	63,000	February	84,000
March	66,000	March	88,000
April	63,000	April	84,000
May	60,000	May	80,000
June	57,000	June	76,000
July	60,000	July	80,000
August	63,000	August	84,000
September	66,000	September	88,000
October	72,000	October	96,000
November	75,000	November	100,000
December	80,000	December	106,664
Total	$785,000	Total	$1,046,664

   Note: The sales forecast for January 1989 is $106,664. This amount is needed to calculate purchases in December of 1988.
   Barbara feels the above forecasts are very likely because of her experience, the business she will be personally bringing to the firm, and her marketing plan.

4. *Purchase (Cost of Sales)*

Cost of sales is 65 percent of each month's sales. Barbara will have to pay 65 percent of each month's sales in the preceding month. For example, in February, sales are forecasted at $63,000. Barbara will have to pay out 65 percent of $63,000 or $40,950 during the month of January. The same procedure will apply to each succeeding month.

5. *Loan Payment*

If Barbara borrows $100,000 through the bank, her monthly payments will be $1,435. In the Cash Budget you will deduct $1,435 as a cash disbursement under Loan Prepayment. Note: When you prepare your Monthly Income Statement you will consider $602 as interest expense (for purposes of this problem).

6. *Estimated federal taxes payable*

In your Cash Budget you will consider $2,500 as tax prepayments in the months of April, June, September and December in the present year. Next year you will budget the same amounts.

7. *Other cash disbursements*

In the first month of this year other disbursements will be heavier because of start-up costs. In the succeeding 11 months they will remain constant.

	January this year	*Each remaining month*
Deposits (utilities, phone, etc.)	$ 2,800	0
Equipment purchase	6,600	0
Insurance (lump sum payment)	7,200	0
Salary & wage group	9,000	9,000
Payroll taxes (12%)	1,080	1,080
Supplies	150	150
Repairs & maintenance	100	100
Advertising	5,000	2,000
Car, delivery & travel	1,000	1,000
Accounting & legal	2,000	350
Rent	2,000	2,000
Telephone	350	350
Utilities	600	600
Miscellaneous	100	100
Total other disbursements	$37,980	$16,730

In the following year the other cash disbursements will be as follows:

a. In January the disbursements will amount to $29,200 exclusive of the loan prepayment of $1,435, which also will have to be considered.

b. In the remaining 11 months the cash disbursements will amount to $22,000 exclusive of $1,435, which also will have to be considered.

8. *New capital purchases*

The company will have to pay for new equipment purchases of $15,000 in December of this year. Bank officers have agreed that if an overdraft does occur they will lend the company additional funds on a short term basis up to 120 days at 14 percent interest.

INCOME STATEMENT ASSUMPTIONS

1. *Sales*

Use sales forecast figures presented in cash budget.

2. *Cost of sales*

You will use 65 percent monthly sales.

3. *Gross profit*

Gross profit is 35 percent of sales.

4. *Expenses*

Expenses for the present year are as follows:

January: $23,182   For the month includes some initial expenses such as additional legal and accounting to set up the business, advertising, promotion and some other items.

Balance of year: $18,532 for each of the remaining 11 months.

5. January through April of 1988 will be $24,425 (to reflect $175 interest expense on a $15,000 loan). The remaining months will be $24,250.

CASE 36

Karen's Delicatessen

Karen Cooper would like to go into business, but has hesitated because of her husband's four failures. Her husband, Lance, first tried a camera shop, but he did not know how to operate many of the cameras or explain their workings to the customers. Second, after getting his credentials, he opened a travel agency. That folded because he would not take time to make contacts and did not know anything about marketing. Third, he decided to open a vegetarian restaurant, even though he was a big meat eater himself. That business was a terrible flop because he never really understood what his customers wanted. The last business he entered was an aerobic dance studio, which he felt was the coming rage and would make him a fortune. However, Lance, who had a sizable paunch, had to depend on others to provide instruction. He underestimated his cash requirements and lost everything, and in time the business closed.

Fortunately, Karen had her own money and never invested in any of Lance's ventures. However, from his mistakes she did learn some basic requirements for success: first, you must have a complete business plan; second, the plan must be well thought out; third, financial resources must be available for short-and long-term growth; and fourth, an owner must be prepared at all times for unknown contingencies or opportunities. Karen also discovered that a background in the business was an absolute necessity, and that the cheapest way to gain experience is to work for someone else.

After careful thought Karen decided that she would like to open up her own delicatessen. She decided against buying an existing business because she wanted to plan everything from the beginning. She did not want to inherit someone else's problems. She knew something about the business because her father had his own successful delicatessen for many years. However, she wanted to get either a part-time or full-time job and learn everything again from scratch.

Karen applied for a job at the best delicatessen in Buffalo, New York. The owner, Bill Heller, was very impressed with her aggressiveness and hired her. Karen started by making sandwiches and salads, working quickly and competently on each task. She talked to the suppliers, found out about pricing, evaluated the types of foods which sold well and which should be avoided, and learned about effective advertising. She even learned how to handle the books, which was especially valuable to her future plans.

After nine months' work at Heller's Delicatessen, Karen felt she was ready to open her own business. Her first task was to determine how much money she would need to invest. She knew from Heller's books what his investments were, but she also wanted to check other stores. She contacted several real estate agents to see if they had any delicatessens for sale. As a possible buyer, she could examine their books to get an idea of sales volume, expenses, and initial investments. She did get the chance to investigate a few and she came up with the following financial information from companies that were doing about $1 million a year in sales:

Balance Sheet

Current Assets

Cash	$ 30,000
Accounts receivable	10,000
Notes receivable	1,500
Inventory	90,000
Other current	10,000
Total current	$141,500

Fixed Assets

Building (net)	$125,000
Equipment (net)	40,000
Fixtures (net)	20,000
Total Assets	$326,500

Balance Sheet (Continued)

Current Liabilities

Accounts payable	$ 32,000
Bank loans	2,500
Notes payable	10,000
Other current	27,000
Total current liabilities	$ 71,500

Long-Term Liabilities

Notes payable (bank)	40,000
Mortgage payable	75,000
Total long-term liabilities	$115,000

Capital

Capital, owner	$140,000
Total liab. & net worth	$326,500

A summary of the income statement for companies whose sales were a little more than $1 million was as follows:

Sales	$1,300,000	100%
Cost of sales	1,014,000	78%
Gross profit	286,000	22%
Less: operating expenses		
Salary (owner)	30,000	
Salaries (others)	91,800	
Payroll taxes (12%)	14,616	
Supplies (bags, etc.)	24,000	
Supplies (office & store)	2,500	
Advertising	15,000	
Legal & accounting	5,200	
Rent*	24,000	
Telephone (including adv.)	3,000	
Utilities	6,000	
Insurance	4,500	
Taxes (real estate, etc.)	1,200	
Depreciation	7,500	
Maintenance & repairs	1,800	
Delivery expense	2,000	
Laundry (uniforms)	2,400	
Shoplifting expense	13,000	
Miscellaneous expense	5,000	
Total operating expense	$ 253,516	19.5%
Total profit before taxes	$ 32,484	2.5%

*If building is leased, $2,000 per month is the average rental; in addition, many owners purchase their buildings in their personal name and rent it back to their company for tax reasons.

Karen took the statements to her accountant to make an assessment of how much she would need to invest into the business. He made the following observations:

a. A total of $201,500 was needed to open up the business presuming she would rent and not buy a building.

b. At least $48,500 in additional capital would be needed for inventory. Suppliers would not extend credit to new owners, and more favorable terms were offered for "cash-and-carry" purchases, which could improve her gross profit from 15 to 20 percent.

c. Operating expenses might need some adjustment, but they could serve as conservative projections. Salary expenses for other employees were based on the premise that three part-time workers would work a total of 17 hours at $5 per hour for 360 days a year, totalling $91,800. The need for help might vary depending on the volume of business and the effectiveness of the employees, but this was calculated on sales volume of approximately $1 million. He also pointed out that she was not making provision for a supervisor or night manager to relieve her from working seven days and nights each week.

d. Finally, he stated that the gross profit could improve if she purchased as much as she could from "cash & carry" wholesalers, rather than from wholesalers who deliver to her door. With close supervision she could probably cut down on shoplifting expenses, but she should watch for employee stealing, which is a particular problem in a cash business.

Karen was very grateful for this advice. Her next task was to secure financing. She contacted Victor Hardfield, a long-time friend, who was on the board of a local bank. She explained what she wanted to do and told him she had about $100,000 to invest into the business and would like a small business loan from the Small Business Administration and the bank. Victor told her she would have to prepare a good business plan to submit to the bank. If the bank felt the proposal had merit, it would approve the loan providing the SBA would guarantee 90 percent of the total loan. Karen thanked Victor for the advice and began to work on the business plan for the bank and the SBA.

Karen found an excellent location in a growing middle-class neighborhood. The landlord offered her a five-year lease at $2,000 per month with an option for another five years. The landlord would give her an option to buy for $250,000 but it had to be exercised within three years. Karen found that the equipment for the delicatessen could be purchased for $50,000. Furniture, shelves, fixtures, and a few customer service tables would cost another $25,000. The outdoor sign would cost $7,500. The accountant itemized her cash investment as follows:

Inventory (beginning)	$100,000
Equipment	50,000
Furniture & fixtures	25,000
Signs	7,500
Supplies (bags, straws, etc.)	5,000

Supplies (other)	1,500
Uniforms	500
Deposits (phone, utilities, rent)	4,000
Start up expenses	6,500
Working capital	50,000
Total capital needed	$250,000

Karen estimated that sales the first year would be:

January	$ 70,000	July	110,000
February	80,000	August	110,000
March	80,000	September	90,000
April	90,000	October	85,000
May	95,000	November	85,000
June	100,000	December	105,000
	Total projected sales for 1987	$1,100,000	

Based on the above forecast for sales the total breakdown of profits or losses for the first year would be as follows:

Total projected annual sales		$1,100,000	100%
Less: Cost of sales		858,000	78%
Gross profit		242,000	22%
Less: Expenses			
Operating expenses	$253,516		
Interest expense	8,796		
Total expenses		262,312	
Estimated net loss per year		$(20,312)	

The profit and loss figure would rise and fall each month and she should plan accordingly. If she runs into a cash problem the bank will usually grant a temporary line of credit to a customer.

Note: For the following year, Karen estimates that monthly sales will increase by 25 percent each month. For example, estimated sales in January 1988 will be $87,500 and in February will be $100,000. For December 1988, when you calculate purchases you will base the figure on January 1989 sales of $109,375. For purposes of this problem assume that all expenses will remain the same except that Karen will add a manager that will cost her $25,000 a year plus 12 percent for payroll taxes. All other expenses will remain as they are at this time (see financial assumptions under question 2).

QUESTIONS

1. Based on the materials presented in this case, develop a business plan to present to the bank. It should include the mission of the business, personal background information (consider yourself the applicant), general business description, description of products and services to be offered, marketing strategy, financial requirements, and the actual loan proposal.

2. The loan proposal will indicate that you will need a loan of $150,000. The amount you intend to invest is $100,000. You are to prepare a monthly cash budget for the first and second year and a monthly income statement for the same two-year period. See financial assumptions below.

FINANCIAL ASSUMPTIONS TO ANSWER QUESTION 2

You will need the following information to complete the cash budget and monthly income statement for the first two years:

Cash Budget

a. All sales are for cash

b. Loan of $150,000 over a 10 year period at 10 percent interest annually will cost the company $1,983 per month. You will have to consider the latter amount in your cash disbursement ($1,983 × 12 = $23,796).

c. Cash outlay for expenses per month will be $20,501 plus the loan repayment of $1,983 per month, or a total of $22,484 ($253,516 total expenses less $7,500 depreciation, a non-cash expense, brings the total cash expenses down to $246,016 plus $23,796 for the loan or a total cash outlay for the year of $269,812. Monthly this amounts to $22,484).

d. Cash expenses for the second year will be increased by $28,000 for the new store manager's compensation ($25,000 plus 12 percent or $3,000 for payroll taxes). Total cash expenses will amount to $246,016 plus $28,000 or $274,016. When you add the loan payment of $23,796 your total will be $297,812 or $24,818 per month ($22,835 for expenses plus $1,983 for the loan).

e. Purchases are to be made each month in advance. The store will pay for all merchandise purchased during the first year at 78 percent of estimated monthly sales 30 days in advance. For example, in February the company is expected to reach $80,000 in sales. If you take 78 percent of this amount you will arrive at the purchase price of $62,400 which will have to be paid in January and considered as part of January's cash

disbursements. The same procedure will be followed in subsequent months.

Note: In the second year the company will be paying only 75 percent of the estimated monthly sales, an improvement of 3 percent. Therefore, you will consider 75 percent in your monthly calculations.

Monthly Income Statement Forecast

a. Total annual expense forecast for the first year is $253,516. For purposes of this problem you will also add to this amount $733 for interest expense on the $150,000 loan or $8,796, bringing the total expenses to $262,312, or $21,859 per month.

Note: We used $733 as interest expense even though the monthly interest during the early years is much more.

b. For the second year you will add $28,000 for the new store manager's compensation. This means that the total expenses will rise from $262,312 by $28,000, or to a total of $290,312, or $24,192 per month.

c. For purposes of this problem we will not consider any other increases in expenses.

3. After you have prepared your cash budget, indicate the months where Karen will need to invest additional funds into the business if she wants to maintain a monthly minimum cash balance of $10,000. If she does not have funds of her own and is not able to borrow money from the bank to make up for the cash deficits, what suggestions would you give her? What will happen if she cannot borrow sufficient money?

4. Based on the cash budget and monthly income statement, would you advise Karen to go into this business? If you still feel that the business does have possibilities, what suggestions would you make?

5. Will Karen be able to purchase the building at the end of the second year, assuming that the bank would be willing to finance $200,000 of the total price and providing she puts up $50,000 as a down payment plus closing costs?

Rockford Boat Builders, Inc.

For more than two years Chris Klark has been looking for a good business to purchase. His main interest has been to get into the boat building business where he can handle repairs and operate a small marina. In searching for the right business, he has found it difficult to find information he can trust. Some cash businesses do not report receipts accurately, hoping to avoid paying taxes. He fears that some also are not straightforward about profits and asset values. Therefore Chris decides that he will only consider purchasing a business operating on an accrual basis, and not one based on cash.

One day a real estate agent contacted Chris and reported he had found the ideal business for Chris in San Diego, California. It was a small marina which would guarantee him repair business throughout the year. The owner, Braxton Rockford, had been making boats for many years. He specialized in making customized sailboats and he was doing quite well. While he did not advertise, he was highly respected. He had a small experienced crew who worked with him in the marina. He wanted $2 million for the business, although the balance sheet submitted indicated the business was not worth that much, as shown below:

	1986	1985	1984
Cash	$ 150,000	$ 200,000	$ 115,000
Accounts receivable	400,000	350,000	225,000
Notes receivable	2,500	5,000	5,000
Inventory	650,000	690,000	650,000
Other current	125,000	250,000	210,000
Total current	$1,327,500	$1,495,000	$1,205,000
Fixed assets	460,000	550,000	600,000
Other non-current	350,000	400,000	350,000
Total assets	$2,137,500	$2,445,000	$2,155,000
Accounts payable	300,000	325,000	235,000
Bank loans	90,000	50,000	125,000
Notes payable	105,000	60,000	40,000
Other current	435,000	350,000	300,000
Total current	$ 930,000	$ 785,000	$ 700,000
Other long term	450,000	550,000	350,000
Deferred credits	10,000	5,000	52,000
Net worth	747,500	1,105,000	1,053,000
Total liab. and net worth	$2,137,500	$2,445,000	$2,155,000
Net sales	$7,000,000	$6,500,000	$6,000,000
Gross profit	1,260,000	1,495,000	1,260,000
Net profit after taxes	140,000	156,000	180,000

Based on these statements, Rockford's net worth was $747,500 in 1986. He wanted $1,252,500 for goodwill. His latest earnings figures showed $140,000 profit for the year, after taxes, and at that rate it would take about nine years just to pay for the goodwill. Yet Chris wanted to pursue the matter since it seemed like an ideal opportunity. The real estate agent, Henry Boswell, reported that the business could be purchased by a creditworthy buyer with a substantial down payment, with the balance financed over a period of time.

Chris examined the statements and asked his accountant to evaluate them and come up with some ratios. Chris also went to one of his long-time banking associates and asked him how much he would loan him for the business. The banker promised that he would have his people review the statements and discreetly inquire about the business.

Chris decided to make an unannounced visit to San Diego. Without any difficulty he visited the entire facility, mingling with the Sunday crowd of boat owners checking on their boats. Chris checked out the placed in detail. Equipment was strewn about the place, but Chris could see that Rockford had all the small and major equipment to handle almost any job. He also looked at the boats being built and talked to one owner who was examining the progress of his 95 foot sailboat, who told him that he had purchased other boats from Rockford and would have no other build one for him. He was, in his opinion, the best in the business. He built them "the old way," taking time to be certain that every screw and bolt was in its proper place and would never come out. Chris was impressed and could see that Rockford took pride in his work.

Buying the business became Chris' primary concern. The asking price was too high so he had to find some way to get it down. The accountant reported that the business was apparently solid, but the net worth had decreased by nearly 33 percent over last year. While sales had risen for 1986, the profits were slipping. Net profits after taxes amounted to 3 percent in 1984, but that was unusual for this type of business. The accountant felt that a fair price for the business would be closer to $1 million. He felt that Chris' projected sales of $10 million might be a little optimistic, but with Chris' marketing plan and production modifications he might achieve those goals.

If Chris expected to make a profit of 2.5 percent of sales after taxes, he would be earning a total of $250,000 on sales of $10 million. Since Chris and his bankers feel that a 20 percent rate of return on investment is minimal, the purchase price should not exceed $1,250,000. Therefore, the accountant concluded that Chris should begin with an offer of $1 million or less and work from that point, not exceeding $1,250,000.

After looking over the the property, tools, equipment, and other assets, Chris' banker said he would be glad to restructure the loan, but the company as it now stands could not handle another loan. The firm had too much debt compared to its total net worth at the present time.

Chris met Rockford, who was very straight and blunt in his discussion. This business was his "baby" and he did not want to sell it, but he was getting older and he wanted to see that his wife and grandchildren were taken care of in case he died. Chris asked Rockford if he would like to stay on in the business even after he sold it. Rockford said he would think about it, and that it might be interesting. When Chris asked about terms, Rockford offered to take 50 percent down and the balance over 5 or 10 years with "a good interest rate."

Chris asked him how much he had in back orders. Rockford said that he had about $3 million in orders that he was currently working on. Rockford financed each contract individually either from the bank or from the owners. Rockford and Chris departed on very friendly terms after Chris told him what a fine business he had and how much he respected his boat building. Chris was afraid the business might be a little too rich for him, but promised to get back to him as soon as possible.

Chris checked with the real estate agent to see how many prospective purchasers had attempted to buy the business, and found that there was only one other. However, nothing had come of it, so Chris decided to take his time in making a decision. He contacted a close friend, Edgar Widkins, who had a sailboat, and asked him if he would approach the agent about the marina for sale. The agent gladly told Edgar all the facts and set up an appointment with Rockford. Just as Chris had expected, Edgar had several meetings with Rockford and finally offered him $700,000 cash for the business. Rockford was furious and quite shaken. Chris sent another friend, but raised the price offered so it equaled the net worth of the company. However, this time the buyer requested that the balance be financed over a 20-year period. The buyer also asked to change the name of the boat line to "Swiggy's Boats." Rockford was infuriated and shocked. He told the buyer to get out.

After waiting a few weeks, Chris asked for another appointment with Rockford. In the meantime, Chris had been able to raise a total of $500,000. After talking boats for hours, they started to discuss the deal. Chris apologized and said he would like to pay Rockford's price of $2 million for the business, but his limited circumstances only allowed him to offer $1 million. He could put $400,000 down and pay the remainder over 20 years. He said he would let Rockford decide on the interest rate. Rockford came back with a final offer of $1,500,000. Chris asked for a few days to think about it.

Chris took some time to calculate how he could handle the deal. He wanted to buy the business now. He looked over his options and proposed this counteroffer to Rockford:

a. Down payment	$ 400,000
b. 20 Promissory notes payable at the rate of $25,000 per year, backed by his personal guarantee and the business	500,000
c. Contract to Rockford amounting to $50,000 per year for as long as he lived but not less than twelve years.	600,000
d. Total amount to be paid to Braxton Rockford	$1,500,000

Rockford examined the proposition and stated that he liked the idea of staying on to work on his boats. He thought he might even teach Chris a thing or two! Chris acknowledged that he was buying the business primarily because of the Rockford name and reputation. Rockford wanted three additional years on his contract, or $150,000 more for the company. Chris realized the amount he would be paying Rockford as salary would be considered an expense item and he would not have to pay interest on that money. Rockford agreed to take the 20 annual notes with an interest rate of 8 percent.

The deal was sealed, and Chris took over the business. Rockford seemed to be very happy with the arrangement, and the entire marina kept operating just as it had in the past. Chris was marketing more and injecting a little more mass production into the building, but quality remained high. Chris was also content, for he was learning to become a master sailboat builder.

After three years, Rockford died. By this time the income statement summary was as follows:

Sales revenues	$15,000,000
Gross profit	3,750,000
Net profit after tax	25,000

Chris had made payments on three notes of $25,000 each and had paid the yearly salary to Rockford as agreed of $50,000. The widow Rockford and her grandchildren were not as thrifty as Mr. Rockford and requested the rest of the money. The total amount owing was as follows:

17 notes at $25,000 each	$ 425,000
12 years salary owing Rockford	
($50,000 × 12 years)	600,000
Total amount owing to estate	$1,025,000

The widow and one of her grandchildren came to visit Chris and asked if Chris could pay several notes in advance because they needed $250,000 desperately. Chris told them that he did not have the money, but he would see what he could do. Chris thought to himself that this might be a golden opportunity to revise the original agreement in his favor. He then made the following proposition:

a. Chris offered to give her a total amount of $350,000 in cash now instead of the $250,000 she requested. In exchange he wanted all the notes canceled as well as the obligation to pay the $50,000 a year management contract to Rockford.

b. He would pay her the sum of $1,000 a month for life with absolutely no guarantees after her death. Bertha Rockford was now 71 years old.

Naturally, the widow and Headley, one of the grandchildren, were outraged. Chris replied that he was not trying to rob anyone and he was willing to keep meeting his obligations as they came due, but raising the cash was putting himself and the business in jeopardy. When the widow had gone to the local bank it would not give her any money on the agreement that Chris had made because it felt he was laden with debt. While his long-term profit picture was great, the short-term picture was not too good. After the bank's refusal, they came directly to Chris. After much discussion the widow decided to accept his proposal. The bank loaned him the $350,000 because he was eliminating a significant part of his total debts. The widow took the money, and Chris had his attorney cancel all the obligations on the original purchase agreement. At the end of the deal, Chris thought back and calculated that excluding working capital of $100,000, he paid only $975,000 for the business ($400,000 down, $350,000 for the widow, $75,000 in notes, and $150,000 in salary). He had paid $675,000 less than the original agreement stipulated, or $1,650,000 ($1,500,000 plus three additional years on the management contract of $150,000). Chris was pleased with the entire transaction.

QUESTIONS

1. Do you think that Chris was an intelligent business person or was he slick and devious? Was he ethical?

2. What did you think about Chris's approach to buying the business?

3. Why do you think that Rockford agreed to the deal when in reality all he was getting was a total of $900,000 plus a management contract which meant he would still have to keep on working?

4. Do you think that Chris could have been a success in this business without Rockford? Explain.

5. When Rockford died and his widow came to Chris for money, do you think that Chris acted properly? Would you have done the same thing as Chris? Is it ethical to do what Chris did?

6. How would you handle the financing of the clients who want to have boats built? Would you take a purchase order from a solid company? Could you get any financing from outside sources to finance the building of customized boats?

7. What kind of insurance should Chris carry if the boats are not built properly? What would you do if a client does not want to pay for the boat after it is built? How do you protect yourself from that contingency?

8. What other lessons did you learn from this case?

CASE 38

Clara's Bakery and Sweet Shop

Brenda Friedman and Judy Marshall were both interested in going into their own business. They preferred to purchase an existing business that was doing well because they felt it would enhance their chances for success. They had lots of energy and enthusiasm to commit to a firm which had great potential but was suffering from weak management or too much conservatism. In addition, they wanted a business they could eventually franchise if everything went as they expected.

Brenda found a bakery for sale. It was only producing about $500,000 a year in sales, and the net profit after taxes was about $20,000. Neither Brenda nor Judy had experience in baking, and the current owner, Clara Burton, had spent most of her time producing her goods for sale. This involvement kept her from expanding into the wholesale business, which was potentially lucrative. Her facilities and space were suited for expansion, but Clara did not want to initiate the process. She was ready to retire and sell the business for cash. She would accept a reasonable price of $100,000.

Clara's records were in good order, and she presented financial statements for the last two years, as presented below.

	1986	1985
Current Assets		
Cash	5,000	11,000
Accounts receivable	12,000	8,000
Inventory	20,000	25,000
Other current	10,000	13,000
Total current	47,000	57,000
Fixed Assets		
Building (net)	55,000	60,000
Equipment (net)	20,000	24,000
Total fixed assets	75,000	84,000
Total assets	$122,000	$141,000
Current Liabilities		
Accounts payable	20,000	27,000
Other current	2,000	19,000
Total current	22,000	46,000
Mortgage payable	25,000	30,000
Total liabilities	47,000	76,000
Net worth	75,000	65,000
Total liabilities and net worth	$122,000	$141,000
Net sales	$500,000	$450,000
Gross profit	250,000	220,500
Net after tax	20,000	18,000

Clara told Brenda and Judy that she wanted to make a quick sale so she was offering the business at a very reasonable price. She thought the building was worth more than the $55,000 valued on the books, estimating that it was worth $75,000 on the market. She invited Brenda and Judy to come in and work with her to see how she managed the store. All invoices were numbered and she kept a record of all her clients' birthdays and anniversaries.

Brenda and Judy had about $40,000 to put into the business, and wondered how to get the balance of the money they needed to take over the business. They talked with some of the local wholesalers who were clients of Clara's. They stated they felt her bread would be a big success and that they would carry it, but they would not be responsible if it did not sell. In other words, they would distribute the bread and take orders on her behalf and collect money on sales made, but bad debt and losses would be their responsibility. Therefore, they would have to raise money for inventory contingencies. They also need sufficient money to enlarge the bread manufacturing facilities. They went to the local bank and they found that the most they could raise on the building was 70 percent of the appraised value, which was $75,000. This meant that they could get a maximum of $52,500 less what was owed on the present mortgage, or a maximum of $27,500. Closing costs would reduce that to about $20,000. With their $40,000 the total amount they could raise would be $60,000. Therefore, they decided to go to the Small Business Administration for a loan of $100,000, which would take care of the purchase price of $100,000 and give them the money for the bread equipment and working capital ($40,000 + $100,000 SBA loan).

Brenda and Judy hired an accountant, and together prepared figures for the SBA. They went to the local bank with their business plan and asked for the money. They were turned down. The bank did not think the business warranted that amount of money. Even if the SBA guaranteed 90 percent of the loan they would not grant it because it could not support two people. The bank did share the confidence that Brenda and Judy had the potential for wholesaling bread, but felt it should be approached on a small scale initially and then gradually built up.

Brenda had served as a nurse in Vietnam for two years. She understood that there were special programs for Vietnam veterans. When she asked SBA officials about this they stated that this was true and that a direct loan could be obtained. Brenda and Judy presented the business plan again to the SBA, and the loan was approved. They were able to convince the SBA of the business potential.

Brenda and Judy decided to attack the business and get it going. Clara remained on for a while until they were proficient in making the bread and other baked goods. They agreed to keep the name Clara's because they felt it was an asset. Now, after three months of operation, they have a problem. Sales of the bread have been going well with the wholesalers, but their accounts receivable are growing each day. They wonder if they should be offering cash discounts or lowering their prices for people who pay cash. Otherwise everything is fine and sales are growing daily. At the end of 18 months sales will probably exceed $1 million. They would like to add a few other lines, but do not have the capital. They have even been approached by a few truck wholesalers who want to handle their products exclusively and even offered to paint the name of the bakery on their trucks. Brenda and Judy are very interested in moving in this direction, but need more money to pursue it. If sales stay at their present pace, monthly accounts receivable will be around $166,666 if everyone pays on a 30 day basis. To be on the safe side, they will need to borrow another $300,000 to maintain sufficient cash flow. Additional equipment, personnel, supplies, materials, and advertising will require another $250,000, thus bringing the total amount needed to $550,000.

They went back to the bank but were denied a loan because of inadequate capital and collateral. Brenda talked to some of her affluent friends. One of the wholesalers, Arthur Wiley, who was handling their products and was friendly with them, made them the following offer.

a. He would put up the $550,000 needed for the business, but he wanted 75 percent of the common stock in return. Arthur felt that the business had promise and he was willing to take the risk, but it had to be on his terms.

b. He would give them 50 percent of the profits even though their stock interest would only be 25 percent, providing sales kept increasing.

c. He would agree to management contracts guaranteeing each of them their current salary for a period of five years.

Brenda and Judy did not particularly like the offer presented by Arthur, but it was the only proposal on the table. They considered other alternatives. Brenda heard of a reliable loan broker in Boise who might help them. They decided to approach him to see what would happen. They wondered if the SBA would loan them more money for their business. They decided to check this out also. They also wanted to explore the possibility of going public and selling stock in their company.

They both feel they have a potential goldmine, but they are confused about which direction to take. They have come to you, a financial expert, for advice.

QUESTIONS

1. Could Brenda and Judy have received more than $100,000 from the Small Business Administration when they asked for their first loan? What would have been required? When you go to the SBA for a loan what must be included in the business plan in order for them to make an evaluation? What happens if the SBA turns your loan down? Can you appeal and if so how do you go about it?

2. While the SBA does have a program for Vietnam veterans, does this mean that every veteran of that conflict is eligible for a loan or will get the loan?

3. How should Brenda and Judy handle the receivables problem? Should they give discounts? Lower the prices to get cash up front? Pay the

wholesalers a bonus to collect when they sell? What recommendations do you have for the two owners to solve the receivable problems if they cannot obtain a loan?

4. Should Brenda and Judy have accepted Arthur's proposal? Do you think they should have made a counter-proposal? What kind of counter-proposal would you have made?

5. What can a loan broker do for Brenda and Judy? Do you think they could find a solution to handle the receivables and obtain other money they need?

6. Will the SBA give Brenda and Judy additional funds because they now have a profitable track

record? How much will the SBA give them and under what terms and conditions?

7. Do you think Brenda and Judy should go public with their stock? How do you go public? Who would handle all the paper work? How much could they obtain? Outline.

8. Do you think Brenda and Judy should get involved with exclusive distributors in their regional area? Would it conflict with their present whole-salers? How could you incorporate these distributors into your channel of distribution without upsetting the established wholesalers?

9. If Brenda and Judy want to expand beyond Idaho into other states, what marketing arrangements would you suggest? What other factors must be considered if they decide they want to expand beyond their present region? Are they ready to expand now?

CASE 39

Paula's Music Center

Music had been part of Paula Van Mornay's life for more than 20 years. Piano was her major instrument. She was highly respected in Sioux Falls, South Dakota, and some years ago was given excellent reviews for concerts she played in New York. Paula could have been a tremendous success in the field, but she decided to marry and remain in Sioux Falls. She gave lessons at home and built up a following of students, but she never made income sufficient to support her and her family. This became necessary when the entire family was involved in a tragic automobile accident. Her husband, Norman, was killed. The two children, Timmy and Donna, were seriously injured and while there was some hope for Timmy, Donna was permanently paralyzed from the waist down. Paula now had to find a way to take care of her family and the growing medical bills. The insurance money and social security were not going to be sufficient.

Paula decided that she should capitalize on her musical ability and looked for a music store where she might sell musical instruments, teach music, and perhaps do some arranging and composing. Paula found a small music store for sale. Its profits were low, but Paula thought she could do better with her skills and reputation. The owner wanted $40,000 for the business, which included the inventory and all assets. The breakdown of the balance sheet was as follows.

Balance Sheet

Current Assets

Cash	$ 600
Accounts receivable	6,000
Notes receivable	150
Inventory	38,000
Other current	1,500
Total current assets	$46,250

Balance Sheet (Continued)

Fixed Assets

Furniture & fixtures (net)	$ 8,000
Equipment (net)	2,500
Total fixed assets	10,500
Total assets	56,750

Current Liabilities

Accounts payable	$10,600
Bank loan	1,500
Notes payable	3,500
Other current	2,000
Total current liabilities	$17,600
Deferred credits	4,150
Total liabilities	21,750

Capital

Owner's capital	$ 35,000
Total liabilities and net worth	$ 56,750

Net sales for the year	150,000	100%
Gross profit	52,500	35%
Net profit	10,500	7%

Paula did not know anything about business and decided to go see an accountant. He examined the books and judged the business worth $40,000, but advised her to offer less. He offered to accompany her to negotiate the price. Paula had a total of $50,000 in capital and would risk it all if she felt the business had potential.

The owner, Elliot Pike, agreed to sell the business for the total cash sum of $30,000. Paula gave him a deposit and arrangements were made to transfer the inventory items in stock. The transfer of the lease was not discussed, but Elliot expected no difficulty. Paula was anxious to take over the business and, in spite of her lawyer's protests about the lease, signed the agreement to buy the business. The monthly rental was $1,000.

Paula had a new sign made announcing that "Paula Van Mornay, former concert pianist," was operating her own music center. Paula did not know what type of inventory to order and when the vendors visited her she depended on them to make recommendations. She soon suspected that all of them were not being honest and were taking advantage of her lack of knowledge when she found herself with excess inventory. However, her music lessons were going well and she hired seven professional teachers to teach various instruments. Paula made a commission on the hourly charge and, of course, students purchased their equipment from the store. But Paula had approximately $15,000 worth of stock that would not sell and she did not know what to do with it. Her vendors advised her to have a special and take the loss, which she did. She lost more than $5,000 on the entire deal. Paula was obviously learning the business the hard way.

Paula's son, Timmy, now nineteen and only partly disabled, attended school to learn the trade of piano tuning. Within two years he was an accomplished piano tuner, which added to the services the center offered. Paula managed to increase sales to $250,000 and was earning $20,000 a year, and was able to count on taking $200 a week out of the business. She was pleased with herself for overcoming adversity and making progress.

A new opportunity arose from Timmy's tuning business. Some people wanted to sell their pianos because they were not being used, and some wanted to purchase used pianos. Paula's real expertise was in piano and she felt she could sell pianos in her store. She and Timmy took a survey and found he could purchase 25 used pianos for $150 to $25,000 each. The average price was around $1,000. Paula estimated she would need approximately $50,000 to buy the used pianos. She did not know what price she would ask for them, but she knew that prices of pianos were constantly increasing and that old pianos in good condition could be sold for a substantial profit. Now Paula had to find a way to finance the purchase of the pianos.

Paula knew she could not afford to buy all the used pianos she needed even if she did obtain the $50,000, so she decided to offer to take pianos on consignment. Fourteen people agreed to sell their pianos this way, allowing Paula to keep any amount over a specified amount. But Paula did not know how to determine prices to ask. There were no published standards, so she just used her best judgment.

Paula knew that before she could start accepting pianos she would have to secure more space. Her present facilities were already cramped. She looked for a location large enough to allow more music studios for teaching and to house the showroom for pianos. Space for a small warehouse would also be desirable. She finally found a good location that would not require much remodeling. After transferring her signs, furniture, and fixtures she could handle the renovation with $10,000. The landlord wanted $2,500 per month and a five-year lease with no renewal options. She wondered whether the piano department could handle the increased rental expense of $1,500 per month. She estimated she could sell from 10 to 15 pianos per month if she had space to show them. However, she felt that sales would be related to the number of children in the area whose parents wanted their kids to be introduced to the musical world.

Paula had to decide how to get the pianos not offered for consignment into her showroom. Some of the pianos were magnificent, and they would attract a great deal of attention because of their uniqueness. She estimated she would need around $40,000 to purchase these pianos, and she wondered where to get the money.

Paula also had to decide what to do if the people wanted to finance a piano—what kind of down payment she should get and how she would finance a piano if she had to pay the owner more than she was getting in down payment. For example, if an owner wanted $7,000 for his piano and the buyer would pay $3,500 as a down payment, then she wondered where she would get the money to pay off the seller. She also wondered what kind of warranty she should offer.

An interesting development took place over the years. As a result of the accident, Paula had learned a great deal about working with the handicapped. Her daughter Donna, who was permanently paralyzed from the waist down, had become an accomplished guitarist. She played before several groups in town and was recognized for her talent. After years of study Paula brought Donna into the organization, and she started to teach with excellent results. People started bringing in their disabled children to see if they could learn to play a musical instrument. Many of the instructors donated a few hours of their time to help teach them. Paula thought this was absolutely wonderful, for her business was doing more than just making money. It was helping others by motivating them to express themselves in music.

Paula's object is not to make a lot of money. Instead she wants to maintain her earnings while perhaps raising enough money to establish an orchestra or other groups such as rock, country and western, and jazz bands. She wants to promote the handicapped musicians who are developing nicely and help them earn a living somehow. Paula has three challenges before her. She must raise money to buy the pianos, find financing to obtain an adequate location, and build funds to support music programs for the handicapped. She has come to you for advice.

QUESTIONS

1. Has Paula chosen the right business to go into? Do you think she approached the business the right way? Did she make any mistakes when she purchased the business? Why do you think she was able to remain in business when others might have failed?

2. What made Paula a success in the beginning? What were Paula's keys to the success?

3. What do you think of her idea of getting into the used piano business? Do you feel that she could make money in this field? What are the pros and cons? Do you agree with her that the greatest market is with children? Identify Paula's target markets for pianos and teaching.

4. Do you feel Paula will make sufficient income in the piano business to afford the increased rental costs? Is location important in this type of business? What are your recommendations for handling the financing of the business? How should

she approach the purchasing of used pianos from present owners so she does not lose money? How should she establish prices for the pianos she is going to sell? How can she get those people with expensive pianos to let her have them or get the money to buy them? Should she have a line of new pianos? Should they be Japanese or American made? Do you think that handling new pianos (assuming that she can get a floor plan for about 25 pianos from a manufacturer) would help her used piano business?

5. Is Paula's goal of setting aside profits for helping fund the handicapped groups a good idea? How much should she set aside for this purpose? Is she too idealistic? Why is it necessary for her to extend herself beyond what the majority of business people would do in the course of their business? Would you put aside 25 to 50 percent of profits from a particular division to aid the handicapped?

Universal Supply House

Paul Burroughs worked for Edwards Technology Inc. as the production manager for one of their divisions. He had been with the company for 30 years and was considered one of their most outstanding managers. However, when the company offered an "early out" retirement program he decided at the age of 55 to make a change. The company agreed to pay his salary and health benefits up until age 62. It was an excellent chance for Paul to own and develop his own business. He wanted something to leave his son and daughter, who soon would be graduating from college. Paul came across a construction supply company which suited his interests in building. It sold builders and contractors lumber and other building supplies.

Paul discovered that the firm, Universal Supply House, was for sale. It was owned by an old friend, Miles Hickcock. As far as Paul knew, the firm was very successful for Miles always seemed to be very affluent. When Paul told Miles that he was looking for a firm like his, Miles immediately asked him to lunch to talk about the matter.

When Paul and Miles met, Miles informed Paul that he had an excellent business with lots of potential, but at this time sales were down, many of his established contractors were not paying, and he owed a great deal of money. In spite of this, he painted a rosy picture of the business, insisting that it had the potential to make millions. Miles wanted $250,000 for the business. Paul asked him to supply financial statements, and the next day Miles submitted them along with the tax statements. Paul immediately focused on the current statement, which indicated that the firm had a deficit net worth of $199,350. Paul was stunned and asked Miles why such a deficit existed. Miles replied that the construction business had been hurting, contractors were going out of business, and he had a lopsided inventory. With interest costs for loans, expenses, and the price discounts he had to give to compete, he could not make a profit. However, he assured Paul that the construction business takes some swift turns—one day you're broke and the next day you're rolling in money. He was confident that better days were ahead.

However, Miles finally admitted that he had not paid anything on his bank loans for a year, even the interest payments, and the bank had four mortgages on his house amounting to twice its actual value. He said the bank had just changed hands in a merger and the new executives wanted something done about the situation. His situation was desperate and he agreed to negotiate a price for the business. Paul said he would talk to his accountant and get back to him within a few days.

The current balance sheet looked as follows:

Current Assets

Cash	$ 650
Accounts receivable	425,000
Notes receivable	75,000
Inventory	275,000
Other current	70,000
Total current assets	$ 845,650

Fixed Assets

Land & building (net)	$ 350,000
Equipment	50,000
Vehicles (cars & trucks net)	85,000
Furniture & fixtures	25,000
Total fixed assets	$ 510,000
Total assets	$1,355,650

Current Liabilities

Accounts payable	$ 375,000
Taxes payable	60,000
Notes payable (current)	600,000
Other	20,000
Total current liab.	$1,055,000

Long-Term Liabilities

Notes payable	125,000
Mortgages payable	375,000
Total fixed	500,000
Total liabilities	1,555,000

Stockholders' Liabilities

Common stock	$ 100,000
Retained earnings (deficit)	(299,350)
Total liabilities & deficit net worth	($199,350)
Stockholders' equity	$1,355,650

The income statement for the same period was as follows:

Total net sales	$1,500,000	100%
Cost of sales	1,200,000	80%
Gross profit	$ 300,000	20%
Less: operating expenses	375,000	
Net loss for the period	(75,000)	

The income statement covered a period of six months and, like the balance sheet, indicated serious problems. However, Paul felt that somehow this business could be turned around because it had been established for a long time, and had a good client base. The accountant, Stan Hertfield, reminded him that as the business now stands, it is worthless. He strongly recommended that Paul stay away from it. But Paul persisted and asked Stan for further assistance. Stan knew of a large financial consulting firm in Raleigh which dealt with a venture capitalist and had literally hundreds of sources of money. He contacted the firm for Paul.

A few days later, a consultant for the firm, Frank Campbell, asked for a meeting with Paul and Stan. Frank said that he felt that the only way the entire deal could be approached would be on a "buy-down" basis. By this he meant that if the secured creditors such as the banks were willing to take less money to satisfy their notes, then he might be able to make the loan. He would offer the unsecured creditors $0.10 on the dollar. The end result would be that assets and liabilities would balance and there would be no net worth. The financial firm wanted to check Paul's references to see if he had the business acumen to manage the business successfully. If so, Frank thought he could find some people in his group of lenders who might be interested in this venture on a "buy-down" basis. There would be charges for the lender, and Frank's company would charge a fee for handling the entire package. Stan and Paul agreed it was worth a try. After several weeks of searching for lenders Frank had a proposal. Frank wanted approval from Paul and Stan before he submitted it to the secured and unsecured lenders. The banks at this time are owed a total of $1,100,000 for notes and mortgages. They have the building, accounts receivable, notes receivable, and inventory as collateral. If the business were liquidated today, the banks could realize a total of $505,000 from the sale of the assets. The accounts and notes receivable were worth $180,000; the inventory, $50,000; the land and buildings, $250,000; equipment, $5,000; vehicles, $15,000; and furniture and fixtures, $5,000. Thus the total assets were worth $505,000. Frank felt that he could not reduce the tax liability of $60,000 and that he could not get the unsecured creditors to take less than $0.10 on the dollar. Excepting the $60,000 tax liability, the unsecured creditors were owed $395,000 ($375,000 in accounts payable and $20,000 in other liabilities). Frank would offer the unsecured creditors $39,500 for what the company owed them. That plus the tax liability of $60,000 to the government would amount to $99,500. Finally, Frank would offer to pay the sum of $405,500 or $0.368 on the dollar to the banks for the total notes and mortgages in the business. This would mean that the banks would lose $694,500 on the total loans. Since the alternative was bankruptcy, he felt they might just accept this offer. Thus, Frank would be paying off a total of $505,000 ($39,500 unsecured plus $60,000 tax liability plus $405,500 to the banks).

Should the proposal succeed, Frank would require the following:

a. Paul Burroughs had to invest $450,000 from his personal assets in the business to get the business moving in the right direction. He could use his house as collateral for a loan, but not the business.

b. The lenders would put up the $505,000 to pay off the bank, the government, and the unsecured creditors. They would secure a first mortgage on the property, and factor the receivables. In addition, they would throw an umbrella or overall lien on the entire business. They would factor the receivables at 5 percent over the New York prime rate and the rate could change if business improved. The mortgage would be at current rates on a five-year basis with payments calculated on a 20-year payout. After all debts were paid and Paul invests $450,000, the net worth would be $450,000.

c. Paul should limit his salary to no more than $35,000 a year the first two years. The company would exercise a strict policy with respect to inventory purchasing and extension of credit. They would have to approve credit extensions on all new applicants, but as long as Paul could keep his receivables within the 60-day limit they would be content. Anything over 60 days they would want immediately paid off.

d. The financial firm would increase his line of credit for receivables and inventory as business progressed.

e. Paul had to obtain a letter of intent from the present owner of the business, Miles Hickcock, indicating that he was willing to sell the business. Paul could pay him anything he wished for the business, but they felt Miles should be grateful to just walk away.

f. The bank and any other lenders who had guarantees from the corporation would have to release all debts and obligations. The entire proposal hinged on acceptance by the bank, Miles Hickcock, and other creditors.

Frank examined Paul's references and financial statements and found them to be satisfactory. Paul had a net worth of over $500,000, and he still had a guaranteed income from his old company. His reputation was clean and all references indicated that he was a conservative person with common sense. The nucleus was there upon which to build a solid business. Frank knew that the suppliers were not going to be happy when they were paid off $0.10 on the dollar and they might not want to do business with Paul in the beginning, but as soon as he established a reputation they would eventually give him credit.

Paul went back to Miles to talk about the business. Miles admitted that the business was insolvent and bankrupt. Paul told him that he was working on a proposition to take over all the loans, but he did not go into detail. He also told Miles that even if he went into Chapter 11 where he would get immediate relief from his creditors, he would still have difficulty staying alive because he did not have the working capital to operate the business. Finally, Paul offered him $25,000 for the entire business subject to resolution of his financial arrangements. Paul wanted his deposit put in escrow in case he could not get everything resolved. Miles protested that Paul was taking over an established business and the offer should be higher. Paul said the offer was final. After a day of thinking about it, Miles agreed to the deal, and Paul had his attorney make up the legal papers. They were approved by Frank.

When Frank brought the proposition to the bankers, they were shocked. Frank reminded them again that the alternative was bankruptcy. The total assets, if sold at liquidation, could bring as little as 10 percent of the total value, or $135,565. A few days later the bankers accepted the offer and agreed to release all their claims, including notes and other obligations on the business. Frank asked for a letter of confirmation.

The next step was to send letters by certified mail to all the unsecured creditors telling them of the situation. The firm would explain that it was prepared to offer a maximum of $0.10 on the dollar for what the company owed them. The alternative was that the company would go into bankruptcy and they stood to get nothing because of excessive debts, legal costs, and the low liquidation value of the assets. Immediately, letters of approval came back, calls were made, and some protested they would rather go to court. Finally, Frank got that matter resolved, and after receiving most letters of approval, he called the banks and gave them a settlement date. Paul completed his deal with Miles, and Frank paid off all the debts owed to the banks and creditors.

Paul put his $450,000 into the business, changed the name to Burroughs Supply Company, and opened for business. He installed computers to handle the inventory, payroll, receivables, payables, and accounting for the firm. He began to build his inventory. He hired a very knowledgeable person to tackle the credit problem.

In the beginning the suppliers would have nothing to do with him. They would not return his calls, but Paul needed materials for his inventory. He contacted all the builders and contractors in the area and tried to develop a relationship with them to get some business. He was careful to exclude those who were slow to pay bills in the past. He wanted to approach the business conservatively and not try to build it up overnight. During the first two months Paul lost money because of his tight credit policy. He could have made additional sales if he had met his competitors' credit policy of granting terms of up to 120 days. But he insisted on 60-day terms, so customers went elsewhere. He knew most of the contractors by now and they assured him that as soon as they got paid (and they stated they had valid contracts with reliable firms and industrial companies), they would pay him, but they needed 120-day credit. He carried a good stock, and charged higher prices than Miles had, although they were competitive with others in the business. It was going to be a challenge to make the business a success.

QUESTIONS

1. Should Paul have purchased a business that was bankrupt? Should he have started his own business?

2. Was Miles unwise not to go into Chapter 11?

3. Why were the banks who lent Miles the money willing to take the buy-down offer from Frank? Should they have let the company go into Chapter 11?

4. Should Miles have sold the business for $25,000? Should Paul have kept Miles around to show him the ropes and point out the problems in the business?

5. Make suggestions on how Paul should handle those clients who claim to have sound contracts with industrial firms or government building projects. How should he handle builders who have contracts to build residential homes for affluent clients? Or who are building for their own account to sell later?

6. Is the financial arrangement Paul has with Frank, where all his assets are tied up, a good one? Do you think that Paul could restructure the financial picture of the company?

7. What other lesson did you learn from this case?

CASE 41

The Great Escape Motel

Simon Tucker has been a successful salesperson for a plastics firm for the last 20 years. He has traveled throughout the country hundreds of times, and he knows every motel and hotel in America. He always swore that when he retired from his position, he would open up his own motel and give people what they really want. He often complained that the beds were too hard to sleep on, the rates were too high, the bar charged too much, and they were poorly operated. He felt motels took your money, and if you asked them a question they were unresponsive. Simon did allow they were all not like that, but on the whole he was dissatisfied as were many other sales people who traveled as he did. They added their complaints to his that televisions never worked, or had poor reception. A store might sell gifts and papers, but they were always closed when you needed them; if you wanted to buy a paperback novel to read at night there were only a few books in stock. The little free automatic coffee maker in the rooms produced coffee that was disgusting, and meals were costly and predictable.

Finally, the day came when the company asked Simon to move to another department, and he decided to quit the firm. He was old enough to retire and in a year he would be eligible for social security. Simon talked to his wife and they decided that he should go into the motel business. He always wanted to do that, and this was the time.

After looking for more than eight months Simon found a nice motel near Tampa, Florida. The owners wanted $800,000 for the entire facility. They produced financial statements which indicated that the business was taking in about $700,000 a year in rentals, and it was making about 2 percent of sales after taxes. The motel had a small bar, a few shops, one of which was vacant, a dining area, a nice lobby, a swimming pool, and a small playground for children. It was located on one of the main highways south of Tampa, and it was quite visible. There were no competing motels within 40 miles, and Simon felt that it represented a great opportunity. The capacity was 100 rooms. They had 50 double rooms that rented for $55 a night, 40 single rooms that cost $40 a night and 10 suites that rented for $90 to $110 per night. Simon calculated that if he could operate at 100 percent occupancy, which was practically impossible, he could bring in total rentals per year of nearly $2 million. This figure did not include the money that could be made from the bar, dining room, and other services which he wanted to include. The surroundings were beautiful. The motel was set back and had a large neon sign right on the highway that was quite visible to all the cars that passed. In addition, there were two billboards on both sides of the street about two miles down the road which alerted tourists and travelers that the "Great Escape Motel," which pampered all their visitors, was a few miles down the road.

The major problem that Simon confronted initially was how to raise the money for purchase, for he only had $100,000. He needed $700,000 plus $100,000 for the working capital, and he did not want to use banks or take mortgages with high interest charges. Simon would rather sell stock in the motel or corporation. Simon found that he could sell two types of stock, common and preferred. He did not want to sell preferred stock, for he did not want to pay out a guaranteed interest dividend each year. Simon therefore opted to have two classes of common stock: type A stock, which would be the voting stock which he would own exclusively, and type B common stock, which would have no voting rights but stockholders would share in the profits of the business. Simon had his attorney, Clarence Burchfield, form a subchapter "S" corporation with the two kinds of stock. He wanted to sell the stock to friends and relatives who were investors in other ventures. Burchfield informed him that there were certain federal and state regulations he should be familiar with and that he would be glad to get the information for him. Simon thanked him and said he had the necessary information.

After the corporation was set up, Simon prepared a prospectus which showed the following income statement forecast for the following year:

Estimated revenues (operating at 70% occupancy)		$1,400,000
Other revenue from other sources		250,000
Total estimated revenue for the year		$1,650,000
Less: operating expenses		
Salaries (owner)	$ 40,000	
Salaries (other)	576,000	
Payroll taxes (12%)	73,920	
Advertising	30,000	
Telephone	15,000	
Utilities	120,000	
Supplies expenses	50,000	
Depreciation	25,000	
Bad debts (including checks)	14,000	
Insurance	85,000	

Property taxes	15,000
Legal & professional	6,000
Licenses & permits	2,500
Miscellaneous expenses	24,000
Total estimated operating expenses	$1,076,420
Estimated net profit to be distributed to stockholders	573,580

Note: An "S" corporation does not pay corporate taxes but each stockholder must pay personal taxes on the profits earned whether or not the corporation distributes profits.

The stockholders' equity section of the balance sheet would look as follows:

Common A stock–1,000 shares at $10 per share	$ 10,000
Common B stock–authorized 150,000 shares, issued	
89,000 shares at $10 per share	890,000
Total stockholders' equity	$900,000

Simon managed to purchase 10,000 shares of the common B stock and thus owned 11.24 percent of the common B stock outstanding. He owned 100 percent of class A voting stock, bringing his total ownership to 12.2 percent. It was estimated that each shareholder would earn approximately $6.37 per share based on Simon's projections for the first year. Thus, their return on a $10 investment would be approximately 64 percent ($573,580 net profits ÷ 90,000 shares = $6.37 per share).

Armed with this information Simon started contacting some of his friends and relatives who might be interested in the stock. He wanted to sell large blocks of the stock but found that some only wanted to buy 100 shares or spend $1,000. A few investors purchased 1,000 shares though, and Simon managed to sell enough stock to purchase the business and raise $100,000 for working capital. All together he had 40 stockholders who owned the business.

Simon moved in and began to make some necessary changes. His wife, Marian, worked the front desk during the day and helped where she could. Simon began advertising, checked with all the travel agencies, attended several of their conventions, worked with the tourist boards of the state, and contacted industry in the surrounding areas to get their business. Simon expanded the motel to include conference rooms with a capacity for more than 50 people, and he had all the video and sound equipment needed to make the rooms useful for meetings. He offered specials and business began to grow. He had not reached the 70 percent occupancy rate, but he had been able to achieve 50 percent and felt that it was a matter of time before he met those goals. In the meantime to provide entertainment Simon started showing movies each night for those guests who were staying over and they seemed to enjoy them. He also made certain that all television sets were functioning properly and any complaints about air-conditioning were taken care of by the engineers, who were on duty 24 hours a day.

However, Simon had to deal with some problems typical in motel management. Some people were registering without luggage and obviously planning a short visit. He was concerned that this might affect the family trade that was busiest on weekends. Then a few guests complained that their wallets were stolen, and this appeared in the local papers. Simon increased supervision of the housekeepers and tried to monitor the visitors of guests. Some salesmen would seek out companionship when they were on the road, and it was difficult to keep track of unregistered guests. Simon was plagued by bad checks, even though he was careful to require proper identification. Some guests complained about persons lingering at the bar who looked as though they were soliciting unsavory business. Simon was considering hiring a house detective.

The first year Simon did not achieve his occupancy objectives. Instead of earning $6.37 per share, stocks only earned $0.65 per share. Immediately there was a great deal of complaints from stockholders who felt they were cheated on their investment. Instead of earning a 64 percent return on their investments as promised, they were earning only 6.5 percent ($0.65 ÷ $10.00 per share = 6.5 percent). Simon reminded them that it was still more than they could get in some places in the current market and promised greater returns in the future.

One day Simon received a call from his attorney, informing him that he had sold stock in violation of the State Securities Law. Simon did not understand what he had done wrong.

QUESTIONS

1. Did Simon violate any federal or state laws when he sold stock to individuals? Can a small business sell stock to raise capital for its enterprise?

2. What other methods could Simon have used to raise money?

3. Do you think that Simon's projections were realistic? What kind of a prospectus should he have presented to prospective investors so as not to deceive or mislead them? Outline the contents of such a prospectus.

4. What should Simon do about the problems he has with his motel?

CASE 42

Angelo's Service Station

Angelo Bandelo has worked as a mechanic for the last 15 years. He is considered to be an excellent mechanic with an instinctive ability to fix and repair cars. Angelo also can do some body and fender work, but prefers the mechanical side of the business. Angelo never had the opportunity to go to college but he did take a few night courses. He barely passed the courses because of his inability to write well, but he felt he had learned a great deal from his instructors. Angelo also attended a few seminars put on by various colleges and universities in conjunction with their Small Business Development Centers, and he also attended some seminars sponsored by the Small Business Administration. After more than a year of classes and seminars Angelo felt he was ready to enter his own business.

He knew that he did not have sufficient capital to go into a complete mechanical operation, but he did find two service stations that were available. Both service stations were operating, but from what he could determine from the owners they were not making money. One was located on the main highway coming in and going out of the town, which was a suburb of Louisville, Kentucky. This location had been operated by several owners, and each eventually went out of business. Most of the major gasoline brands were represented within a radius of about two miles. Price competition was fierce. When Angelo checked out the distributor prices and how much the service station earned per gallon, he found that on regular gasoline they were lucky to make one penny per gallon. The profit on unleaded and premium gas was slightly higher. The owner wanted to sell the property as well as the business, but agreed that he would lease the business to Angelo for 18 months after which time Angelo could purchase the building or the present owner would have the option to sell the property to someone else. The location included a nice building with a small office for the owner and a storage room for cigarettes and parts, batteries, and other items needed to handle quick service for their clients. The service section had room for three bays where cars could be fixed or where other parts could be stored.

The owner of the station wanted $25,000 for the business plus the value of the inventory on a dollar for dollar basis. He would rent the entire site, which included approximately three acres, for a total of $3500 per month. He wanted the first and last month in advance plus one month security. The owner, Ted Marcos, reported he purchased gasoline from all sources, including the major refineries and other independent dealers who would call and have a tank available at certain prices. The problem all gas station operators have, according to Marcos, is having sufficient cash on hand to buy tanks of gas cheaply when they are available. As long as Angelo maintained a solid cash position he could make a nice profit and compete. If his cash position became tight he would suffer because he would have to buy from the distributor at higher prices, although they would give him some credit terms which would help.

The second gas station which was available was away from the main highways and back in the interior of the city. The station had no competition and was located close to a small shopping mall. The gas prices were much higher because of the lack of competition, and instead of making a penny on each gallon of regular gas the owner made five cents per gallon. However the volume was not as great and certainly did not compare to the tremendous volume of the other operation. The site was smaller but attractive. There was an office, a storage room and two bays for repair work. In this operation the owner also had a tow truck which added to his income. Since he was located in a neighborhood area he had developed a nice clientele and he knew most of them.

The owner of the second station sold a major brand of gasoline products which he purchased from the local distributor. He had six gas pumps and could have used a few more, especially when traffic was busy. The owner, Ray Stokes, wanted $250,000 for the site and the total operation. Angelo lacked the money to buy the location outright, but Stokes suggested he go to one of the local banks to see how much of a mortgage he could get on the building. Angelo contacted a local Savings and Loan Association and after appraising the location they said they would come up with a mortgage of $175,000 for the property, which included two acres. Angelo had personal resources of $45,000. Angelo was still short $30,000 for the purchase price, and he needed working capital to buy gasoline, parts and accessories for the station. Angelo's wife, Maggie, contacted all her relatives who had money to see if they would help Angelo get started. Maggie only managed to scrape up $25,000 from her relatives who each demanded a share of the business. The specifics of the profit sharing were not spelled out. Angelo went back to Stokes and told him the amount he had managed to raise. Stokes finally agreed to accept a second mortgage on the building and their personal guarantee for the $30,000. He wanted the amount paid off at the rate of $1,000 a month plus interest of 15 percent per year.

Now Angelo had two locations to consider. The first station could be purchased for $25,000 plus the stock, and he could rent for $3,500 per month. It was located on the main highway and promised tremendous volume compared with the little operation inside the town. However, the highway location produced very low profits in the face of intense competition. Angelo felt that his mechanical expertise would not be as useful in that high volume, transient situation. So he decided to take the second location because it did not have competition and he could build up the business in other profitable areas, including repair.

Angelo assumed the business, and the major brand distributor gave him all the cooperation he could to get him started. Business was not too brisk, but after a while Angelo got to know his customers. It was a small area and there was a limit to sales of gasoline and oil. He also found that he was losing out on some of the cheap purchases of gas because of his franchise agreement with the refinery and the distributor. He was making a greater profit than he would have on the main highway, but his possibilities were limited. The stockholders wanted to know when they were going to get some profits. Angelo did not know what to tell them or how to determine what they should get. To make matters worse, the twelve owners of the business were coming to the station and charging all the gasoline purchases and repairs to their accounts. When Angelo tried to collect, they told him to take the money they owed him out of profits. He called an accountant who was a customer and asked him to take care of his books on a monthly basis. Perhaps he could determine an equitable distribution in accordance with the terms of the corporation. According to his accountant, Angelo was making just enough to take care of his loans and bills. He was only keeping $800 a month to live on. When he worked as a mechanic he was making $25,000 a year.

Angelo tried to determine what profit centers he should develop to make additional money. Possibilities included automatic car washing; used tires; used car rental for people having their cars fixed; buying used cars for parts sales much as a junk yard; major repairs such as transmissions; expanding the muffler business; accepting body and fender work; a special emergency sales package for people in the neighborhood which would take care of road repairs, tows, breakdowns and other needs; upholstery work including seat covers; and expanding into complete air conditioning repairs. Although these would take some additional capital, Angelo thought he could manage to handle some of them. However, he did not know which would produce the greatest return on his investment.

Maggie's relatives were not likely to invest more money. In fact seven wanted to withdraw a total of $20,000 invested. Others were willing to remain and told Angelo to pay them what he could when he could. However, those who were willing to stay felt they should be able to continue to charge their purchases at the station.

The accountant informed Angelo that the total initial investment was $70,000 ($45,000 from Angelo and $25,000 from relatives). Based on those figures, Angelo owned 64.28 percent and his relatives 35.72 percent of the business.

Angelo had to come up with the $20,000. Maggie and the family were fighting bitterly and she would not talk or associate with most of them under any circumstances. He did not have the money and did not know what to do.

QUESTIONS

1. Did Angelo make the right decision to purchase the off-beat station instead of the one on the highway? Do you think he would have been successful in the highway location? Would he have been able to compete with the others surrounding him if he elected to buy the location?

2. Is it a good idea to borrow money from relatives? What mistakes did Maggie make when she borrowed the money? How could it have been corrected at the time she accepted the money?

3. What direction should Angelo take to increase his sales and profits? Select those profit centers

you feel would make his business more productive.

4. How would you market your products in a location like Angelo's? What recommendations would you make? Do you think he should lower his prices to be more competitive with those on the highway? Do you think that people in his marketing area are patronizing the service stations on the main highway to save money on gas and repairs? What are your recommendations?

5. What should Angelo do about his relatives who charge their purchases at his station? Do you think

they have a right to do so? How can he stop it without causing more trouble?

6. How is Angelo going to pay back the $20,000? Assume the banks have turned him down because he is a new business and he has no other alternative except his accountant, who also happens to be a client. The accountant offers to give Angelo the entire amount of $25,000 to pay off all the stockholders, but he would want 49 percent of the business in exchange. However, he promised that he would not make any purchases on credit, would take care of the books without charge and would not demand profits be distributed until the business became profitable. If Angelo does not take the accountant's offer, what can he do? Should he accept the accountant's offer?

7. Another person has approached Angelo and wants to purchase the business. He is willing to pay off the mortgage with the bank, the balance owed the former owner, and give Angelo and his relatives their entire investment back. Angelo's former employer has told Angelo that he would like him to come back and work for him as service manager. He would pay him $30,000 a year plus a percentage of profits in the service department. Do you think Angelo should take up the offer and sell the business and go back to his old job?

Management
Problems

Robinson Brothers Company

Larry Robinson and his two brothers started a small auto parts and accessory store many years ago and gradually built up a small chain of four stores. Sales last year totaled $18 million and gross profits on those sales amounted to 29.7 percent or $5,346,000. After-tax profit on those sales amounted to 1.1 percent or a total of $198,000. These figures have been worrying Larry for some time. The cost of the merchandise should be getting cheaper because of their higher volume, but they actually appear to be paying more, for their gross profit has slipped from 33 percent of total net sales to 29 percent. Larry has checked with the purchasing agent for the company, and he has been informed that many of the suppliers have been increasing their prices little by little, pleading higher costs of labor. However, Larry is not convinced by that explanation, for Robinson Brothers has also increased their prices slightly and one should offset the other.

Larry asked for invoices and Orson Washburn, the vice-president of purchasing, supplied him with everything he requested. They sat down together and went over specific prices. After a very intensive examination Larry told Orson to start looking for new suppliers. There must be other firms who want their business and will give them better prices. Orson immediately started sending out letters to new vendors asking them for prices and discounts. He also asked them to send their salespeople to visit with him to discuss their company, their policies, and, in general, what they could do for him. Within a short time numerous vendors appeared and Orson gave each of them all the time they wanted to present their wares and the information he needed to make a proper evaluation of their respective companies. Orson did indeed find out that he could get better prices, and he told Larry he was surprised that there was such a difference. Larry pointed out that based on present sales a 1 percent increase in gross profit would be $180,000 higher. If the company could get back to its former gross profit which was approximately 4 percent higher through more efficient purchasing, gross profits would be increased to $720,000 assuming sales remain the same. Orson, who was Larry's brother-in-law, had been with the firm for eleven years. He agreed that perhaps they had taken those old firms for granted and assumed that they would continue to be competitive. Larry suggested that Orson give the old suppliers an opportunity to meet the prices of the new vendors. Nearly all of the regular suppliers made the necessary adjustments without delay. Orson decided to give some new vendors an opportunity, but to only give them a token amount of business and build volume slowly. Orson knew them to be reliable and he did not want Larry accusing him of not giving new vendors an opportunity to participate in the purchasing function. However, Orson did not find it necessary to drop any of the established vendors.

Larry was extremely pleased with Orson's handling of the situation. Orson took the opportunity to discuss his compensation. He asked that his salary of $25,000 be raised, but Larry refused. He felt that since Orson's wife owned 25 percent of the company, she was making sufficient profits for both of them to share. He also was afraid that if they started taking more out of the business, then other executives in the company would want a raise also. Orson could not persuade Larry and was not happy about the situation. Larry could not understand that Orson disliked going to his wife for money because it made him feel like a beggar who has to explain every nickel and dime. Mable was tight with money, and going to her hurt Orson's pride.

Gross profits for the next several months improved as expected, and then they started to slip by 1 percent and then 2 percent. Larry called in Orson and wanted to know what the problem was. As a matter of fact, he was actually screaming at Orson for letting the prices get away from him. Finally, Orson had enough and handed in his resignation. Larry tried to dissuade him, but Orson was adamant. Years of resentment at being dependent on Robinson money and management surfaced. Even though Larry apologized and offered Orson a $100 a week raise, Orson would not come back. Then he told his wife he was leaving her as well as the business.

A few months later Larry found out that Orson had opened up his own business selling the same products. He wondered immediately where Orson got the money to start the business. He understood that it was large and was doing quite well. Larry felt that the only way he could have accumulated enough money to start a business was by taking kick-backs from his suppliers. Larry felt Orson must have, in effect, been stealing from his business for years. He wanted revenge for what Orson had done. Larry has come to you for advice and wants you to advise him on how to keep this from occurring again.

QUESTIONS

1. Do you think Orson was wrong stealing money from the company?

2. What can Larry do to prevent this from happening again? Design a system to keep on top of this area. Are there any signs other than a decrease in gross profit to alert a business owner that a buyer for the company might be taking kick-backs from vendors?

3. What action should Larry take against the suppliers who made those arrangements with Orson? How will Larry be able to determine those suppliers who made kick-back arrangements with Orson and prove it in court?

4. If Larry can prove that some of the suppliers were giving Orson kickbacks, can Larry take them to court?

5. Do you think Larry should report his former brother-in-law to the IRS?

6. Would a bonding policy have helped Larry if he is able to prove that kickbacks were made to Orson?

7. Do you have any other recommendations to offer Larry?

8. Do you think Larry should forget the entire matter and just cut off the vendors who are guilty of giving kick-backs?

Evergreen Lawn and Garden Equipment, Inc.

Evergreen Lawn and Garden Equipment Company distributed their products over seven states, including North and South Carolina, Kentucky, Tennessee, Alabama, Mississippi and Georgia. In 10 years they have developed a substantial business that is averaging $14 million in sales per year. They have 150 people working for them in many departments, including production, packaging, shipping, traffic control, accounting, personnel, purchasing, customer service and marketing. They have just installed a data processing department. The company is considered progressive, but problems have been developing throughout the organization. Lilly Wellman, the former Human Resources Manager, did an excellent job for the company but was offered a much better position elsewhere and left the company. Vincent Walcott, the president of the company, had hired Edwin Clurman for the job and while he did not have the experience Lilly had, he does have an M.B.A. in Human Resources Management and a few years experience in the field. One problem the company is now experiencing is high personnel turnover among new employees hired since Clurman took over the job. The company hired 25 people and 21 were found not fit to remain in the company. Clurman insisted he was following approved techniques and interviewing procedures, but something must be wrong.

Another problem is that the company union has been very active filing complaints and claiming that they are getting no assistance from Clurman. They feel he does not really listen and understand them. When they bring grievances to him he takes a firm management point of view and will not budge. Clurman has stated in his defense that when Lilly left the company she took three of the best employees in that department and left him with only a secretary. He feels that given time he will be able to develop his new people into a viable and effective group.

The next thing was that one of the workers complained that she was being discriminated against because of her race. She had been with the company ever since they opened and had always received outstanding reviews. This year she received a very poor one, and as a result she was fired. She immediately contacted the Equal Employment Opportunity Commission, and they are now inside the company taking affidavits from present employees, gathering facts, and checking for other violations.

A fourth problem is a formal complaint that the company is not acting as an Equal Opportunity Employer. Several female applicants were denied employment after having been asked if they are married, which is a clear violation of the law.

Clurman thinks that one reason why he is having many problems is that there is no personnel planning. He indicated to the president that he did not receive a copy of the sales forecast and was not aware that the company expected to increase sales by 20 percent this year. Had he been aware of the forecast he would have contacted the managers to ask what their personnel requirements were going to be. As it now stands, when department managers need people they come in and tell Clurman that they need five bodies yesterday. This makes it difficult to select the best people for the job and also could have something to do with the Affirmative Action Recruitment complaints.

The appraisal system needs review. The union has pointed out that few people in the organization have ever been rated as outstanding unless they are related to the president or have a close friend in the top executive ranks. They stated that most people are usually rated satisfactory, adequate, or good. They claim the rating system is structured to keep incremental increases in pay down to a minimum. The managers do not have the time to fill out the forms and do not like the confrontation that they must face each year at evaluation time.

Also the recruiting program has not been too effective and mainly has been limited to local advertising or posting vacancies on the bulletin board. Anyone who recommends a person who is hired gets a $50 bonus. There is no orientation program, and when people are hired they are thrown right into the job after meeting the supervisor. In most cases the supervisor takes them aside and assigns the new employee to an experienced worker who teaches them the ropes of their new job.

Another complaint by Clurman is that the job descriptions and job specifications are inadequate and have not been brought up to date for years. In some cases when an employee leaves, their work is temporarily assigned to someone else. That "lucky" person ends up with additional work, but no increase in compensation. Clurman thinks that if the job descriptions and job specifications are brought up to date, his success ratio will improve dramatically. Every time he has tried to get updated position descriptions data from the department managers he gets absolutely no cooperation.

The union is complaining about compensation and has requested that talks begin before the old contract expires in six months. The grapevine reveals that they intend to be very tough, and if they do not get what they want they will strike the entire operation. According to the information Clurman has received, they want at least a 15 percent increase in wages, more benefits, and a better performance appraisal system. Some people in the union want opportunities to advance. During the last five years not one employee from within the company has been hired for an executive position even though they had the credentials.

Vincent Walcott, the president, feels that while it is easy to blame Clurman for all the problems the company is experiencing there might be a kernel of truth to Clurman's complaints. Some of the procedures should be rectified. He knows that the union will be demanding all sorts of ridiculous things in their new contract, but he thinks that Clurman can handle the difficulties coming.

The members of the Equal Employment Opportunity Commission have reported that they have found enough evidence in the discrimination case brought by Janice McDermott, who was fired because of the poor appraisal she received, to bring suit against them. The officer handling the case informed Walcott that he could either try to make a settlement with the complainant or they would go to court. The officer also stated that their recruiting practices were not consistent with an equal opportunity employer. They can definitely prove that the interviewer who supposedly asked the female applicant if she was married did so in several cases. The compliance officer wants those people reinterviewed or he will take them to court. He also insists on an updated affirmative action plan because they are selling products to the government. These will be challenges for Clurman.

QUESTIONS

1. Do you think that Clurman is responsible for all Human Resources problems in this company? Do you think the interviewers were properly prepared to handle interviews successfully? Do you think Clurman should have supervised this function more carefully?

2. Do you think Clurman has a prejudice against unions? Do you think he will be an effective labor negotiator?

3. What should he do to work more effectively with the union?

4. How would you handle the discrimination complaint? Would you try to make a settlement, or would you let the matter go to court? (The backlog of E.E.O. discrimination cases is nearly three years.)

5. What type of personnel planning should Clurman institute in the company? Do you think that Clurman should meet with all the managers in the company and insist on job descriptions and specifications? Do you think that Walcott is backing Clurman sufficiently?

6. How do you explain the fact that the managers are not grading outstanding employees as outstanding?

7. Are the managers handling the performance appraisal system incorrectly? Does there have to be a confrontation each year? What type of performance appraisal program would you recommend for the management of the company?

8. How would you expand the recruiting program to make certain requirements of being an Equal Opportunity Employer are being met?

9. What changes would you make in the orientation program for the company? Do you think that the managers should submit some sort of a training program for new employees who enter their department?

10. The union is talking tough regarding the new contract. What can Clurman do to prepare himself for the labor negotiations which will be coming up in the near future?

11. What other changes would you make in the Human Resources Department of this company?

Romano Supply Company

Mario Romano owns and operates the Romano Supply Company in Tampa. The firm has been in business for 26 years and specializes in plumbing, heating supplies, and fixtures. It also offers pipe valves and fittings, water heaters, pumps, and faucets. Romano boasts of having the most complete showroom of bathroom fixtures and air conditioning systems in the entire area. The company sells mainly to industrial, commercial and residential consumers.

Romano will not install any of the products he sells. Instead, he will supply residential customers who request installation a list of all the plumbers and other contractors who buy from him. The latter policy has helped him considerably because the plumbers and contractors do not feel threatened by the supplier.

Mario has experienced fluctuations over the years, but, in general, has made a great deal of money. He is, however, concerned because last year's sales were flat and the trend seems to be continuing. At first he thought that the local market might be drying up, but he found that business was moving along as briskly as ever. No new competitors were on the scene, so he concluded that the problem must lie within his own organization.

In Mario's opinion, he pays his employees well and has always treated them as if they were family. At the end of each year he gives each employee a turkey or a ham, and a bonus of $10 for every year they have worked for the company up to a maximum of $100. The employees have always seemed to be satisfied. He goes out of his way to lend small amounts of money or cosign on bank loans if they ask him to. Mario is always careful to praise people when they do something special and, if necessary, he will admonish them if they do something wrong. However, when he does scold them, he always does it in private.

Mario keeps tight control and does not have any managers. His experience years ago with several managers was unsatisfactory. He found that they took too long to make obvious decisions, and needed too much training before they could work independently. In general, he always found it necessary to step in to get things done. He also found that his employees preferred to take orders from him rather than the managers because they trusted him and felt comfortable with him. As a consequence Mario fired all of the managers and has been running the business himself since.

When Mario goes on vacation, his son Peter usually takes over the business, signing checks and taking care of everyday problems. Although Peter grew up in the business, he does not like working for his father. This has led to some violent arguments, but Peter has stuck to his guns and informed his father that he wants to become a lawyer when he graduates from college in June. Mario has pointed out to Peter that he could make an excellent living from the company and even make it much bigger than it is at this time. But Mario has accepted that his son will never take over the business, although he hopes he will change his mind or fail in law school. When Peter is not able to work in the business and Mario has to leave on business or vacation, Mario always calls each day and talks to employees of the various departments, checking to see if everything is all right.

Recently Mario has noticed problems with the company that he has never seen in the past. Absenteeism is higher than usual. People are leaving the company and obtaining employment with some of his competitors. Mario cannot understand why this is happening since he feels he has been good to his employees. He has tried talking to them as he used to do in the past, but they just listen, agree, and promise to try to do better. Perhaps, Mario feels, they are just burned out.

Mario decided to contact a good friend who has a much bigger business. When his friend listened to Mario's problems, he suggested that Mario try participative management. He explained to Mario that by getting his employees to participate in decision-making, they would become more involved. When they become part of the problem-solving process, a better organization results. Mario always believed in a restricted type of democracy, giving employees the right to make small decisions such as where the water cooler should be located, but not permitting them to be involved in more important matters. However, Mario respected his friend's opinion, and so decided to try this new approach. If he were not satisfied with the outcome he could terminate it at any time.

Mario called a special meeting of the employees one evening after work. He had a catering firm provide food and drinks to make the meeting somewhat of a business-social function. Mario started the meeting by telling the employees that sales were stagnant. He told them he was not happy with the absenteeism and sick days and he felt that they could be doing a better job. He told them he had always tried to take care of them as if they were his own family and he called them together to see if they could help him solve all the problems as a family. Mario explained the new concept of participative management. He would like the entire staff to select six people who would form a committee to study the problems he mentioned during the meeting and come up with their own recommendations for making the company more viable and successful.

Mario pledged that he would give their recommendations the highest consideration. He also asked that the committee meet as soon as possible, and he promised to be available for any questions. His employees were surprised at Mario's plan. Several of the more outspoken employees questioned his recommendation respectfully and asked if he really wanted a very frank and honest viewpoint from them about the direction the company should take. Mario assured them that was what he was looking for and said he would be extremely disappointed if he did not get their complete cooperation. After the meeting many of the employees shook his hand, telling him that they would work even harder to make things better. Mario was pleased that he had taken his friend's advice.

During the next few weeks the committee asked for various kinds of information, which Mario immediately supplied. Mario noticed that all the members of the staff were showing up for work earlier than the regular time and many were working longer than usual. Sales were up for the last few weeks, and Mario was pleased with the turnaround. The committee called a special meeting of all the personnel on a Friday night and asked to see Mario in his office Monday to discuss recommendations the employees had formulated.

On Monday the committee began by expressing their sincere appreciation for the confidence Mario had given them and then proceeded to present their recommendations which were as follows.

1. As the company was structured, no opportunity for advancement existed. There were no managers and employees could advance no further than their present positions. Therefore, the committee suggested that Mario hire a general manager, sales manager, office manager, and a warehouse manager immediately. In addition to their desire for advancement, the company needed newer methods to deal with competition. The company should have a sales force that is better supervised and product lines should be expanded to take care of the different types of industries that were coming into the area. They also asked that Mario consider the present staff to fill those vacancies, but stated that if Mario felt other people were more qualified they would accept his better judgment. However, they hoped that Mario would give them every consideration because of their loyalty over the years.

2. Secondly, they requested that after the managers were appointed, that Mario give them the responsibility and authority to do their jobs. They pointed out that everyone knows Mario is an exceptional leader and he could use his expertise to develop and mold the managers into an efficient team. They felt that Mario should discuss with each manager the job responsibilities, and then together agree on the goals to be accomplished for the year. If he would do this, then the managers would know what was expected of them and they could be held responsible for their performance. They asked that Mario deal directly with the managers and not go directly to the employees since this would weaken the position of the managers. They pointed out that when the company did have managers it was confusing dealing with two bosses.

3. The committee recommended that overtime be paid when the employees worked extra hours. While they enjoy working for Mario, they feel they should be paid for all the time they spend on the job. They asked that the hospitalization benefits be improved and that the present life insurance policy of $5,000 be increased to $50,000 or $100,000. The insurance representative informed them that a group term policy for the entire organization would not cost much more for the higher limits.

4. Finally, they requested that Mr. Romano do away with the present annual year-end bonus program and instead establish a profit sharing program for all the

personnel where they could eventually purchase all of his stock over a period of time. They felt that since Peter does not want to come into the firm and since Mario has no other family members who are interested in the business, those who have worked for him should be given the opportunity to buy him out at a fair price. If Mr. Romano did eventually sell all his stock to them, they would like to retain him as chairman of the company and also keep the name Romano Supply Company out of respect for him.

The committee members concluded their recommendations and again thanked Mario for giving them the opportunity to present their views. They ended the meeting by saying that they felt the company could make great strides and that they would do everything they could to make it more successful.

Mario was shocked and outraged. What he was confronted with, in his opinion, was not a solution but a revolution, and he was the author of the revolt. If only he had followed instincts and just cracked heads and solved his own problems or if his son would change his mind and come into the company, this would never have happened. Now he was up against a united front with all his employees asking him to approve a program that would strip him of authority and destroy his business. Mario decided to stall for time to come up with a new strategy to deal with this uprising.

Mario sent a letter to the committee members thanking them for their input and assuring them that he would give all their recommendations serious consideration. He promised to get back to them as soon as possible. Privately Mario was determined to deal with them differently and from now on there would be "no more Mr. Nice-Guy."

As the weeks passed, it became obvious to the employees that nothing was going to happen. Mario had changed his style of management. As a result of the tougher management style, several of the employees privately told Mario that they could see he was upset, for which they did not blame him. They had been against the recommendations made at the final meeting, and had fought bitterly to have working conditions remain the same. They told Mario which employees had pushed for the recommendations. Mario thanked them for their loyalty and promised confidentiality.

Mario hired people to replace the committee members, and then fired them. He told them they were disloyal, and that he would not give them recommendations for future positions. Most of the members knew what was coming and some were in the process of looking for other jobs. However, they all took it hard and were shocked that Mario could turn on them for only following his instructions. When they left, Mario changed all the locks and proceeded with business as usual.

Meanwhile, the rest of the employees were frightened. Mario held another meeting and told them that he would continue with his old style of management, and if they did not like it they could leave. Morale was down and sales and profits started to decline each year. Ironically, the people who were fired landed positions with several competitors and were doing well. Several of Mario's longtime employees also left for better positions. Mario was losing some of his clients because he did not have good personnel, and what was once a thriving business was gradually moving into decline.

Then Mario had a massive heart attack. Peter, contrary to his prior intentions, came into the company as the chief executive officer. He informed all the personnel that he was permanently taking over the company. He called a special meeting to tell employees he would do everything in his power to bring the business back to its former status. The employees responded positively to Peter's remarks and pledged their cooperation and loyalty. Peter knew it would be a long, hard task to get the company back on a positive track, but that the basic nucleus was there to start improving. He regretted the loss of the committee members and other employees and wished he had them at this time. He took out their list of recommendations and read them with interest.

Peter wants to succeed. He has 65 people in the organization. Morale is low and motivation is nonexistent. There is no management and communication is weak between owner and employees. Employees are afraid of committees. No job descriptions exist, absenteeism is reappearing, and above all confidence is lacking in the Romano word.

QUESTIONS

1. What style of management should Peter follow in reorganizing the company?

2. What can Peter do to motivate the employees? How can morale be improved?

3. Should Peter disregard the committee recommendations? Do they make sense now that Peter had taken over the business? Should he consider a profit sharing plan which would mean selling stock to employees?

4. What other recommendations would you suggest to Peter to solve the company's problems?

CASE 46

Swiss Catering Service

Swiss Catering has been in business for seven months. During that time they have been quite successful. The owner of the business, Marie de Fand, was born in France and studied gourmet cooking for a number of years until she reached the point where she was declared a master chef. Although she did not need to work because of her family background and affluence, Marie wanted to do something challenging, and she loved cooking unusual specialties. When she came to America, she decided to enter the catering business in Dallas, Texas. She loved Dallas, and she felt that there was a target market for her type of catering which placed emphasis on quality food and the manner in which it was served.

Marie followed the European approach to catering, and it was a smashing success. Each of the people who worked for her had to be impeccably clean and dress accordingly. She even taught them useful French phrases and expected them to use them when serving guests. All the wines were imported from Europe, but she was careful to make certain that the steak came from Texas. Her prices were outrageous, but it seemed that the consuming public did not seem to care. She kept raising her prices but her customers did not mind a bit, and as a matter of fact it only increased her sales. When good clients called her and asked what type of wine they should use at a small gathering, Marie would send a few bottles of the appropriate wines to their house free of charge. Marie did not advertise. She did not believe in it and felt that her reputation was the best advertising she could get. It did not cost anything but exacting service from her and her employees.

In the beginning, Marie did all the cooking. Eventually she had to start training and supervising others in the art. She tried to employ some of her chef friends from France, promising them excellent wages and bonuses but with no success. In any case she struggled to do her best with her personnel. She had some employees who refused to learn French and she had to fire them.

In the beginning she was not afraid of firing people, for she knew she had to have perfection. However, she was developing a larger full-time staff and she was afraid of a union. Marie had catering group supervisors who would promise to do things her way, and then when they went out on a job would change specifications. Then she had problems with some of the waiters trying to fraternize with the guests. It was a known fact that her clientele were the best and were extremely wealthy so it was to be expected that a few of the younger employees might use their charms to attempt to become friends with some of the guests. Marie did not have a tip program for the employees who did the catering. They were paid a flat $10 per hour for their services and the bill to the client was a total bill with no provision for tips. Sometimes the clients did give tips to the waiters, but Marie made it clear to her clients that they were only obliged to pay the bill and that a tip was not necessary. The waiters did not like this because they were used to a different system.

Marie was also having a problem with appearance. It was the responsibility of each supervisor for a catering group to check on employees' appearance, whether they were clean, whether they had any body odor, and in general to make certain that each member had everything in place and had not forgotten their white gloves. Each supervisor was to bring with him/her the cleaning materials to clean uniforms, shoes or gloves. This policy was not being carried out and Marie did receive a few complaints.

Marie was also starting to get complaints that the food was not hot and that the waiters were speeding up the meals and drinks. She also received complaints that the bartenders did not mix the drinks properly or they were purposely trying to get some people drunk. In one case a client reported that the host for the party was drunk thirty minutes after the affair began. While he did manage to stay on his feet, he collapsed on the table when he was making a toast to the Ambassador from Holland.

Marie was trying desperately to straighten out the employees, but they did not seem to want to work with her. She had less difficulty with the women, but she wanted men to balance the staff. She was also having difficulty with the cooking. In one affair a very important client in the oil business ordered Beef Wellington for all the guests and instead of getting what they ordered they received "Arroz con Pollo" (rice with chicken). The cake, which was to have been something special cooked by Marie, was mixed up with a small cake that was inscribed on the top "Happy Birthday Milagros." The affair was a complete bust and Marie was furious. It was obvious that the supervisor had taken the wrong cake but she could not understand the meal confusion, for she did not have any orders that day for Spanish cooking. The guests however, did enjoy the meal, but Marie apologized and did not charge them for the entire catering party.

The work was piling up on Marie, and she knew that something had to change. She was determined to get the right people for the catering force. A friend of hers told her that maybe she should have a profit sharing plan, but she flatly refused that recommendation. Finally, the supervisors approached Marie and told her that they could not take her treatment of them. They resented her screaming and shouting and her fussiness about cleanliness. They also resented the compensation program, especially the no tip policy. They also complained that the hours were too long. If she did not change they were all going to walk out of her business when she least expected it. Marie was burning inside. She never had employees talk to her in this manner, and yet she did not want to lose her temper until she obtained some advice. Marie told them she would get back to them and thanked them for their candor. She felt everything could be arranged to their satisfaction.

Marie did nothing about the situation for a week. One evening she received a call at her private number which she only gave to her most important clients. It seems that T. R. Sanders was furious because at a reception he gave for his daughter the bartenders were nasty and crude and kept mixing up the orders. His little daughter Mandy Lou, who does not drink, was given Shirley Temples with gin in them, and she threw up all over the dining room table. The waiters started swearing at some of the guests, and when he complained, the waiter went over and dropped an entire dish of hot creamed soup over his pants. The entire party was a complete failure. Further, he threatened to sue for getting his daughter drunk and for the injuries he suffered. He was going to tell everyone in Dallas and Fort Worth that they should discontinue using her services until she managed to get things back to their original standards. Marie pleaded with T. R. and he managed to calm down after she told him about all her problems. He finally offered to put some of his management experts on her case to see what they could do to help her. He added, "Marie, we like you and we need your type of service in Dallas but not the version we saw tonight." However, he said, "I will do everything in my power to help you even if I have to send my managers over there to run the place. If that doesn't work, I'll buy the place from you at any price and make you president." However, he assured her not to worry.

Marie was relieved, but now it was final. She had to come to grips with her catering force which now numbered 245 people including chefs.

QUESTIONS

1. Why do you think Marie's business was such an instant success?

2. Do you think that Marie grew too fast? Do you feel she should have grown at a slower pace? Why?

3. What seems to be the basic problem with Marie? Why won't her supervisors and other employees do what she asks? Do you think it was wise for her to demand that they learn French phrases? Do you think she was right to check them out for body odor?

4. Do you think that Marie needs a better training program for her employees? What other type of programs would you recommend?

5. Do you think that her program dealing with the tips was satisfactory, or do you think that she should have made some other arrangements?

6. What changes, if any, should be made in the compensation program?

7. What should Marie do about the cooks? Should she bring master chefs from Europe who have been trained for years, no matter what the price? How would you approach that problem? Should Marie spend more time in the kitchen? Do you think in a short period of time Marie can train chefs in this country to be as good as the French?

8. What other recommendations would you make to Marie to not only get the organization straightened out but to get back those clients who were disappointed in her service?

CASE 47

Stephen's Department Store

Stephen Korzinski owns and operates Stephen's Department Store in Providence, Rhode Island. Korzinski has been in business for more than 40 years. He started the business as a small general store that sold no more than 100 products. Gradually the complexion and image of the store started to change, and because Stephen had a parsimonious style the store grew and progressed through the years. Today the store is selling more than $10 million a year and Stephen expects that if he expands into some of the suburban areas he can double or triple his sales. The one thing that has him worried is credit sales. All through those 40 years Stephen's policy has been to sell for cash. Because of his prices and the quality of goods he sold, he was able to get cash. It was a unique situation and many of his competitors felt that Stephen was a "miracle man," for they were burdened with a variety of costly credit plans.

Stephen finally realized that he would have to change his policy. While it went against his entire value system, he knew that to survive and grow he would have to extend terms to his customers. Yet, he was determined that it was going to have strict requirements for eligibility. Stephen examined all the credit card companies, but did not like the idea of having to pay a percentage to the companies. Stephen decided to set up his own credit department. He was quite aware that according to Dun and Bradstreet Industry Norms for 1985–86 department stores with industry assets over $1 million were averaging only 1.3 percent net profit after taxes. Since Stephen was making about 2.5 percent it was all the more reason not to give away a percentage of his sales to credit card companies. He could depend on Dun and Bradstreet for credit reports on business firms and Equifax could be used for individuals.

Stephen hired Tabatha Plasket as manager for the new department and outlined the requirements for a new system including:

a. a credit application that was complete and nondiscriminatory, but one that would go beyond the usual three credit references. He was especially interested in their credit history, occupations, and address or location where they could be found in case of nonpayment.

b. a grading system where each client would be assigned an appropriate credit limit and the conditions that would be necessary to increase that limit.

c. a system that would weed out marginal accounts.

d. a revolving credit program established for approved accounts that would charge the maximum interest rate allowed by the state.

e. an installment credit program for big ticket items, which would be financed over a period of not more than three years. He wanted all installment contracts discounted with the bank on a non-recourse basis. (This means that if the client does not pay, then the bank loses the money and cannot come back to Stephen.) Included in the installment program were requirements for down payment, criteria for establishing the length of the contract, and the administrative procedure should be firmly established and clear to the customer.

f. a fast and rapid evaluation procedure that is effective and will not cost the company sales because the customer gets tired and loses interest waiting for the credit department to approve his credit worthiness. However, he would rather lose an account than approve a client who is not up to his standards.

g. a system where all accounts receivable are aged, and Stephen can obtain a perfect view at a glance of how much credit is out on the street. Stephen suggested that Plasket get a computer in the department that would provide all the information he needed, when he needed it.

h. a system where active accounts who pay their bills on time are sent their bills with the envelopes stuffed with advertising brochures, inserts, and other promotional items which will increase sales.

i. a procedure for collection of all accounts over 45 days past due which did not resort to collection agencies or use of the company's attorneys unless he so directed them.

j. a means to identify that the person using the card is authorized to do so.

Tabatha pointed out that it was important for the accounts receivable subsidiary ledger to be up-to-date daily. If a client had a credit limit of $700 and the accounting department was 10 days behind in posting invoices, then a client could exceed the limit before they would catch it. She also pointed out that billing should take place without delay, for if the bills are not out then payments are not received on time.

This was a major challenge for Tabatha. It was clear that Stephen held her responsible for credit sales. She called her staff together to design a system which would meet his requirements.

QUESTIONS

1. Design a credit application that meets Mr. Korzinski's expectations. Remember that it cannot violate any existing credit laws and cannot be discriminatory.

2. Design a grading system in order to assign clients a credit limit. How would you handle a client who wants a greater limit than you have determined should be granted? Would you extend credit to students or young people who are just out of school and working, or would you consider them marginal or undesirable accounts? What additional conditions would make them acceptable?

3. What would constitute an undesirable client? What are the characteristics of an acceptable client?

4. Set up an options revolving credit plan for Stephen and explain how it would work.

5. Do you think that all big ticket items should be financed for a period of three years? What factors would determine the time period you would finance a product?

6. Do you think that interest charges on goods purchased on credit should begin from the day the goods are purchased? What would be some of the determining factors in making your decision?

7. How will it be possible to get reports checked out quickly when Korzinski expects so much?

8. How would you make certain that the holder of the credit card is really the person authorized to use it?

9. Why do you think that Stephen feels that an account over 45 days old is lost? Do you agree with him? What collection procedure would you follow to successfully collect a past due account? At what point would you feel that the account is lost? What would you recommend doing about it? Why do you think that Mr. Korzinski does not want to use a collection agency or his own attorneys?

10. Do you think that a computer will help in this department? How and in what manner?

11. What can Stephen do to make sure that all accounts receivable records are posted daily so that people will not exceed their credit limit and that all bills are paid on time?

12. Do you have any other recommendations that would enable this department to be more successful?

Zepke's Colonial Furniture Store

Rodney Zepke had owned and operated the Zepke Colonial Furniture Company for the last 20 years. During that time Rodney made a good living and managed to have a few exceptional years where he did make a substantial amount of money. The average year produced profits that amounted to about $25,000 a year after taxes. Rodney withdrew $65,000 a year for himself.

Rodney's son, Danny, was now working for him, and he was adding to the company enthusiasm manifesting itself in increasing sales. However, Rodney could see that while Danny was doing a good job and was a hard worker, it would be some years before his company could compare with some of his more successful competitors in the area of Rutland, Vermont.

Then Rodney met Kurt Glaser at a furniture convention in New York. He was impressed with Glaser's charming personality, his approach to what he termed "magnified retailing," and his record of achievements in the furniture field. Rodney thought Kurt Glaser was a genius. Rodney met with him several times and after listening to him discuss his successes in turning other stores into high profit operations, he asked him if he would be interested in coming to Vermont and working for him. Kurt replied that at the present time he was employed, but he would entertain anything that represented an improvement. Kurt agreed to visit him and evaluate the opportunity.

Within a few weeks Kurt did come, and Rodney showed him the entire operation and the financial figures. The financial statements at that time were as follows:

Balance Sheet

Cash	$ 60,000
Accounts receivable	160,000
Notes receivable	10,000
Inventory	300,000
Other current	35,000
Total current assets	$ 565,000

Fixed Assets	
Building (net)	$ 170,000
Furniture & fixtures (net)	20,000
Equipment (net)	25,000
Total fixed assets	$ 215,000
Total assets	$ 780,000

Balance Sheet (Continued)

Current liabilities

Accounts payable	$	75,000
Bank loans		10,000
Notes payable		30,000
Other current		80,000
Total current liabilities	$	195,000

Long-term liabilities

Mortgage payable	$	65,000
Deferred credits		5,000
Total long-term liabilities	$	70,000

Stockholders' equity

Common stock 40,000 shares $10 par value	$	400,000
Retained earnings		115,000
Total stockholders' equity		515,000
Total liabilities and net worth	$	780,000

Net sales for the year	$1,200,000	100.0%
Gross profit	450,000	37.5%
Profit after taxes	24,000	2.0%

Kurt pointed out that the net profit was too low and that he was earning only a 4.7 percent return on his investment, which was ludicrous. Kurt also thought that his image was too conservative. Rutland needed a new, sharp, and highly aggressive furniture discount house which sold not only colonial furniture but contemporary furniture as well. He argued that to make money he must spend money, and he felt he could easily generate sales of $5 million a year with net profits after taxes of 6 percent. This would provide net profits of $300,000 and a return on his present investment of 58 percent minimum.

Rodney was excited with these figures and showed them to his son, telling him what Kurt promised to do with their business. Naturally, Danny was taken aback because he felt the business was going to be his. He did not relish working for an outsider, particularly one that looked as slick as Kurt did to him. He listened to the proposals of Kurt and questioned him, but left the matter up to his father. However, he told his father that Vermont is not going to accept the high pressure tactics used in a large city, and he did not feel completely confident in Kurt. Rodney dismissed the statements as pure jealousy and made a deal with Kurt.

The agreement was as follows:

a. Kurt Glaser would have complete authority to operate and manage the business of Zepke Colonial Furniture Store and would be appointed to the positions of vice-president and general manager of all operations.

b. Kurt Glaser was to receive a salary of $75,000 a year plus a bonus of 2 percent of net sales of the company, providing the total net sales for the company reached $5 million in a one year period.

c. Kurt Glaser would be provided with a car of his choice and given a housing allowance plus expenses to operate the business.

d. As long as Kurt Glaser maintained a sales pace that was leading the company to annual sales of $5 million or more, then Glaser would have complete authority in the business and the owner would not overrule any of Kurt's decisions.

e. This contract is indefinite, but the agreement can be terminated by the owner at any time for just cause which would include: not reaching sales quotas of $5 million, embezzlement, or if the corporation itself was in jeopardy because of Kurt Glaser's management. In the event the contract was terminated, then the owner would have to pay Kurt Glaser one year's salary plus his bonus of 2 percent on sales made up to the date of termination. In the event of termination, Kurt Glaser agrees not to compete either directly or indirectly in the same business within a radius of 100 miles.

f. Bonuses will be paid promptly on January 15 of each year by the owner, Rodney Zepke, to Kurt Glaser. If the owner cannot make those payments when due, then Glaser will have the option to convert his bonus into common stock of the firm at the book value determined by the auditors at the end of the year.

Kurt was pleased with the agreement as was Rodney, and for the first time in years he felt that he had a chance to become one of the important business firms in the area. He also felt that in the long run Danny would understand and be pleased, because the business was really being built up for Danny.

Kurt attacked the business with a vengeance, and sales were made at a very rapid pace. Sales were not only coming from Rutland, but from all over the state. Clients were also coming from out of state. If Kurt was able to maintain the pace, sales would easily reach $6 million the first year. Danny left the business at his own request and started working for a real estate agent in town. Rodney was terribly disappointed but had complete confidence in Kurt. As he pointed out to Danny, Kurt was delivering and producing sales and increased sales meant increased profits. Kurt, however, was using high pressure tactics such as no down payment, five years to pay, and no credit limits. He made arrangements with finance companies to handle all the conditional sales contracts and chattel mortgages he had signed from his clients. The finance companies were even paying rebates on the financing, and this was an extra source of profit for Rodney. The people in Rutland were surprised to see that Rodney had changed his image. Many of the old clients would not come back to the store, for the sales force was entirely geared to the hard sell. Kurt had brought in a line of cheap furniture which appealed to lower income levels.

Kurt finished the year with sales of $6 million and was totally satisfied. He promised Rodney that next year he would double those figures. The accountant was now calculating the year end figures and eventually came up with the following internal statement:

Balance Sheet

Cash	$ 30,000
Accounts receivable	1,100,000
Notes receivable	100,000
Inventory	950,000
Other current	50,000
Total current assets	$2,230,000

Fixed assets

Building (net)	$ 145,000
Furniture & fixtures (net)	18,000
Equipment (net)	60,000
Total fixed assets	$ 223,000
Total assets	$2,453,000

Accounts payable	$1,700,000
Notes payable	150,000
Loans payable	200,000
Other current	190,000
Total current liabilities	$2,240,000

Long-term liabilities

Mortgage payable	$ 62,000
Deferred credits	15,000
Total long-term liabilities	$ 77,000

Stockholders' equity

Common stock (40,000 shares at $10 par value)	$ 400,000
Retained earnings (deficit)	(264,000)
Total stockholders' equity	136,000
Total liabilities & stockholders' equity	$2,453,000

Net sales for the year	$6,000,000	100.0%
Cost of sales	4,600,000	76.7%
Gross profit	1,400,000	23.3%
Less: operating expenses	1,779,000	
Net loss for the year	($ 379,000)	

When Rodney examined the figures, he just could not believe what he was reading. The firm started off with a retained earnings figure of $115,000 and when he subtracted the loss of $379,000 the firm's deficit in retained earnings was $264,000 ($379,000 – $115,000). The loss also wiped out part of paid-in capital to the extent of $264,000, bringing down the total net worth or stockholders' equity to only $136,000 ($400,000 – $264,000 = $136,000).

When Rodney presented these figures to Kurt, Kurt acknowledged that while he achieved the sales goals, in the first year of his program there were heavier expenses due to his own salary, the increase in sales personnel, administrative personnel, and tremendous advertising and promotion costs. However, if Rodney would let loose with some of his personal capital and inject some more money into the business then he could assure him that the situation would be turned around next year. He would concentrate not only on sales and expenses but earning a profit of at least 6 percent of total net sales. Rodney pointed out that he had promised profits last year. Kurt replied that he had overestimated the profits picture, but it was not his fault. He had had to revamp the store's image, and he found it impossible to meet those goals. The foundation stones were in place, and Rodney could now expect the results he promised. Kurt demanded his 2 percent bonus on sales, or $120,000, and Rodney told him that he did not have the money. Kurt replied that he would take stock, or he would sue and take over the company.

Rodney was now in a terrible dilemma. He had the personal capital to straighten out the business, but he was not certain whether he wanted to keep Kurt at the helm. He was sorry for his son Danny who was doing quite well in the real estate business. Rodney's attorney advised him to go into Chapter 11 because he would get immediate relief from all creditors. He felt he could present an equitable plan for the creditor's acceptance. Kurt would become just an ordinary creditor and could not take over the business. He also pointed out he could get rid of Kurt without paying him a year's compensation. Somehow the thought of filing for Chapter 11 did not sit well with Rodney. He was New England born, and was proud of his heritage and reputation. If he was going to have to "take it on the chin," he would do it, for he believed in paying his debts and paying for his mistakes. And he was still not completely turned off on Kurt as were his son, the attorney, and the accountant. He and Kurt got along fine, but maybe he should try to come to some agreement where he came back into the business and worked with Kurt.

In the meantime the suppliers were asking for their money, and when the auditors examined in depth, the accounts receivable proved to be worth about 40 percent of the book value. The notes receivable of $100,000 were from former accounts receivable that would not pay and were converted to notes. When this asset was evaluated, the auditors stated they were worthless. The inventory was mainly contemporary, and on the whole was not the quality or type that Rodney purchased when he operated the store. Rodney estimated that the inventory was in reality worth about 50 percent of its book value. Therefore, in summary, when he calculated the value of the accounts receivable, notes receivable, and inventory, he came up with an adjusted total realistic value of $915,000 versus the figure of $2,150,000 which was their stated value on the books ($1,100,000 in accounts receivable + $100,000 in notes receivable + $950,000 in inventory). Therefore, Rodney had to consider after the adjustments of $1,235,000 his total current assets were only worth $995,000 ($915,000 plus $30,000 cash plus $50,000 other current). When he subtracted total adjusted assets of $1,218,000 ($995,000 current plus $223,000) from total liabilities of $2,317,000 Rodney actually had a deficit net worth of $1,099,000. Rodney suddenly realized that he was bankrupt. Rodney could not understand how Kurt could have permitted the company to get into this position. Kurt had not given him all the relevant facts. Rodney could not understand how a company doing $6 million in sales could lose money. Rodney knew he had to make some quick decisions.

Fortunately all the notes of the business were not personally guaranteed by Rodney. Rodney could just let the business go into bankruptcy or he could make some other arrangements. He wondered if Kurt could really pull the business out from the hole that was now so deep.

The attorney and the accountant suggested that Rodney do the following:

1. Go into Chapter 11 and present a reorganization plan where he would pay everyone $0.25 on the dollar. This was more than they would get in bankruptcy over a period of five years.

2. Go into Chapter 11 and present a plan for complete payment of all debts but ask for up to 10 years to pay back all the debts. Under the plan, Rodney would not accept any salary or compensation, but he would ask his son, Danny, to head the company and receive a salary of $35,000 per year.

3. Invest sufficient capital into the business to pay off the debts and bring the bills current, and then let Danny take over the business.

4. If he feels responsible for the management contract to Kurt, then he could pay it off or make some other settlement. The attorney believes strongly that Glaser acted improperly and, in fact, was grossly negligent in mismanaging the business and should be sued.

5. Let the business go into liquidation and have the court appoint a trustee to pay the creditors what they could.

QUESTIONS

1. Should Rodney have made the arrangement with Kurt Glaser? Why do you think he bypassed his son to permit a stranger to take over the business? If you were Danny would you have been more vocal? Do you think that Rodney's wife should have taken a position with her son in this matter?

2. Do you think the contract between Kurt and Rodney was fair? What flaws did you find in the agreement and what type of contract would you have made with Kurt?

3. Do you think that Rodney should have been alerted to the situation sooner? Do you think that

Kurt knew what he was doing? Do you think that he could have eventually turned the corner with the business, for he did manage to increase sales up to $6 million?

4. Why do you think there were so many receivables that were uncollectable? Why do you think Kurt converted worthless accounts receivable to notes receivables and kept them on the books? Do you feel there was a solid credit policy in this organization? Do you think there is a relationship between sales and the large receivables on the books?

5. Why do you think the former clients in Rutland would not patronize Rodney's store? Would you buy from this store?

6. Why was it that clients were coming from Canada and other states to purchase furniture from Rodney?

7. Now that Rodney is aware that the company is in such bad shape, what advice would you give him to solve the problems? Do you think he should invest his own money into the business and give Kurt another opportunity? How should he handle Kurt?

8. If you were Danny, would you want to go back into the business after Kurt left? Do you feel that Danny and Rodney can rebuild the company to its former position?

9. What other lessons did you learn from this case?

Gruber's Material Handling Systems Design, Inc.

Eric Gruber was an engineer who specialized in material handling equipment such as industrial cranes and sophisticated conveyer systems. Gruber had worked for Von Mag Handling Systems, Inc. in Memphis, Tennessee, for the last 19 years and was earning $52,000 per year. Everything was going well for Gruber when suddenly everyone in the organization was notified that the company was closing at the end of the week. Gruber as well as the other employees were shocked. No one had seen this coming. Because he was 48 years old, Gruber saw all sorts of obstacles to seeking employment with another firm. He went home in a state of depression and shock. He could not understand how a large firm like Von Mag could close up and so suddenly. Elsa, his wife, was also surprised, but assured Eric that perhaps it was for the best, for he always talked about getting his own business. She suggested that Eric take a few weeks to think about what he wanted to do in the future.

After several weeks Eric decided it was time for him to start his own business or look for an existing business in the field of handling systems. He had several real estate agents and his banker look for the right opportunity. In the meantime Eric contacted some of Von Mag's clients and did manage to get some freelance business from them. Although it did not amount to much, it did keep him in the field. Finally, after nine months of looking, Eric started to get very nervous. He and Elsa were feeling the strain of uncertainty. But, at last an opportunity came up and Eric was quite excited. The Cornell Materials Handling Center was for sale, and could be purchased at the right price.

Cornell's handled casters, fork lift trucks, industrial conveyers, hand trucks, dockboards, ladders, and other small products for the materials handling clients. The firm did not engage in designing systems for industrial companies because it did not have the expertise nor the equipment to handle that aspect of the business. Cornell thought that he could have increased sales dramatically if he had had that systems designing capability. As it was, Cornell concentrated on selling and servicing German made fork lifts and the other equipment. Cornell stated that he wanted to sell the business because his son did not want to take over the company. Cornell had been in the business for nearly 25 years and wanted to retire.

Cornell was asking $486,000 cash for the business. However, he would be willing to consider terms if the buyer was creditworthy. Eric asked him for some financial figures and Cornell gave him the following:

	1986	1985	1984
Sales	$1,750,000	$1,500,000	$1,350,000
Gross profit	315,000	270,000	216,000
Net after taxes	33,250	13,500	12,150

Balance sheet figures were as follows:

Cash	$ 21,500	Accounts Payable	$ 45,000
Accounts receivables	125,000	Notes payable bank (floor plan)	295,000
Notes receivable	20,000	Other current	15,000
Inventory	395,000	Total current	$355,000
Other current	10,000	Stockholders' equity	286,500
Total current	$571,500		
Fixed assets	70,000		
Total assets	$641,500	Total liab. and stockholders' equity	$641,500

Eric was impressed with Cornell as well as the business and felt that it was just the opportunity he was looking for. Eric discussed the matter with Elsa, and she was concerned that the business was not engaged in exactly the same type of activities as his former employer. Eric pushed that opinion aside, and replied that he understood all the equipment the business was selling. He could use the company as a base and within a few years develop the business into exactly what Von Mag had been doing. After hours of fruitless discussion, Elsa could see she was not going to get Eric to reason, weighing all the pros and cons as he should. It looked to her that he was going to risk their life savings without sufficient thought. Elsa also thought that Cornell wanted too much for the business. To recuperate the $486,500 based on earnings in 1986 of $33,250 it would take Eric nearly 15 years, and by that time he would be 63 years old. Eric was adamant, however, and told Elsa that it was his decision to make and that he would take it whether she liked it or not. Elsa and Eric fought bitterly but finally worked out a compromise. First, he would try to get the business for less money and secondly, he would put Elsa in charge of the office. While Elsa did not have much experience, she had worked as a file clerk many years before.

Eric asked his lawyer for advice. The lawyer suggested that he not buy the corporation itself because of unknown contingent liabilities. Rather he should try to purchase just the assets he wanted and assume those liabilities he wanted to assume. Under no circumstances should he buy the stock of the corporation. He could include the name of the corporation in the purchase if he wanted. Eric preferred to use his own name, for he had been in the trade for a number of years and was well known.

So Eric and Cornell negotiated the price of the business, and after hours of discussion Cornell agreed to permit Gruber to purchase assets and assume all the liabilities of the business for $350,000. However, Gruber must make his decision and give him a deposit immediately. Cornell would not finance any part of the purchase price and wanted the balance of the money at closing in no more than 30 days. Cornell told Eric that the purchase price obviously did not include the cash or the name of the business. Cornell explained the floor plan arrangements he had with the bank and reported that the bank would be glad to handle his inventory for him. Cornell also explained that the bank handled the financing or installment selling of the equipment to the consumers under the following plans:

1. *With recourse.* Under this plan the unpaid balance after deducting the deposit or trade could be financed through the bank. The bank would advance Eric the unpaid balance, and as long as the industrial consumer paid the monthly payments everything would be fine. However, if the consumer did not make the monthly payments, then the amount owing would be charged to Gruber and the equipment would be returned to him. He would then have to resell the equipment to get his money out of the repossession. Cornell warned him to be careful under this arrangement, for when equipment comes back it is usually in bad shape. However, the bank did rebate as high as 3 percent of the interest charges on the total unpaid balance if the consumer paid the amount in full. Therefore, if Gruber charged 14 percent on an unpaid balance of $15,000, under this plan the bank would rebate to him 3 percent of the $15,000, or $450 per year for each year financed. Equipment was usually financed from three to four years. Cornell had only four repossessions in the last five years and did not use this plan very much.

2. *Without recourse.* Under this plan the unpaid balance owing on the truck is remitted to Gruber, and the bank assumes all responsibility for the transaction if the consumer does not make the monthly installments. Under this plan Gruber would only earn 1 percent on the unpaid balance.

Cornell also stated that the lease for the building had only two years remaining, and the monthly rental was $3,500. He expected that the landlord would give him the same lease and the renewal option at $4,000 per month at the expiration of the lease. Eric was pleased with the terms and gave Cornell a deposit of $10,000 on the purchase.

Eric went back to Elsa and told her that he forced Cornell to lower the price by the total amount of $136,500. The new purchase price was $350,000. Elsa asked Eric where he was going to get the money. Eric proposed they would sell their stock and use the money they had saved. He also thought they might have to mortgage the house, which was free and clear of any liens. Elsa was very reluctant to go along with Eric's plans. Eric told her that he had already given Cornell a $10,000 deposit for the business which they could lose if they didn't follow through. Elsa thought that her husband was jeopardizing everything. Eric took her to meet Cornell, and she had to admit she was impressed with the business. Reluctantly, Elsa agreed that he could go ahead as long as she could be part of the business. Eric agreed and proceeded to raise the money for the settlement scheduled in two weeks. The bank granted Eric a mortgage sufficient to give him an additional $50,000 for working capital. Cornell had agreed that if the net worth was more when Gruber took over the business, the purchase price would remain the same. This seemed especially fair to Eric.

Finally, the closing came and Cornell delivered the lease approved by the landlord under the same conditions; only now the lease read "Gruber's Material Handling Systems Designs, Inc." Cornell also delivered letters of intent from the manufacturers he represented, indicating that they would accept Gruber as their dealer for the present. They reserved the right to make a change if they felt he was not acceptable. The attorney for Gruber protested this point, for he stated that the lines were vital to the success of the business. They needed more assurance. Cornell thought Eric would have absolutely no difficulty retaining the lines, for Eric had experience and was taking over a competent personnel group. Cornell assured Eric that he would give the cooperation he needed if there was any difficulty. He would not assume any liability, however, if any of them failed to deliver their lines. Eric's attorney advised him that he should not accept the company on that basis, but Eric insisted that it would be all right. He felt that Cornell's cooperation was all he needed.

The sale went through and the new balance sheet looked as follows:

Cash	$ 50,000	Accounts payable	$ 35,000
Accounts receivable	105,000	Notes payable (bank)	325,000
Notes receivable	25,000	Other current	10,000
Inventory (fork-lift truck)	325,000		
Inventory (other)	73,000		
Other current	10,000		
Total current	$588,000	Total current	$370,000
Fixed assets	70,000	Stockholders' equity	400,000
Intangible assets (goodwill)	112,000	Total Liab. and stockholders'	
Total assets	$770,000	equity	$770,000

The bank had approved Gruber for floor plan financing and gave him a line of credit up to $500,000 subject to review. However, the agreement included a proviso that inventory in stock for 90 days would have a curtailment charge of 10 percent which would have to be paid by Gruber. There would be additional curtailments of 10 percent per month until the sixth month when the unit would have to be paid in full. Thus, if a fork lift cost Gruber $15,000 and it was in stock 90 days Gruber would have to pay $1,500 in 90 days, another 10 percent or $1,350 on the unpaid balance in 120 days, $1,215 in 150 days, and the balance of $10,935 at the end of 180 days. Thus, Gruber would have to see that all stock moved quickly and make certain that the models ordered were popular. Otherwise he could be stuck with high inventory costs.

Eric and Elsa took over the business, changed the name, advertised in all the newspapers, and sent out direct mail letters to all their clients. They advised them of the sale and described the new services the company would be able to offer in systems design engineering. The employees of the company settled down after a few weeks except in the office where Elsa had replaced the office manager. Eric called together his sales, service, and parts managers. He told them that he had full confidence in their ability and expected them to perform their jobs as competently as they had for Cornell. He would devote most of his time to developing the engineering side of the business. This would eventually help all the other product areas increase their sales. He expected each manager to report any problems and the progress that was being made. He was clear with the sales manager that all trucks should move out as quickly as possible because he did not want to pay curtailment fees on trucks. Eric believed in delegation and he would support his managers completely as long as they produced.

For the next few months business was brisk. Eric confined himself to the engineering side of the business while the various managers worked hard to develop more sales. The only problem area was the office. Because Elsa had assumed leadership there had been several changes in personnel and Eric was not able to get the information he needed to keep abreast of financial matters. Every night, even after a satisfying day, Eric and Elsa would argue. She complained that the parts manager was buying too many parts or the sales manager was not trying hard enough to make sales. She felt the service manager could be doing more business than he was at the time. Eventually, Eric stopped listening to Elsa. One day the bank called Eric and informed him that the corporate account was overdrawn. The bank found it necessary to bounce his checks. Eric was stunned. He managed to scrape up sufficient money to handle the overdraft in the account, but the suppliers were nervous about his checks bouncing and threatened to put him on a C.O.D. basis.

Eric called in a respected accounting firm to bring the books up to date so he could get an immediate grasp of his financial position. Since his problem was cash flow, the accountants immediately worked up the following: an aging of accounts receivable; a breakdown of inventory into the units on floor plan; the units that were paid from the floor plan and which Gruber owned if there were any; the inventory of other stock; an aging of notes receivable; and an aging of accounts payable. Within a few days the accounting firm came up with the following data:

1. Aging of accounts receivable:

Total	0–30 days	31–60 days	61 days & over
$210,000	$95,000	$40,000	$75,000

2. Aging of notes receivable:

Total	0–30 days	31–60 days	61 days & over
$25,000	$15,000	$3,000	$7,000

3. Fork lift inventory:

On floor plan with the bank	$275,000
Owned by the company (paid off)	125,000

4. Inventory of other stock:
    Total inventory of $125,000, up from the $73,000 amount when Gruber took over the business. Thus, there was an increase of $52,000.

5. Accounts payable:

Total	0–30 days	31–60 days	61–90 days	91 days & over
$140,000	$35,000	$25,000	$30,000	$50,000

6. Contingent liability as a result of financing trucks with the bank on a with-recourse basis:
    a. Fourteen trucks were financed with recourse and the aging of those trucks is as follows with respect to their payment

Total	Current	30 days past due	60 days past due	90 days past due
14 trucks	5 trucks	1 truck	2 trucks	6 trucks

    b. The six trucks which are past due have a total balance owing on them of $84,000, which will have to be paid by the company if those accounts are not brought up to date. When Eric asked the sales manager why he approved those clients on a with-recourse basis he was informed that, in spite of his objections, Elsa had approved them because they stood to make a 3 percent interest rebate from the bank on each transaction. The sales procedure was to route all sales contracts through the office to be submitted to the bank. When Cornell owned the business, he rarely accepted a sale on a with-recourse contract. In addition to these problems, Eric had a payroll of $18,000 to make this week, and he did not have the money in the bank to pay the employees.

When Eric compared the business today with the business when he took over the company, he noticed the following changes:

	Started	*Today*	*Change*
Cash	$ 50,000	$ 1,000	$ −49,000
Accounts receivable	105,000	210,000	+ 105,000
Notes receivable	25,000	25,000	0
Inventory			
Trucks on floor plan	325,000	275,000	−50,000
Trucks owned by comp.	0	125,000	+ 125,000
Stock other products	73,000	125,000	+ 52,000
Accounts payable	35,000	140,000	+ 105,000

Eric was at a loss to understand how all this could have happened in such a short time. His receivables were excessive but sales had increased dramatically in all the departments. The sales manager was pushing very hard to sell the trucks he had to pay off, and while he was having difficulty selling some of them, he did have some possible deals working which might reduce the stock. Gruber told him to sell the trucks they owned at any price to get some cash. The inventory of other products increased because the parts manager said they were losing too many sales because of the lack of basic parts which Cornell would never stock. He pointed to increased sales to show that the additional inventory had paid off.

According to the accountant the credit policy of the company was not uniform as it should be. Decisions were made by any of the managers including Elsa, the office manager. Credit policy was something Eric was not involved with at his former place of employment, and he did not understand sales or inventory procedures. He knew engineering and that was the only area that showed improvement.

At this point Eric had numerous designs underway. In several cases, they needed only little more work before he could sell them to clients. He tallied up his back orders and had approximately $300,000 of engineering systems sales pending. These would be completed when the parts and materials he ordered arrived. The gross profit on these sales averaged 40 percent of the sales figure. But Gruber knew he must give attention to other parts of the business immediately but does not know where to begin.

The bank recommends that you advise Gruber on rectifying the present state of affairs. You have agreed to take on the account and have agreed upon a fee.

QUESTIONS

1. If you were an employee working for the firm, would you start looking for another job?

2. Would you advise Gruber to go into voluntary bankruptcy? What advantages would that have for him at this time? What would be the disadvantages?

3. What immediate action would you take to meet the payroll?

4. What other action would you take with respect to the rest of the assets and liabilities? Be specific and indicate how you would handle each asset or liability.

5. Would you fire Elsa? Do you feel it was wise for Eric to bring his wife into the firm? Do you feel she was responsible for any of the problems?

6. Do you feel Eric should be phasing out the lift truck business and the other areas and concentrating more on the engineering?

7. Do you feel Eric gave this business sufficient examination before he purchased it? What mistakes did he make before making his decision to purchase?

8. Would you have signed the purchase agreement if the lines or manufacturers were not firm in their decision to allow Eric to represent them?

9. Do you think Eric was prepared to go into business for himself? Did he delegate too much authority to his managers? How would you have handled the managers?

10. What should Eric do in the future, assuming you are able to straighten this mess out, to see that this does not happen again?

CASE 50

Hunter's Security Systems, Inc.

Henry Hunter owns and operates Security Guard Service in Buffalo, New York. He has more than 400 security guards working for him, and he has some of the largest and most respected companies in Buffalo as his clients. Henry was a former detective, and when he retired he decided to put his background to use and opened up his own security service. Because of his reputation and contacts he had made over his 25-year career with the police force, his business quickly became a success. He mainly hired retired police officers who had a good grasp of the problems likely to be encountered. The firm provided other services including surveillance work, security systems design, and private investigating, but the major emphasis was on security service. The only problem Henry had was with his office. He did not have any background in that particular area and his office manager, Danny Leahy, had died a few weeks ago. Henry was having difficulty finding a replacement.

Henry's wife, Lydia, suggested that he give their son Albert an opportunity to take over the office. Henry was not particularly keen about the proposal because he thought Albert was lazy and not particularly intelligent. His wife pointed out that although Albert had failed at two tries at college, he did complete a correspondence course in accounting with a "B" average. Finally, to keep peace at home Henry decided to give his son a chance. Henry had a talk with his son indicating his expectations and outlining his responsibilities. Albert promised he would do a great job and took over the office.

During the first month or so, it appeared that Albert was getting a good grasp on procedures and he was getting along well with Edna, the office clerk. She also helped with the petty cash, but it was up to Albert to handle the accounting. They only used an accounting firm once a year to perform an audit. Albert had little experience in office management but decided to arrange a system which would make the company more effective. At the end of the third month he presented his father with an income statement, as follows:

Sales and all revenues		$100,500
Less: purchases		12,000
Gross profit		$ 88,500
Less: expenses		
Payroll expenses	$218,400	
Advertising	15,000	
Petty cash expense	1,500	
Rent	6,000	
Telephone	8,000	
Uniform expense	24,000	
Miscellaneous	2,000	
Total expenses		$274,900
Total loss for the period		($186,400)

Albert informed his father that the bank balance was $175,000 and that the company had a total of $600,000 in accounts receivable. The breakdown of the receivables was as follows:

Total Amount	*0–30 days*	*31–60 days*	*61–90 days*	*91 days and over*
$600,000	125,000	155,000	135,000	185,000

Henry asked for a breakdown of the payables and Albert informed him that it was not complete but he estimated that it was about $300,000. When Henry looked at the above figures, he knew that something was very wrong. When Danny was handling the books, they always showed a profit. He could understand what Danny submitted to him, for it always followed the same pattern. But with Albert's records nothing seemed to make sense. He knew that sales were incorrect because he averaged $200,000 in sales a month. When he questioned his son about this, Albert said they were accurate because he only received $100,500 in cash. He claimed you could not consider anything a sale until it was collected. Henry told him that was ludicrous and asked to look at the accounts receivable book.

When Henry went through the books, he discovered that not all the sales were recorded. When he questioned Albert, he told him that Edna could not get out all the bills on time so they left those sales out of this statement. Henry asked why the customers were not billed. Albert replied that he had taken a course in accounting and knew what he was doing.

When his father checked out the purchases on the income statement he found that they were actually purchases for a client's new security equipment, not ordinary supplies. Henry asked where the supplies expense was entered, and

Albert told him that Edna did not get all those bills recorded, but they would be on the next statement. When Henry checked the payroll, he found it was the only thing that was right with the exception of one employee who was just hired. Henry asked him if the new employee was paid, and Albert said he paid him from petty cash. Henry asked Albert if he recorded the payroll taxes of approximately 12 percent, but Albert replied that because he had not paid payroll taxes yet he did not record them on the books. However, he again assured his father that when they were paid he would see they were properly noted on the next income statement. Henry asked about the rent, which was $4,000 per month, and said he should have recorded $12,000 on the statement. Albert stated he had not paid the rent yet, but he would get around to it. Henry also thought that the advertising item was too high and asked for an explanation. Henry examined the charges to the account and found that Albert was charging all travel expenses to advertising. His father explained that 95 percent of the amount was not advertising expense, but travel costs incurred when the company had to use a bus to transport a group of security guards to the stadium or some other location. Albert was asked about petty cash and told Henry that he always made out a check to petty cash for $500 when he needed money or felt the supply of cash was getting low. When Henry asked him how much he had in the petty cash box at this moment, Albert counted a total of $765, which was in excess of the $500 limit. The uniform expense was the same as reported on the last statement.

Henry could not understand the amount of cash he had in the bank and asked Albert how he arrived at that amount. Albert told him that he just called the bank officials and they gave him the daily figures. He just adjusted his check book for that amount. Since the bank always kept accurate records they were probably more correct than his own balance and that is how he arrived at a figure of $175,000. Henry knew this was not correct because his average daily balance was around $25,000. Although Henry did not know much about keeping books, he knew that his office was totally disorganized and that something had to be done.

Henry also found it extremely difficult to check on files. Instead of filing invoices by name or company, Albert organized them by billing date because he felt that it made more sense. Albert also filed all correspondence that came in and went out in two folders. He felt it saved space when everything was filed by date—all he had to do was look for the date he sent out a letter or bulletin and he could easily find it. Another thing Henry noticed was that the invoices were no longer in numerical order and that the checkbook had some checks missing. Albert explained this by stating that if he or Edna made a mistake in invoicing, they threw out the form. If they made a mistake writing a check, they merely voided it and threw it away.

Henry knew that Albert was honest and would not steal anything, but he needed help fast in getting the books in order and the office reorganized the way it was when Danny was alive. He called his regular auditor but because it was his busy tax season he was not available to restructure the system or advise his son.

So Henry has come to you and wants you to set up an accounting system for Albert and reorganize his office procedures.

1. If you were called in to reorganize the office for Henry, where would you start? Outline your procedures.

2. What accounting journals and ledgers would you install in the company? When would you suggest that each be used and in what manner?

3. Assume that the chart of accounts the auditor had set up were as follows:

100	Assets
101	Cash
102	Petty cash
103	Accounts receivable
104	Notes receivable
105	Supplies
106	Security equipment
107	Accumulated depreciation
200	Liabilities
201	Accounts payable
202	Salaries payable
203	Taxes payable
204	Notes payable
205	Notes payable (current)
300	Capital
301	Henry Hunter, capital
302	Henry Hunter, drawing
400	Income
401	Sales
402	Miscellaneous income
500	Expenses
501	Salary expense
502	Payroll taxes
503	Supplies expense
504	Interest expense
505	Purchases expense
506	Depreciation expense
507	Advertising expenses
508	Travel expenses
509	Telephone expense
510	Entertainment expense
511	Miscellaneous expense

Set up a sample page for the sales journal and give an example of how a transaction should be recorded when a sale is made. Do the same for the following:
a. cash receipts journal
b. cash disbursements journal
c. purchase journal
d. general journal

What special ledgers should be set up for daily use? Set up a general ledger, an accounts receivable subsidiary ledger, and an accounts payable ledger and indicate when they should be used. Also give an example of how a transaction is to be recorded and how the ledger acts as a check on the control account in the general ledger.

4. Outline your procedure for setting up a proper and efficient filing system that will provide prompt and accurate information to Henry or others. Make certain your system is still effective even when Albert and Edna are not working.

5. Outline a daily plan or a financial checklist which should be rigorously followed to see that all the data is recorded properly and on time, and is available to management when needed.

6. Outline the basic format that should be followed to reconcile the bank statement with the company checkbook monthly. What procedures should be followed to give Henry an accurate daily cash balance?

7. Should Albert and Edna be fired? What would you do? Do you think it is a good idea to hire members of your own family? If you elect not to fire Albert, where would you put him?